AF478083

DIRECT DEMOCRACY

CARIBBEAN
STUDIES
SERIES

Anton L. Allahar and Natasha Barnes
Series Editors

DIRECT DEMOCRACY

COLLECTIVE POWER,
THE SWARM,
AND THE LITERATURES OF THE AMERICAS

SCOTT HENKEL

University Press of Mississippi / *Jackson*

www.upress.state.ms.us

The University Press of Mississippi is a member
of the Association of American University Presses.

First printing 2017

∞

Library of Congress Cataloging-in-Publication Data

Names: Henkel, Scott, author.
Title: Direct democracy : collective power, the swarm, and the literatures of
the Americas / Scott Henkel.
Description: Jackson : University Press of Mississippi, 2017. | Series:
Caribbean studies series | Includes bibliographical references and index.
Identifiers: LCCN 2016054686 (print) | LCCN 2017015361 (ebook) | ISBN
9781496812261 (epub single) | ISBN 9781496812278 (epub institutional) |
ISBN 9781496812285 (pdf single) | ISBN 9781496812292 (pdf institutional)
| ISBN 9781496812254 (hardback)
Subjects: LCSH: America—Literatures—History and criticism. | Democracy in
literature. | Democracy—America. | Democracy and the arts—America. |
Social movements—America—History—19th century. | BISAC: LITERARY
CRITICISM / Caribbean & Latin American. | SOCIAL SCIENCE / Ethnic Studies
/ African American Studies. | SOCIAL SCIENCE / Black Studies (Global).
Classification: LCC PN846 (ebook) | LCC PN846 .H46 2017 (print) | DDC
809/.897—dc23
LC record available at https://lccn.loc.gov/2016054686

British Library Cataloging-in-Publication Data available

CONTENTS

ACKNOWLEDGMENTS

A tremendous number of people helped me and contributed to producing this book. My siblings, Richard Henkel, Breena Scharrer, Kelly McIntyre, and Ronnie Hecht, have been a constant source of love. My mother, Kathryn Henkel, put me on my life's trajectory, for which I always will be grateful; my father, Ronald Henkel, had a witty way with language that may be in some of these pages; their memories and their struggles are for me a great source of pride and inspiration.

My colleagues in the departments of English and African American and Diaspora Studies at the University of Wyoming have given me an intellectual home, a challenging and nurturing community that is as valuable to me as it is rare in the profession. I appreciate especially Peter Parolin, Julia Obert, Vanessa Fonseca, Mike Edson, Susan Aronstein, Susan Frye, Caroline McCracken-Flesher, Caskey Russell, Jeanne Holland, Andy Fitch, Mike Knievel, Joyce Stewart, Cliff Marks, Arielle Zibrak, Rick Fisher, and Maggie Bourque. The writing group of critical race studies scholars led by Kerry Pimblott and Tracey Patton, including Erin Forbes, Peter Fine, Marcus Watson, Darrell Jackson, Ekaterina Alexandrova, Molly Marcuse, Amanda Stow, and Irlanda Jacinto, is a model of rigorous, cooperative academic exchange, one in which I am very grateful to participate.

The ideas here have been improved by comments and questions from many audiences. Among these, I appreciate the scholars who gathered at the International Slavery Museum in Liverpool in 2013 for a conference on the seventy-fifth anniversary of the publication of C. L. R. James's *The Black Jacobins*. The opportunity to test out these ideas with an audience including Nick Nesbitt, whose book *Universal Emancipation* made it possible for me to write this book, Selma James, Rachel Douglas, Christian Høgsbjerg, Robert A. Hill, Selwyn Cudjoe, Raphael Dalleo, and Philip Kaisary propelled this project forward at a crucial stage. April Herndon and Lindsay Weinberg read an early draft of the manuscript and offered critical advice. Ed Folsom and peer reviewers at the *Walt Whitman Quarterly Review* provided an excellent forum for my early thinking about *Democratic Vistas*.

Special thanks go to the mentors who saw this project through its early stages: Scott Michaelsen, Ellen McCallum, Salah Hassan, and Zarena Aslami. Likewise, I owe special gratitude to Sid Dement, who ran with me and talked about gardening with me; and to Andreas and Emily Pape, who are friends beyond what I can describe. David and Kelly Werner, Chris and Laura Bishop, and Deanne Westerman and Matt Johnson fed me and supported me. Liz Rosenberg walked and talked with me, a process that always led me to greater clarity. Justin Rogers-Cooper pushed my thinking in very valuable ways. Taylor Hagood's friendship and advice, as well as our walks together, are kindnesses I will never be able to repay. Priscilla Wald's scholarly rigor and generosity are examples to which I aspire.

While at Michigan State University, my colleagues in the English Department and my fellow activists in the Graduate Employees Union helped to shape my theoretical views and political commitments. My thanks and solidarity go especially to Duncan Woodhead, Jenn Nichols, Jacque Lloyd, Brian Holcomb, Brian Thomas, Julie Hartman-Linck, and Ernesto Mireles.

Colleagues in the Working Class Studies Association—Christie Launius, Tim Strangleman, Michele Fazio, and many more—have helped me to find a scholarly home.

Many other friends and colleagues helped me in innumerable ways. In particular, my thanks go to Matt Applegate, Basheer Bergus, Stephen Cormier, Adam Laats, Bob Micklus, Stephen Paushter, Christina Pullano, Benita Roth, Hiroki Sayama, Paul Shovlin, Dorothy Tortugal, Al Tricomi, Al Vos, Brian Wall, and Jim Zeigler.

I appreciate the support of the Caitlin Long Excellence Fund at the University of Wyoming.

Vijay Shah at the University Press of Mississippi supported this project from the start, which I appreciate very much. Many thanks are also due to Lisa McMurtray at the press, as well as to the peer reviewer for thoughtful and insightful criticism.

And most importantly, I am deeply grateful to my love, Kelly Kinney, whose intelligence, commitment, and criticism made this book far better than it otherwise would have been.

PROLOGUE

In conversations about the hopes for a more democratic future, the Haitian Revolution and the contribution that C. L. R. James's book *The Black Jacobins* makes to our understanding of it deserve prominent attention. Between 1676 and when the revolution began in 1791, approximately 911,000 Africans, mostly from the Bight of Benin and West Central Africa, were stolen and transported to what was then known as the French colony of Saint Domingue.[1] Approximately 773,700 of them survived the Middle Passage. Until the revolution destroyed the regime, the colony was the largest disembarkation center for slaves in the Caribbean and one of the greatest generators of wealth the world had ever seen. At its peak the colony produced two-thirds of France's overseas trade, especially sugar, indigo, cotton, and tobacco—all of this in 10,714 square miles, a geographic space similar in size to the state of Maryland. As James writes in an elegant but terrible sentence, "If on no earthly spot was so much misery concentrated as on a slave ship, then on no portion of the globe did its surface in proportion to its dimensions yield so much wealth as the colony of San Domingo."[2] This wealth came at a high cost of life, and it showed a tremendous exertion of power, both the power to work and produce and the power to dominate and coerce those workers.

From 1791 to 1804, a mass of insurgents led by Toussaint Louverture and Jean-Jacques Dessalines, both ex-slaves themselves, threw off their former masters, resisted recolonization attempts by France, Spain, and Britain,[3] abolished slavery, and renamed their new independent nation Haiti, taking that name from the native Taino peoples who had been exterminated by colonists centuries earlier. Many aspects of the Haitian Revolution are subjects of continuing debate—about the ethics of decolonial and racial violence, the bases of human rights, the role of the state in consolidating struggles for liberation, and more. Both radical and reactionary writers have claimed its legacy.[4] Furthermore, as Sibylle Fischer writes, "Slavery shows that we cannot neatly separate the social from the political, and that we cannot theorize liberty without thinking about liberation and what kind of liberty ensues from what kind of liberation."[5] Yet in these conversations it is also difficult to overemphasize the following facts: the Haitian Revolution was a successful national slave rebellion during an era when the abolition of slavery seemed like an impossible goal; it was fought and won by the people who had been enslaved; and it led to the founding of a state based on what Nick Nesbitt calls universal emancipation, rather than on the privilege of a few.[6]

In 1802, however, two years before the revolution's end, the outcome of these events was uncertain. The French colonial forces had adopted a strategy to remove or co-opt the revolutionary leaders; the strategy was built on the assumption that depriving the revolution of its leadership would end the resistance and provide the opportunity to reinstate slavery. On June 6, Toussaint, the first and most important of the revolutionary generals, was captured and then exiled to France, where he spent the short remainder of his life jailed in squalid conditions.[7] Dessalines at this point was aligned with the French.[8] Yet in a remarkable turn of events, "the insurrection became general," as James writes, and this put Charles Leclerc, who was Napoleon's brother-in-law and also the French official tasked with quelling the rebellion, "into a mortal terror."[9] On August 25, 1802, Leclerc wrote a letter to the French minister of marine stating, "It is not enough to have taken away Toussaint, there are 2,000 leaders to be taken away."[10]

Directly after quoting Leclerc's letter, James notes that "the women were now fighting side by side with the men," and that "the little local leaders not only beat off attacks but maintained a ceaseless harrying of the French troops, giving them no peace."[11] In this time Leclerc was publicly stating that his intent was not to restore slavery, but rather to restore order, an argument that found some purchase among the big leaders but which nearly no one else believed.[12] The specter of reenslavement fueled the general insurrection, and in response to the general insurrection, Leclerc went to nearly genocidal ends, ordering the murder of every ex-slave over the age of twelve.[13] During these months, an outbreak of yellow fever began; it would eventually kill Leclerc and more than half of the European soldiers.[14] During the months from June 1802, when Toussaint was captured, until October, when Dessalines switched back to attacking the French, the situation in Saint Domingue was highly unstable, and the revolutionary leadership was mostly absent, for a variety of reasons. Yet in this period, the revolution adapted and grew substantially; women and men continued the work of freeing themselves from slavery, and did so with remarkable success. It had taken eleven years of effort, organizing, struggle, and fighting to get to this point; within fifteen more months, the revolution would be won and independence declared. But even eleven years is too short a framework for an adequate understanding of these events; as Carolyn E. Fick and others have pointed out,[15] the participants in the Haitian Revolution built upon a long and diverse tradition of resistance, including sabotage, marronage, and guerrilla tactics. If, as Fischer suggests, the kind of liberty is related to the kind of liberation, the liberty in question here was made by the 2,000 leaders who fought for it, and by many more who, in previous generations, put in place the foundations for such a struggle.

Leclerc's letter notwithstanding, therefore, 2,000 is not an accurate headcount. James promotes the 2,000, calling them "little local leaders," but this is not accurate either.[16] Elsewhere, James shows that these insurgents are acting in a network of resistance: he describes the insurgents as a swarm, using this metaphor five times in *The Black Jacobins*, writing, for example, that "the road from the heights ran along the sea-shore, and the sailors who remained in [the French] ships in the harbour could see [the insurgents] hour after hour swarming down to Le Cap[. . .] It was the end of white domination in San Domingo."[17] Every time, as in this instance, James uses the metaphor of the swarm to describe a particular type of collective power, one strong enough to terrify Leclerc. The swarm metaphor has a long and complicated history: it is as common to see writers use it, like James, to describe a logic of collective action as it is to see it used by colonial thinkers as part of a vocabulary meant to dehumanize what it described. The various uses of this metaphor will be one of the major lines of investigation in this book, but for now I wish to note that this metaphor and the dynamics of power it describes speak to some of the major themes of James's career, and also to some of the most enduring problems of democracy, labor, and slavery in the Americas during the long nineteenth century.

⑥   ⑥   ⑥

In a series of lectures he gave to the Institute of the Black World in 1971, James stated that if he were to rewrite *The Black Jacobins*, he would focus on the 2,000 and the implications of their example, drawing to a greater degree on primary texts produced by the participants in the revolution.[18] In the intervening years, a number of scholars have responded to this call, notably Carolyn E. Fick, in *The Making of Haiti*, and Laurent Dubois in *Avengers of the New World*. This archival research has done a great deal to add to our understanding of who the 2,000 were, what they observed, and what they thought about these events. Much of the scholarship notes that the events of the summer and fall of 1802 were remarkable—Leclerc's comment about the 2,000 leaders is itself quoted frequently—but how this general insurrection could sustain itself has been difficult to explain. If a stable leadership structure is indispensable, the Haitian Revolution ought to have folded, or at least faltered, in 1802, but it did not. The 2,000 ought to have been reenslaved, but they were not. Rather, the revolution altered its dynamics and grew into a sustained general insurrection that the Atlantic world's colonial powers were unable to suppress, even at great cost.

James's comments in his "Lectures on *The Black Jacobins*," together with his existing representations in the book and the subsequent scholarship, suggest that the 2,000 present a compelling topic for further research and therefore provide the starting point for my argument. Yet the 2,000 are not the only ones to display such a logic of collective action, nor are they the only people to have valued the power of cooperative resistance to domination and exploitation. This power is in the way enslaved people resisted their enslavers directly, it is in the way union activists in the eight-hour workday movement took greater control over both their labor and their leisure time, and it is in the way that people form bonds of mutual aid for collective resistance against a repressive regime, rather than appealing to that regime for leniency. Such power is not unique—it is, rather, part of our shared human experience—although the examples that follow show it particularly clearly. For reasons to which I will now turn, I call this power direct democracy; its history is the subject of this book.

DIRECT DEMOCRACY

INTRODUCTION

This book is a literary history of direct democracy in the Americas during the long nineteenth century. My primary argument is that direct democracy can be understood as a complex and collective type of power. What is evident in the example of the 2,000 leaders in the Haitian Revolution is that they possessed a considerable amount of power—an amount sufficient to end a centuries-long slave-labor regime and to found a new nation. What I hope to show over the course of this book is that they also possessed a particular type of power, one that is likewise shown in the literary representations of slaves, women, and workers in the texts throughout this era. The term *democracy* comes from the Greek and suggests a situation where a *demos*—people—have *kratos*—power, rule, or authority. Much of the relevant scholarship, for example, Giorgio Agamben's *Homo Sacer: Sovereign Power and Bare Life*, emphasizes the problems of rule and authority, in other words, how people are governed. But in the etymology of democracy, there is also power, and thinking about democracy as a type of power presents a challenge to common, often bureaucratic and limited interpretations of the term and opens an alternative archive, one that includes James's *The Black Jacobins*, Walt Whitman's *Democratic Vistas*, Lucy Parsons's speeches advocating for the eight-hour workday, B. Traven's novels of the Mexican Revolution, and Marie Vieux Chauvet's novella about Haitian dictatorship, *Love*.

My secondary argument is that each of the writers considered here recognized the power I call direct democracy, even though they used various other terms for it, and they represented its physical manifestation as a swarm. Whether these writers use the swarm metaphor as a compliment, as an insult, or merely to describe the phenomena they saw, their use of the metaphor points to the presence of the power I call direct democracy. The metaphor of the swarm has a complicated history—the United States Declaration of Independence refers to "swarms of British officers"; recently, British Prime Minister David Cameron referred to European immigrants as a "swarm of people coming across the Mediterranean."[1] Peter Linebaugh and Marcus Rediker use the metaphor repeatedly in *The Many-Headed Hydra: Sailors, Slaves, Commoners and the Hidden History of the Revolutionary Atlantic.*[2]

Michel Foucault writes in *Discipline and Punish* about the "swarming, howl-ing masses."[3] Edward Said writes in *Orientalism* of the "swarming, unpredict-able, and problematic mess in which human beings live.[4] A major part of the work on this project has been to track the metaphor's use in various contexts. The observable trends suggest that the metaphor is used in a variety of ways, but it is most often used to describe a group, a movement, or a community—it is a metaphor for multiplicity and complexity, and it conveys ideas about a collective type of power. What these examples show, I argue, is that direct democratic power is not just under capitol domes. It is on the plantations where people in Haiti fought for their liberty and independence, in streets full of union picketers like Lucy Parsons, and in the textile factories that B. Traven shows as the incubators of dissent during the Mexican Revolution. In each of the cases here, the swarm metaphor is like a signpost, pointing to the presence of direct democratic power.

The goal of this book is to construct a literary history of the characteristics, problems, and possibilities of direct democracy in several related situations, in order to produce a comparative analysis. This focus and approach, as I hope to show, allows us to see the struggles against domination and exploita-tion in a new light, and how the metaphor of the swarm makes a contribution to the body of scholarship on assemblages like crowds, mobs, masses, and multitudes. The long nineteenth century—which I define as the era from the Haitian Revolution until the United States occupation of Haiti, roughly from the 1790s through the 1930s—was the era in which crowds and other assem-blages of people were first studied in a dedicated, though insufficient way. Also during this era, constituted powers like states and corporations used particular philosophical and material structures to engage with those crowds. These facts are not unrelated. In the history of the problems and possibilities of democracy, what John Plotz calls the "great century of crowds"[5] was a par-ticularly tumultuous and creative era, one in which systems of domination and exploitation expressed tremendous power, as did the people and move-ments who struggled with those systems.

This introduction builds the groundwork for the book's argument, and does so in two parts. First, I situate my argument in relation to ongoing con-versations in the scholarship, with a particular attention to the terms of the debate. To paraphrase Roger Scruton's comment about Spinoza's methodol-ogy, these interpretations help to clarify terms that will be used throughout this book; I use some of these terms in ways that are different from how they are normally used, and I wish to be as clear as possible.[6] Second, I provide a context for the various ways in which authors during the long nineteenth century used the swarm metaphor. The many uses of the metaphor help to illustrate this project's main concerns, including the problems of democracy, slavery, and labor, the dynamics of racial repression and resistance, and the issues of power that run throughout these problems. I close this introduction with a brief schema for the book's argument.

Problems of Democracy and Power

As mentioned above, the English word *democracy* comes from the Greek and suggests a situation where a *demos*—people—has *kratos*—power, rule, or authority.[7] Several readings of the term's etymology are possible. The first issue is the interpretation of the *demos*—who counts as a person? Here, it is useful to remember Agamben's comment that "[e]very interpretation of the political meaning of the term 'people' must begin with the singular fact that in modern European languages, 'people' also always indicates the poor, the disinherited, and the excluded."[8] One must also add to this the particular status of the enslaved, and the many social and juridical ways in which the slavocracy's defenders attempted to strip the humanity of enslaved people. Issues about democracy's *demos* will surface throughout this book.

The second issue, the problems of *kratos*, is this book's primary concern. From *kratos* there are several logical paths to follow, two of which are parallel. First, if one follows a path of people plus rule and authority, this leads, as it does for Agamben and many others, to the problems of forms of governance, ranging from the traditional to the radical, from representative democracy to what Spinoza calls absolute democracy. I will return to a discussion of that path in this book's conclusion. But second, if one follows a path of people plus power, the question becomes about the type of power. It is not simple to distinguish between types of power and the forms of organization they take, but neither is it correct to assume they are indistinguishable. This is why I wish to suggest that the etymological distinction here, between an understanding of democracy as a form of government and democracy as a type of power, is like a fork in the road leading to different but parallel paths.[9]

The first aspect of the problem of *kratos* is that English has only one applicable word for power, whereas other languages have two or more. Latin, for example, has *potentia* and *potestas*; Haitian Kreyol has *pwisans* and *pouvwa*; French has *puissance* and *pouvoir*; Spanish has *fuerza* and *poder*; Italian has *potenza* and *potere*; German has *Macht*, *Vermörgen*, and *Gewalt*. The first of these terms generally speaks to the power of ability, the agency to act. This power is in learning, striving, and in producing—it is the power inherent in human capacity. The second of these terms speaks to a relation of power. This is the power to influence, guide, or teach another, and also to overpower, to control, to dominate another—it is the power inherent in human interactions. Perhaps the clearest statement on this point comes from Ursula K. Le Guin, who writes that the "word power has two different meanings. There is *power to*: strength, gift, skill, art, the mastery of a craft, the authority of knowledge. And there is *power over*: rule, dominion, supremacy, might, mastery of slaves, authority over others."[10] Much English language scholarship uses the term *agency*, which may be a synonym for the power of ability; its use may have grown because it marks the distinction I outline here, but it invites the misconception that it can be an institutional form of power, as in a *federal agency*, for example, rather than a type of power intrinsic to the body. English also has the term *force*, which is often used synonymously with the power to overpower, especially in physical or military terms, but to be precise, force is more closely aligned to a measurable phenomenon. In my use force is a quantitative term, a problem of physics; power is a qualitative term, a problem for literary theory and political philosophy.

The distinction between these powers is not always clear. For clarity I will call them the two modes of power, but to use Spinoza's terms, they are *non opposita sed diversa*; in other words, there is a distinction between them, but while they can be opposed to one another, they are not necessarily opposed. One can think here about how intellect, a characteristic intrinsic to the body and thus an example of the first mode of power, can be used to mentor another and is thus an example of the second mode of power; likewise, physical strength is intrinsic to the body, but it can be used to dominate another.[11] Both modes of power share common traits: they are both, to varying degrees, *complex*, by which I mean they are made up of many interacting parts, each of which influences their composition; the resulting whole can become more than the sum of those parts.[12] In this technical sense, complexity is not a synonym for difficulty but is, rather, a synonym for multiplicity. These modes of power are composites of diverse elements that at times cohere but at other times conflict. For example, the sailors, slaves, and commoners of Peter Linebaugh and Marcus Rediker's many-headed hydra are multiple and diverse—in the author's terms, they are motley.[13] Ruling powers in modern states rely on a mix of tradition, patriotism, religious superstition, economic inequality, nationalist ideologies, and more to rule. These powers are also *adaptive*, meaning that they are responsive to a particular context, and able to change and evolve when desired or necessary. The first mode of power wants to change, to grow; the second mode of power wants to relate— but they are not constant. Rather, in some cases they evolve, to a degree, in response to the environments in which they operate and in response to each other; in other cases, usually revolutionary situations, they are altered in substantial ways.

Either mode of power can be radical or reactionary in content, although one tends to see the power of ability emphasized by political movements seeking some change, and the power to overpower emphasized by reactionary responses to those movements. In these cases it is difficult not to make moral judgments about injustice, nor is this something I think from which serious scholarship should refrain, but on these questions, I follow an ethical line that Spinoza drew, understanding ethics not in correlation to what is good or bad, but in terms of the things that either increase or decrease our power to act. Gilles Deleuze writes that Spinoza's "ethics presents itself as a theory of power, in opposition to morality as a theory of obligations."[14] Such a framework points to a politics of radicalism and reaction, not a correlation to what any given community or era finds palatable or unpalatable. It is not useful to describe either mode of power as universally praiseworthy and the other as universally objectionable. This ethics of power has "nothing to do with a morality," Deleuze writes; "If you do not know beforehand what good or bad you are capable of; you do not know beforehand what a body or mind can do, in a given encounter, given the arrangement, a different combination," it therefore makes better sense to treat the effects of these types of power in more nuanced ways.[15] The reason for this is that not only do these types of power often overlap, but also both modes of power are part of the human experience; both can be put to a variety of uses.[16]

But even though the two modes of power overlap, not to make a distinction between them, especially in English-language scholarship, may mistakenly suggest that power is a singular concept, or that it is a zero-sum game, something that, when possessed by the state, by capital, or by another system of domination, leaves little power left over. At worst, the lack of multiple applicable terms in English for the different modes of power can lead people to believe that they are powerless, especially when compared to others who are stronger, but this is a mistake. As Agamben, citing Aristotle, notes, "the *kithara* player keeps his ability [*potenza*] to play even when he does not play, and[. . .] the architect keeps his ability [*potenza*] to build even when he does not build."[17] These abilities and powers are intrinsic, and they are empirical phenomena, easily observable whenever a person learns or grows stronger, whenever people cooperate for mutual benefit, or when one person acts upon another. Even in desperate situations, several examples of which will appear in these pages, these intrinsic powers can be severely restricted or misdirected, but wherever there are people, so too there will be these powers.[18] There are no situations where people are powerless.

There are many situations, however, where the type and degree of power people possess may or may not be adequate to alter the situations in which they find themselves. This is one aspect of Marx's comment, which James quotes three times in the first hundred pages of *The Black Jacobins*, that people make their own history, but only such history as it is possible for them to make.[19] The systematic domination of the Atlantic world's colonial slavery depended on this inequality of power. As Linebaugh and Rediker have shown at length in a diverse set of circumstances in *The Many-Headed Hydra*, these are stories about exploitation and the resistance to exploitation, about cooperation among different kinds of people for contrasting purposes of profit and survival."[20] Like the people in Linebaugh and Rediker's history, some of the people and characters we meet below could not resist in effective ways, given the tremendous power to overpower wielded by the slave trade, but others could resist and did so given what power they could wield in their particular situations.

⑥　⑥　⑥

The problems of democracy's *kratos* appear in the work of still other historical and contemporary writers, including Emmanuel Sieyès, Marx, Walter Benjamin, Carl Schmitt, Hannah Arendt, Antonio Negri, and Jacques Rancière. Each writer attaches particular nuances to their terms, some of which I hope to capture here as they are relevant, in order to situate my terms in relation to them.

Gabriel Ash, in the translation to Frédéric Lordon's book *Willing Slaves of Capital: Spinoza and Marx on Desire*, writes that the "English word 'power' has two meanings that French (and Latin) distinguish with two separate words. *Puissance* (Latin *potentia*) can be thought of as inherent power (ability, power of acting, doing), whereas *pouvoir* (Latin *potestas*)[. . .] stands for relational, differential power (power over, social power, political power, etc.)."[21] In his notes on the translation of Gilles Deleuze and Félix Guattari's *A Thousand Plateaus*, Brian Massumi writes

> *puissance* and *pouvoir* are associated with very different concepts[. . .]. *Puissance* refers to a range of potential,[. . .] a "capacity for existence," "a capacity to affect or be affected," a capacity to multiply connections that may be realized by a given "body" to varying degrees in different situations.[. . .] The authors use *pouvoir* in a sense very close to Foucault's, as an instituted and reproducible relation of force, a selective concretization of potential.[22]

From the *Grundrisse* to the end of his career, Marx used the German *Arbiets-vermögen* to describe the concept most English scholarship either calls "labor power" or "labor capacity"; both terms are appropriate translations, and they both speak to the nature of the thing that Marx describes, an empirical phenomenon, intrinsic to the body, analogous to the French *puissance* and the terms other languages have for what I have called the first mode of power. In Samuel Moore and Edward Aveling's English translation of *Das Kapital*, Marx writes that "Labour-power exists only as a capacity, or power of the living individual."[23]

In English-language scholarship, or in work that has been translated into English, the most common terms used to describe the two modes of power are *constituent power* and *constituted power*. Of the many examples, among the most interesting is, as Agamben writes in *State of Exception*, the conversation—sometimes direct, at others, indirect—between Carl Schmitt and Walter Benjamin in several texts, including Schmitt's *Dictatorship*, which has only recently been translated into English, and Benjamin's "Critique of Violence," which, due to Benjamin's complex use of terms, is a text that is notoriously difficult to translate.[24] As Agamben notes, both texts were written in 1921, and when placed together, provide an invaluable insight into the problems of power. In *Dictatorship*, Schmitt generally renders the first mode of power in German as *Macht*, and when he names the phrase, he does so in French as *pouvoir constituant*; his term for the second mode of power is generally rendered in English translation as "constituted forces," in German as *Gewalten*, and in French as *pouvoir constitué*.[25] In Schmitt's work after *Dictatorship*, he largely drops the distinction between these powers, in effect hiding the existence of constituent power; this move raises confusion about the two modes of power, a confusion that serves Schmitt's purposes. Benjamin's concepts of lawmaking violence and law-preserving violence are analogous to Schmitt's concepts in method, perhaps, and motivation, but not always in their results.[26] The German title of his essay *"Zur Kritik der Gewalt,"* for example, points to the complexity of the situation: *walten*, one of his major terms, simultaneously means "to be powerful" and "to depose power." *Walten* is the root verb for violence, *Gewalt*, which explains why his terms are most often translated as lawmaking violence and law-preserving violence.

These problems of power likewise motivate Antonio Negri and Michael Hardt, who favor the terms *constituent power* and *constituted power* and often note that they build these terms from the distinction between *potenza* and *potere* in Negri's first language, Italian. In his explanation of these terms, Hardt suggests to think of the concepts not as referring exclusively to a noun, a constitution, a formal legal document, but rather as referring to a verb, to constitute, to cause to come into being.[27] Many things beyond legal documents can be constituted: communities, economies, associations. Priscilla Wald's book *Constituting Americans: Cultural Anxiety and Narrative Form* is among the best extended examinations of this concept.[28] As Hardt writes in his introduction to Negri's *Insurgencies: Constituent Power and the Modern State,*

> constituent power names the democratic forces of social transformation, the means by which humans make their own history. [It is] animated by the power not only to rebel against and overthrow the current order but also to create from below new democratic forms of social organization. Constituted power, in contrast, defines the fixed order of the constitution and the stability of its social structure. [. . .] Constituent power animates the constant activity of resistance and organization, rebellion and political innovation that arises within and against the constituted order.[29]

In *Homo Sacer*, Agamben sketches a debate between what he calls "constituting power" and constituted power; in more recent work, he reinterprets constituting power as "destituent power" in order to take fuller advantage of the nuances of Italian grammar.[30] Jacques Rancière simply and elegantly calls his interpretation of constituent power "politics" or "dissensus"; his term for constituted power is "the police."[31]

All of this has not been to suggest that these authors mean precisely the same ideas with their terms, but rather to show that a broad range of work has built upon the relations between what I call the two modes of power. Each of these writers constructs their terms in order to convey particular nuances, and a reader can consult their texts for an elucidation of those nuances, work which is not possible here. But for clarity, and as a way of providing an overview for the broad conversation into which these writers enter, the following schema may be useful.

What I call the first mode of power and the second mode of power are not meant to imply an order or precedence, although Schmitt does explicitly state a progression: he writes that every constituted power is in place because an earlier constituent power was able to constitute itself through some act, usually, as Jacques Derrida writes, through an originating act of violence.[32] This, of course, is the crux of the conversation for many of these authors. As they show, the logics of these two modes of power perhaps present themselves most clearly when they come into conflict. Consider William Lloyd Garrison's comment in *The Liberator* of August 1, 1856: "Unquestionably, every existing government on earth is to be overthrown by the growth of mind and

Figure 1: A Constellation of Concepts for Power		
First Mode of Power Power of ability/ "power to…"	{English}	Second Mode of Power Relational power/ "power over"
potentia	{Latin}	*potestas*
potenza	{Italian}	*potere*
pwisans	{Haitian Kreyol}	*pouvwa*
puissance	{French}	*pouvoir*
fuerza	*{Spanish}*	*poder*
Macht/Vermögen	{German}	*Gewalt*
constituent power	{Schmitt/Hardt and Negri}	constituted power
lawmaking violence	{Benjamin}	law-preserving violence
constituent/destituent power	{Agamben}	constituted power
dissensus/politics	{Rancière}	the police

moral regeneration of the masses."[33] This is perhaps more questionable than Garrison makes it seem, but his comment gets at the gist of the situation, and in his public speeches in the years before the American Civil War, he had a particularly strong way of illustrating the fact: as he reached the crescendo of his speeches, he would burn a copy of the United States Constitution.[34] Constituent power, as I write above, wants to grow, to change; constituted powers want to conserve, to perpetuate the relations they have over the people they govern. As Garrison knew well, constituted powers do not yield easily. Constituent powers may want to overthrow a regime, and that regime will not want to be overthrown. The outcome of the moment when they come into conflict makes all the difference: paper constitutions can be burned and governments can nevertheless stay in power, or governments can be overthrown and new constitutions written.

In the essay "Force of Law," Derrida, building from Georges Sorel, Benjamin, and others, describes the situations where such conflicts take place. His primary example is the moment when a general strike continues past the point of being declared illegal.[35] In that scenario, if the strikers prevail, they possess what Benjamin calls lawmaking violence; if the police prevail, they reinforce the fact that they possess law-preserving violence. Derrida therefore calls this the revolutionary situation—a constituent power in this scenario could show that it has sufficient force to overthrow and supplant a constituted power, or the constituted power, usually through its police or military, could show that it has sufficient force to conserve itself. What Derrida calls the revolutionary situation takes legal form in many countries under different names, but in English it is commonly known as the situation in which a group of people are read the Riot Act.

To be read the Riot Act is to be warned that constituted power is on the cusp of using force to conserve itself. For Derrida, Schmitt, and other theorists, the moment is important because in it the distinction between constituent power and constituted power comes into comparatively clear distinction. Schmitt in particular writes about the British law as a model and about the analogous laws of Weimar Germany, but it should be noted that riot acts are common features of legal frameworks in many states—Sedition Acts, for example, have been part of the United States legal code since 1787. The Haitian constitution of 1801 states, "There cannot exist in the colony corporations or associations that are contrary to public order.[. . .] All seditious gatherings should be dissolved immediately, first by way of verbal order and, if necessary, by armed force."[36] The language, intent, and implementation of these statutes may differ, but the logic of the situation in which they are enforced follows a common path: when a person in authority reads the text of the Riot Act, the group to whom it is read must disperse; if the crowd does not disperse after having been read the Riot Act, it becomes an unlawful assembly and can then be dispersed by force. Schmitt writes that the "whole idea of this regulation is that all the initiatives and directions rest with the local authorities—elected as they are by the citizens—and that the military commander is only an obedient executive."[37] This, ultimately, is a moment when the logic of political representation shows itself. As Nick Nesbitt writes, the system of representation itself is not designed to bring a constituent power to the point where it can flourish, but the reverse: "'representation' is another name for the alienation of one's power to act, its delegation to another party.[. . .] How one might mitigate that tendency toward alienation in a modern, large-scale democratic state is a political dilemma to which representation is not the solution, but the problem itself."[38] But to Schmitt, this was no dilemma—the issue for him is that sovereignty rests on the notion that the people have, at some point, consented to be ruled, and thus the representatives are, in Schmitt's words, "bearers" of constituent power.[39] It is a point that Schmitt asserts throughout his work: the representatives are both the holders of constituted power and the bearers of constituent power, and can thus use the prior consent of the people as a basis for the whole range of its activities, from daily administration to the maintenance of order, even if that order includes acts of state violence against those people.[40] When this consent was given expressly, by whom, exactly, and under what conditions, is obscure, but for Schmitt, it exists, and it lives on in perpetuity, or at least until it is overthrown by a new constituent power in an act of constituting itself.

Schmitt was not unaware of the cynical uses of repression. Earlier in his text, citing Montesquieu, Schmitt notes, "Unlimited power was exercised under the pretext of restoring order, and what, in the past, had been called 'freedom' was now called 'uproar' and 'disorder.'"[41] He also writes that "it may be the case that the exercise of the people's *pouvoir constituant* is inhibited and that the actual circumstances demand the removal of these obstacles to begin with, so that the constraint inhibiting the *pouvoir* is eliminated. The people's free will can be enslaved through contrived methods and external constraints, or by causing general confusion and disorder in the conditions."[42] This leads Schmitt to a conversation about how far the "bearer" of constituent power can go to confront such crowds and, if necessary, use lethal force against people to end a state of emergency.[43] Schmitt is careful on this point— his position is that the laws for the state of emergency must be spelled out, in order to stop dictatorship from evolving into totalitarianism.[44] Given those conditions, however, the representatives of the regime continue to operate as the bearers of constituent power and, as such, are within the law to take measures including, in Schmitt's example, the use of "poisoned gas against cities if, in a given case, this is the necessary measure for the restoration of security and order."[45] Having articulated this logic, Schmitt finds it highly problematic that the Weimar Constitution is silent on the situation. He writes that it "is absurd to reassure the president of the Reich that he can, say, allow the official authorities to ban newspapers when he can theoretically advance against cities with poison gas and threaten the death penalty or allow extraordinary commissions to impose it. The right over life and death is *implicite* [implicit], the right to suspend the freedom of the press is *explicite* [spelled out]."[46] These are Schmitt's stated objectives: to protect the sovereignty of constituted power, even if doing so includes state terrorism within that state's territory, against its own citizens. The parameters of the state's available actions, he strongly advocates, need to be spelled out explicitly in that state's constitution.

As this example and others in the next section suggest, it is not a clash of reason one finds in the revolutionary situation, but rather, when the Riot Act is read, a clash ensues between the relative force of constituent power and constituted power. Schmitt writes that the "theory of the *pouvoir constituant* is incomprehensible simply as a form of mechanistic rationalism. The people, the nation, the primordial force of any state—these always constitute new organs. From the infinite, incomprehensible abyss of force [*Macht*] of the *pouvoir constituant*, new forms emerge incessantly, which it can destroy at any time and in which its power is never limited for good."[47] The root problem at issue, for Schmitt, is the possibility that a crowd, a new form of constituent power, could destabilize a constituted power. It is the main theme of his career, and in the works that follow *Dictatorship*, he calls it the problem of sovereignty.[48]

To inhibit or halt this destabilization was Schmitt's major contribution to the history of political thought; for Schmitt, the issue is how to maintain constituted power through such states of emergency. He writes that the "justification for dictatorship consists in the fact that, although it ignores existing law, it is only doing so in order to save it."[49] One must understand Schmitt's argument here clearly: in such a situation, a dictatorship is not a form of government that operates in opposition to democracy. In his terms, a commissarial dictatorship seeks to restore an older constitution after a revolutionary situation, and a sovereign dictatorship seeks to make new law that is nevertheless in keeping with an older regime. In either case, Schmitt's view is that a constituted power, whether called dictatorship or democracy, continues to be the "bearer" of constituent power through the process of representation.

For the moment, it is apparent that the collapsing together of constituent power and constituted power has been a contortion and assimilation of constituent power by constituted power. This is not to devalue the concept of constituent power, but rather to show that it can, as Schmitt suggests, be enveloped into the orbit of constituted power.[50] It is logically the case—with notable exceptions—that a previous constituent power, having been successful, having constituted itself, having transformed itself from an insurgency into a new government, for example, would then seek to conserve itself against future threats of some subsequent new constituent power. As Agamben writes, several theorists, perhaps most prominently Benjamin in "Critique of Violence," have attempted to find a way out of the dialectic of constituent power evolving into constituted power ad infinitum—this is the problem of a so-called permanent revolution.[51] I leave that problem for another project; to sum up the situation here, it will have to be sufficient to share an anecdote from the contemporary Occupy movement—one that may be a fiction but that nevertheless puts this problem clearly—in which a crowd of protesters, assembled to register their displeasure with a range of grievances, were told by police, "Disperse, in the name of the People of California!" To which the protesters responded: "We are the People of California!"

⑥   ⑥   ⑥

The terms *constituent power* and *constituted power*, Schmitt notes, come from democratic theory.[52] The distinction is useful, but with the exception, however, of Rancière's versions—"politics" and "the police"—in English-language scholarship, the terms are a bit clumsy. The two forms of the verb to constitute suggest a relation, as Schmitt notes: every constituted power is the result of some previous constituent power that successfully constituted itself.[53] But not every constituent power is successful in constituting itself—movements are ignored, rebellions are crushed, protests often seem temporary, even if they send out resonances. But this does not mean that the movements, rebels, and protesters are powerless. To the contrary, such people show their power even when they do not achieve their goals, a fact that the term *constituent power* seems unable to convey. It does not make sense, therefore, to call some examples constituent powers, because they do not result in constituting anything. There are times when a constituted power is sufficiently strong to reject any challenge to it. This does not mean that the power that presented the challenge was powerless, it means only that it lacked sufficient force to be a successful challenge. Movements may be ephemeral or unsustainable, but because they do not develop into powers that can force themselves on others does not render them invisible or unimportant. Perhaps Benjamin's terms *lawmaking* and *law- preserving* violence show the issue most clearly. Lawmaking violence seeks to make new law, of course, and law-preserving violence seeks to conserve it. Yet there are situations where violence is used as a just means but makes no new law, either literal or figurative.

The contributions that the writers noted above make to the democratic theories of power are substantial, but I wish to expand the scope of their conversations. Agamben, for example, writes of the American Civil War but makes no mention of slavery; he refers to the French Revolution but does not mention the Haitian Revolution, even though it would add more substance to his already significant analysis.[54] Little of this work mentions race or slavery, which is a curious omission, because, in many cases, race and slavery illustrate quite well the themes of exclusion, power, and violence that this set of thinkers so productively analyze. Negri's book *Insurgencies*, which is among the longest recent interventions into questions of constituent power, is nearly completely blind to issues of race and slavery. Therefore, these thinkers are often silent about the particular problems of the larger Atlantic world and its intersectional characteristics of racial domination, transnational circulation, and economic exploitation. Put another way, the scholarship on the modes of power comes largely from a continental perspective, which is useful but not fully adequate for an analysis in other contexts.

Furthermore, in English-language scholarship the word *constituent* usually refers to enfranchised participants in an electoral body—elected representatives refer to "their constituents," meaning the people who can vote in their districts or jurisdictions. "Constituent power," therefore, seems unable to convey that such power is found in all people, not just the enfranchised.

Most groups under consideration in this project, like the 2,000 in the Haitian Revolution, were resisting enslavement. Part of the apparatus of Atlantic world slavery in the long nineteenth century was the denial of their humanity. Therefore, inherent in their struggles was the assertion that they were human beings, regardless of the laws and cultural norms that they resisted. It is for these reasons, and to convey nuances that hopefully will become increasingly clear over the pages of this book, that a different, though analogous, term is necessary here.

Lucy Parsons, whose work is one subject for analysis in this book's second chapter, writes that the "introduction of new ideas into a man's mind is not accompanied by the use of a specially coined word, but by the adaptation of old words to broader uses."[55] In my view, interpretation is reinterpretation—it is not the creation of something from nothing, but rather the act of establishing a new meaning for an existing concept. The term *direct democracy* is commonly understood as a more immediate form of organization or government, usually drawing some inspiration from the government of ancient Athens. There are many admirable studies that examine worker cooperatives, participatory communities, political movements, or maroon colonies, which, in their various ways, exemplify functioning direct democracies.[56] This book could be seen as a companion to those volumes—it certainly participates in the same larger conversations—but I do not mean to convey what is usually meant by this term.

As I hope the prologue above makes clear, my intent is to theorize a concept of direct democracy from alternative materials; rather than rebuild ancient Athens, I mean to evoke the personhood of even those who have traditionally been excluded from the *demos*, and to link it to the modes of power suggested by *kratos*. As Agamben points out, those kept from legal inclusion in the *demos* are what he calls "bare life," those who are included only by virtue of being excluded.[57] Slaves, women, those without property, prisoners of war, prisoners of the state, and captives in various places and eras have been excluded from citizenship and—in the most dangerous cases—treated as inhuman, without any rights that a state need respect. Yet they are included as well because, among other reasons, their labor is necessary to produce wealth for others who can exercise power over them. In addition to a far more inclusive interpretation of *demos*, I wish the term to convey the nuances expressed in this section—the dynamics of the modes of power, their complexity and adaptability.

In my interpretation, direct democracy is the power of ability when multiplied by cooperation. In what follows I retain the term *constituted power*—it is apt, and it provides a link back to the conversations I have sketched here.

But while my interpretation of direct democracy is analogous in some ways to how constituent power has been interpreted, the differences mentioned above make a distinction necessary. My interpretation follows what I have called the first mode of power through a particular path, from innate capacity to cooperation, and ultimately to the emergent, collective properties of that power. Whether rendered as *potentia*, *puissance*, *Macht*, or another term, the first mode of power is innate to the body—abilities atrophy or increase with neglect or practice, of course, but the builder does not lose her ability when she is not building; the player does not lose his ability when he is not playing. As Spinoza wrote, cooperation with others increases this power,[58] and as Marx wrote, in particular conditions, when workers cooperate, their *Arbeitsvermörgen*—their labor power, or labor capacity—shows "not only . . . an increase in the productive power of the individual, by means of co-operation, but the creation of a new power, the collective power of the masses."[59] In such situations, the capacities of each person may be multiplied by the capacities of every other person, and the group's collective power is therefore an emergent property of that cooperation. Put more simply, in certain situations, a group's power can add up to more than the sum of its parts. There are many situations where people increase their power to act when they cooperate, and when they do, I call it direct democracy.

Uses of the Swarm Metaphor

The previous section situated my interpretation of direct democracy in conversation with other critical work; this section begins to sketch a history of examples for this interpretation, a history that will continue in the chapters to follow. As mentioned above, this book's secondary argument is that many writers in the Americas during the long nineteenth century recognized the power I call direct democracy, even though they used a variety of other terms to describe it, and when they did, they used the metaphor of the swarm. Much of the work on this project has been to track the metaphor in many different texts; the examples in this book show that when a reader sees the language of the swarm in the contexts under consideration here, the metaphor is like a signpost, pointing to the presence of direct democratic power.

The political use of swarm metaphors is both common and complicated, and its interpretations have always been contested. Some of these perspectives show the common scientific beliefs of their eras, some show their political aspirations or superstitions. Given the perspective of different writers, the use of the swarm metaphor gives us information about the workings of this collective power, whether merely to describe it, to praise it, or to denigrate it. The insults, perhaps, prove the point best: used in this way, the swarm metaphor often shows that a writer has judged that a swarm of people, protesters, or picketers has sufficient power not just to be noticed, but to be dealt with in some way. The representations of the swarm metaphor run a range from the bigoted, as in Arthur Herzog's book *The Swarm*, with its myth of the hyper-aggressive "Africanized" bee, to the revered, as in Hilda M. Ransome's book *The Sacred Bee in Ancient Times and Folklore*.[60] The Bible notes that swarms are both leaderless and a model for industriousness.[61] A significant amount of recent work has studied the remarkable collaborations of actual swarms to see what lessons could be learned for the dynamics of human communities, as for example, in James Surowiecki's book *The Wisdom of Crowds: Why the Many Are Smarter than the Few and How Collective Wisdom Shapes Businesses, Economies, Societies, and Nations* and Peter Miller's book *The Smart Swarm: How to Work Efficiently, Communicate Effectively, and Make Better Decisions Using the Secrets of Flocks, Schools, and Colonies*.[62] I wish to note briefly one important aspect of these studies: the command over labor is one of the most important features of both slavery and capitalism—without dictating to workers the terms and conditions of their labor, there is no profit in either system.[63] The enslaver and the capitalist view this hierarchy as natural and normal, even beneficial to the worker. The scholarship on more horizontal forms of organization like swarms is presenting a challenge to that idea. There are some situations best handled by small groups of experts, situations where particular specialized knowledge and expertise is required; there are others where a broad array of perspectives allows a group to see solutions that one person could not have seen alone. One of the tricks that capitalism and other forms of hierarchy play is to pretend that such hierarchies are necessary where they are not.

My task here is to show that the swarm is most often used as a metaphor for a type of collective power. A particularly insightful example is how John Brown attempted to persuade Frederick Douglass to join the raid on Harpers Ferry. Brown said, "Come with me, Douglass; I will protect you with my life. I want you for a special purpose. When I strike, the bees will begin to swarm, and I shall want you to help hive them."[64] In Brown's plan, his attack on Harpers Ferry was to have triggered a broader set of rebellions against slavery, taking the shape, in Brown's most ambitious imagining, of a sustained guerrilla war against the slavocracy, striking from bases throughout the Appalachian Mountain range into the Cotton Kingdom. As the attacks were to have progressed, Brown and Douglass were to have continually freed people from the plantations on which they were enslaved and recruited them into this army for subsequent attacks.

While John Brown's use of the metaphor shows its most common employment, as signifying a type of collective power, the metaphor has always been in contention—how that power is organized, the purposes to which it has been put, tend to show the political thinking of the era in which the metaphor is used. In *The History of Animals*, for example, Aristotle states that every bee hive has more than one king. A "hive goes to ruin if there be too few kings," he writes, "not because of the anarchy thereby ensuing," but because the king contributes to the procreation of the next generation.[65] A hive will also go to ruin, he suggests, if there are too many kings—this situation would lead to "faction." These were widespread beliefs, and they held, according to the best of anyone's knowledge, until the seventeenth century, when several researchers, including Jan Swammerdam, in his *Historia Insectorum Generalis*, reported that the king had ovaries.[66]

The king therefore became the queen bee, and her personification continued along these royal and gender lines, aided by work such as Charles Butler's book *The Feminine Monarchie*, published in 1609, which was the standard text on beekeeping for more than two centuries, and Joseph Warder's book *The True Amazons: Or, The Monarchy of Bees, Being a New Discovery and Improvement of those Wonderful Creatures*, published in 1712.[67] In orderly Enlightenment style, the title page of *The True Amazons* states that the book will show: "I. That they are all governed by a QUEEN. II. The amazing Beauty and Dignity of her Person. III. Her extraordinary Authority and Power. IV. Their exceeding Loyalty and unparalleled Love to their Queen." It seems that Warder wanted both to flatter the court and to attract a wider audience, because he concludes his book with a recipe for "how to make the English WINE or MEAD, equal, if not superior to the best of other Wines."[68]

On the other hand, to thinkers like John Burroughs, the swarm provides a model of a cooperative society, a functioning democracy. Burroughs writes in "The Pastoral Bees" that the

> notion has always very generally prevailed that the queen of the bees is an absolute ruler, and issues her royal orders to willing subjects.[. . .] But the fact is, a swarm of bees is an absolute democracy, and kings and despots can find no warrant in their example. The power and authority are entirely vested in the great mass, the workers. They furnish all the brains and foresight of the colony, and administer its affairs. Their word is law, and both king and queen must obey.[69]

As these examples suggest, the anthropomorphization of animals is fraught territory.[70] From a scientific perspective, many studies of the dynamics of actual swarms include a literary caveat: the queen is an example of a situation where our understanding of the thing has outgrown the language that we still use to describe that thing.[71] The fact that swarms of bees—and ants, as well as certain schools of fish and flocks of birds, to name just a few—do not only exist but thrive without a leader is an uncontroversial statement in the scholarship.[72] So while the anthropomorphization of bees is no surprise, its history reveals two interesting assumptions that are still apparent in the language we use: first, because one bee was larger, that it must be male, and second, that this larger bee was in charge. A hierarchy of royal bees and worker bees made intuitive sense to people who were familiar with hierarchical political and social structures. Such assumptions still carry weight in many situations: it is common to hear that order comes from hierarchy, and that without it, no form of organization, no community is possible, that the absence of hierarchy is mayhem. Yet the democracy of worker bees also makes sense to writers with alternative views. It is perhaps for these reasons that the swarm is one of Michael Hardt and Antonio Negri's favorite metaphors, appearing frequently in several of their works.[73] Hardt and Negri write in *Multitude* that the "swarms that we see emerging in the new network political organizations[...] are composed of a multitude of different creative agents.[...] The members of the multitude do not have to become the same or renounce their creativity in order to communicate and cooperate with each other. They remain different in terms of race, sex, sexuality, and so forth."[74] Here, the metaphor stands for a certain diversity in what Hardt and Negri call the multitude, and a rebuttal to much of the thinking on mass movements that suggests that those movements have a homogenizing effect on their participants.

But while Hardt and Negri see diversity in the metaphor, Frantz Fanon, in *The Wretched of the Earth*, writes that the

> terms the settler uses when he mentions the native are zoological terms. He speaks of the yellow man's reptilian motions, of the stink of the native quarter, of breeding swarms, of foulness, of spawn, of gesticulations. When the settler seeks to describe the native fully in exact terms he constantly refers to the bestiary.[...] The native knows all this, and laughs to himself every time he spots an allusion to the animal world in the other's words. For he knows that he is not an animal; and it is precisely at the moment he realizes his humanity that he begins to sharpen the weapons with which he will secure its victory.[75]

As Fanon states and as Michael Lundblad affirms in *The Birth of a Jungle*,[76] there is a long history in which to make a person an other, to remove people from the *demos*, is not just to exclude them from a particular political community, but also to remove them from humanity: in other words, to dehumanize

groups of people has often been to animalize them.⁷⁷ These ideologies have
had material consequences; the most relevant examples for this study are laws
and cultural norms denying the humanity of enslaved people as a basis for
their continued bondage. Furthermore, as studies like Andrew S. Curran's
The Anatomy of Blackness: Science and Slavery in the Age of Enlightenment
show, scientific discourse during the era did much to make the political use
of animal metaphors seem natural and normal.

Much like Fanon, in a letter to Arnold Ruge, later collected in the *Deutsch-
Französische Jahrbücher*, Marx writes that

> people who do not feel that they are human beings become the property of their
> masters like a breed of slaves or horses. [. . .] The philistine world is a *political
> world of animals*, and if we have to recognize its existence, nothing remains for
> us but simply to agree to this *status quo*. Centuries of barbarism engendered and
> shaped it, and now it confronts us as a consistent system, the principle of which is
> the *dehumanised world*.[. . .] [W]hen homage is paid to [these masters] and they
> survey the swarming mass of these brainless beings, what is more likely to occur
> to them than the thought that Napoleon had at the Berezina? It is said of Napo-
> leon that he pointed to the crowd of drowning people below him and exclaimed
> to his companion: "*Voyez ces crapauds!*" [Just look at these toads!] This is prob-
> ably a fabrication, but it is nonetheless true. Despotism's sole idea is contempt for
> man, the dehumanised man, and this idea has the advantage over many others of
> being at the same time a fact. The despot always sees degraded people.⁷⁸

Such exclusion and dehumanization, Marx suggests, did not spring, fully
formed, from the earth, but were produced over time in the service of for-
tifying and maintaining hierarchies of various sorts. In Fanon's context the
hierarchy is of colonizer and colonized, and in other contexts is part of an
ideology supporting the global slave trade, or to buttress racial, class, or gender inequalities. One could choose to believe that such hierarchies are natural
and normal, but the hierarchical world, Marx suggests, has been achieved
by centuries of systematic, institutionalized force. Such a hierarchical system
may seem natural or normal because it is ubiquitous, but that appearance
is a constructed veneer. That a hierarchical world exists, or that such ideas
exist in the world, may be a fact, but it is not an immutable one. Such a view
produces a tiered understanding of human relations, where masters look with
contempt at those below them, and those who look up from below seem to
have lost their humanity.

The dehumanization Fanon and Marx describe was one of the ideological
pillars of the slave trade and of the dominant political forces in the Atlantic

world in the revolutionary age. Writers like George Fitzhugh, who belonged to the liberal, paternal wing of proslavery opinion, interpreted democracy and equality in ways that aligned with their views, rather than opposing them. They understood democracy as the rule of the best of the people and equality as equality of type to type: men were equal to men, women to women, and slaves to slaves, but unequal across types. Fitzhugh's project was to advocate for a hierarchy that he thought would be a stopgap against poverty and unnecessary suffering. In a community where there are leaders and led, he believes, where people are fit for their station in life, conflicts are lessened and people prosper according to the direction they provide or receive.[79] A community without slavery and the order it brings would be barbaric; he states that such towns would "swarm with paupers and misery."[80] For example, Fitzhugh writes, "We agree with Mr. Jefferson that all men have natural and inalienable rights." He continues:

> To violate or disregard such rights is to oppose the designs and plans of Providence, and cannot "come to good." The order and subordination observable in the physical, animal, and human world show that some are formed for higher, others for lower stations—the few to command, the many to obey. We conclude that about nineteen out of every twenty individuals have "a natural and inalienable right" to be taken care of and protected, to have guardians, trustees, husbands, or masters; in other words, they have a natural and inalienable right to be slaves. The one in twenty are as clearly born or educated or some way fitted for command and liberty. Not to make them rulers or masters is as great a violation of natural right as not to make slaves of the mass. A very little individuality is useful and necessary to society—much of it begets discord, chaos and anarchy.[81]

Fitzhugh does not argue against democracy and its ideals as such, but rather against a deluge of democracy, an excess of liberty. Fitzhugh's use of the language of the US Declaration of Independence may seem self-contradictory, but it was actually a common and strategic act of appropriation: rather than defining slavery as an anomaly within a democracy, he states that slavery is entirely consistent with an understanding of democracy. His use of the swarm metaphor is like many in the long nineteenth century, linked to the denigration of crowds and mobs. Fitzhugh's book, *Cannibals All! Or, Slaves without Masters,* reads like a threat to anyone who would challenge the relations between masters and slaves: without such a hierarchy, our communities would degenerate to the point where people would eat one another.

Fitzhugh writes that the "Reader will thus see that Abolition contemplates the total overthrow of the Family and all other existing social, moral, religious, and governing institutions."[82] Fitzhugh's metaphor of swarms of paupers and slaves is intended to provoke a fear of change and a justification for maintaining a political system he saw as just. Without hierarchy and the particular forms of order it maintains, many feared that mayhem would rule. For thinkers like Fitzhugh, any challenge to hierarchical order was a slippery slope leading to general disorder, and it required force to stop it.

⊚   ⊚   ⊚

Fitzhugh's use of the swarm metaphor combined with the state violence that he calls for to suppress such swarming is no accident. In the history of animal metaphors used to dehumanize people, *Schwärmerei* has a particular place. The term is used often in nineteenth-century writing, particularly in its German original, and in rather well-known places, including *The Communist Manifesto* and in Kant's writing about enlightenment. *Schwärmerei* is meant to describe people who act irrationally—the term is most often translated from the German as "enthusiasm" or "zealotry." Alberto Toscano notes that the term was coined by Martin Luther, who used it to castigate the peasant revolts that Engels would later write about in *The Peasant War in Germany*.[83] Andrew Poe's recent dissertation, "The Sources and Limits of Political Enthusiasm," considers *Schwärmerei* and a related concept, *Enthusiasmus*, at length. Both concepts, he argues, were used to describe situations where people were operating outside the bounds of rationality—the Brothers Grimm, to give just one interesting example, defined *Schwärmerei* as "the mental state of heresy and a foggy confusion of concepts."[84] Poe takes a more nuanced approach than has traditionally been taken, building from recent work on political affect. "Many view the use of political emotions generally—and enthusiasm in particular—as perilous to democracy, preferring instead to encourage the rationalization of interests because of its predictability," Poe writes. "Such concern for emotions that motivate political closure seems salient, especially in the context of new and developing democracies, where allegiance formations have proved vulnerable to hyper-nationalism. But [. . .] not all political emotions need motivate closure. I elaborate an analytic and behavioral distinction between enthusiasm (which, I argue, leads to open allegiances) and fanaticism (which results in closure)," concepts that correlate, in Poe's reading, to *Schwärmerei* and *Enthusiasmus*.[85]

The metaphor can be turned on its head, and used differently, as Marx and Engels do in the *Manifesto*, writing: "*Sie hat die heiligen Schauer der frommen Schwärmerei, der ritterlichen Begeisterung, der spießbürgerlichen Wehmuth in dem eiskalten Wasser egoistischer Berechnung ertränkt*," which, in most translations, including Robert C. Tucker's anthology *The Marx–Engels Reader*, is translated as "It [the bourgeoisie] has drowned the most heavenly ecstasies of religious fervour, of chivalrous enthusiasm, of philistine sentimentalism, in the icy water of egotistical calculation."[86] Here the metaphor conveys irony. In most other situations—often related to arguments for reading the Riot Act to a group of protesters or revolutionaries—*Schwärmerei* is part of a vocabulary and a logic that precipitates state violence. Kant employs it in his essay "What Is Orientation in Thought?" and does so to link it to what he calls a "lawless use of reason" and "civil coercion," which is his term for the repression an authority will undertake when reasoning has gone beyond the limits set by that authority. As Warren Montag writes, the situation "can only provoke the authorities who, seeing that reason cannot govern itself, will impose their government upon it to the detriment of all."[87] Thus, *Schwärmerei* is the euphemism for reason that has dared to go beyond the limits set for it by an authority or a constituted power. Put more directly, this "lawless use of reason" presents a radical threat to constituted power. It might be said, from a certain perspective, that *Schwärmerei* alters Kant's famous dictum and says instead, argue as much as you want, and disobey when necessary. But constituted powers generally do not tolerate such threats for long. As Montag notes, this is the foundation for the argument that constituted power makes that those who cannot govern themselves must be governed by others. From the perspective of constituted power, arguments or action against it are often seen as irrational; if one sees a constituted power as rational, any radical challenge to it will be seen as irrational, and the judgment from that perspective brings consequences.

The writers we will see use the metaphor in this way, most prominently Carl Schmitt, Thomas Carlyle, and Thomas Gray, participate in a tradition of writers who, in their defense of a particular constituted power, deny that others who critique or act against that power have any rationality. One has to walk carefully, of course: that the interpretation of rationality is made to serve constituted power here does not justify jettisoning the concept *tout court*. As Nesbitt writes, for many writers, including Spinoza, "reason stands opposed to 'prejudice,' 'superstition,' and 'fanaticism.'"[88] But the writers who employ the concept of *Schwärmerei* deny the alternative rationality of others as a justification for defending a constituted power with force.[89] As Michael Hoelzl and Graham Ward write in their translators' introduction to Schmitt's *Dictatorship*, Schmitt believed that the "romantic individual[. . .] was incapable of making decisions," because such a person was motivated by impulse, not reason.[90] Schmitt writes that the

> constructing artists of the state viewed the mass of people that needed to be
> organized into a state as an object that had to be shaped, like a material, by their

will. According to humanist belief, in people—the uneducated masses, the var-iegated animals, [. . .] the 'many-coloured beast with many heads' as Plato calls it,[. . .]—there was something irrational that needed to be governed and led by reason. But, if people are irrational, then one cannot negotiate with them or forge contracts; rather they must be mastered through cunning or violence. In this case reason cannot make itself evident, it does not argue; it dictates.[91]

The logic is quite cunning, actually: as Marx noted above, the despot always sees degraded people. This despot in question here demands that a critic remain within the bounds of what the despot considers to be rational, and when the critic moves beyond those bounds, the despot calls foul. That boundary breaking is then grounds to use force against the critic—to oper-ate with a different understanding of rationality is to invite the despot's force. But reacting with force shows the despot's hand and further cultivates the dehumanized world that Marx says the despot seeks. Force, not reason, fol-lows the reading of the Riot Act; force is the foundation upon which such a dehumanized world is built.

In gentler language, this is what Michel Foucault, in *Fearless Speech*, calls the "aristocratic thesis": because in a democracy, the people are the most numerous, and include the worst citizens, the best citizens are overruled. Therefore, what is best for the *demos*, the people, cannot be what is best for the *polis*, the city.[92] Schmitt repeats this logic in condensed form in several strategic moments of his book, stating simply: "reason dictates."[93] If the *demos* are irrational, and one cannot negotiate with irrationality, the conclusion must be that such irrationality must be confronted with force. To thinkers like Schmitt, who view a particular constituted power as rational and just, the use of force becomes not only rational, but also justified. To walk through this logic carefully is one of Schmitt's main tasks in *Dictatorship* and, therefore, why he places such emphasis on the Riot Act.[94]

Schmitt is a careful, methodical thinker, so therefore he does not reference to any great degree the contemporary and substantial body of popular work on the madness of crowds, but these writings reach strikingly similar conclu-sions, even if they differ in the seriousness of their methods. It is worth not-ing, even briefly, their similarities. The worst iterations of this line of thinking are represented in the popular psychology of the era. As Gustave Le Bon writes,

What constituted a people, a unity, a whole, becomes in the end an agglomera-tion of individualities lacking cohesion, and artificially held together for a time by its traditions and institutions. It is at this stage that men, divided by their interests and aspirations, and incapable any longer of self-government, require directing in their pettiest acts, and that the State exerts an absorbing influence. With the definite loss of its old ideal the genius of the race entirely disappears; it is a mere swarm of isolated individuals and returns to its original state—that of a crowd.[95]

Le Bon and his co-thinkers strike an emotional note, so there is good reason why Schmitt makes no reference to this body of work, although he clearly agrees with its gist: there is very little logic or evidence to be found in Le Bon's work, but there is ample bigotry, veiled as pseudoscience. As John Plotz writes in *The Crowd*, a sustained effort to rebut this bigotry is a futile endeavor.[96] Plotz states that Elias Canetti's book *Masse und Macht*, translated into English as *Crowds and Power*, is the best book in this tradition, yet he cannot imagine arguing with it: the book offers no proof for its claims. Plotz writes that "it is possible to be moved by [Canetti] (he moves me), but it is not possible to be educated. For that reason, the notion of a rebuttal, even an engagement, came to seem hopeless."[97] For my part, I can only echo Plotz: reading through Le Bon's unveiled bigotry against the working class, toward women, and toward colonized people makes his writings, and the work of his epigones, lose all credibility.[98]

But one note might be made in parting from this group. As Le Bon writes, correctly, crowds have the power to destabilize any form of authority—a point that Schmitt also recognizes.[99] The fact that so many other writers have chosen to call upon the language of swarms suggests that the metaphor has both creative potential and destructive power, that it is a valuable tool in a political vocabulary. So, to paraphrase Marx, what separates the worst of architects from the best of bees is the capacity to imagine, to think abstractly. We humans have the creativity to imagine that another world is possible; without that ability and the urge to act upon it, political change would be impossible. Part of this ability is the capacity to learn, to rethink old ideas in new ways. The metaphor of the swarm is linked to the constituted and colonial powers that Fanon and Marx critique, but to some degree, the language of domination can be put to new purposes as a tool for liberation. Such is the case for Linebaugh and Rediker—as they state about the body of people who make up the mythology of the many-headed hydra, they first "had to translate it out of the idiom of monstrosity."[100]

Schmitt's view that reason dictates, that some are fit to rule and that others are fit only to follow, finds its rebuttal in alternative appeals to rationality, as when Nesbitt writes that the "Haitian Revolution scandalized the North Atlantic Enlightenment powers because it was essentially an affirmation of true democracy: the proper and logical right of anyone, absolutely anyone, to rule."[101] If the assumption is that there are some people who do not possess the autonomy required to rule themselves, they will need to be ruled by others. If the reverse is true, it leads to revolutionary possibilities. If all are autonomous beings, capable of self-governance, the ideological bases of slavery crumble, as does the line of thought that finds its fullest expression in Schmitt. At times, these powers play out in the revolutionary situation, but not always. The power I call direct democracy interacts with constituted power in ways that can be spectacular but can also be subtle. Large acts of rebellion and repression get more attention than quieter interactions do, but both can show the dynamics of the modes of power.

In this book's chapters, I show how the problems and possibilities of democracy's *kratos*, what I call direct democracy, play out in several related situations throughout the Americas during the long nineteenth century. For this task, I wish to echo Cedric Robinson's objective in *Black Marxism*, namely, that "as a scholar it was never my purpose to exhaust the subject [of a black radical tradition], only to suggest that it was there.[102] Chapter 1 analyzes what is, in my judgment, the single best example of direct democratic power, the 2,000 leaders in the Haitian Revolution. How, this chapter asks, did the revolution's participants succeed in freeing themselves from slavery when their leadership structure became unstable? When James, in *The Black Jacobins*, describes people acting together as a swarm, what does he convey with this metaphor? James, perhaps to a greater degree than any of the other authors included here, is able to recognize direct democratic power. This chapter explores how he was able to do so.

Chapter 2 more fully substantiates the concept of direct democracy by showing a transnational debate between Thomas Carlyle, Walt Whitman, and Lucy Parsons. In his essay "Shooting Niagara: And After?," Carlyle has contempt for "swarms" of working-class activists, women, and recently freed slaves seeking to be included in the electoral franchise. In *Democratic Vistas*, Whitman responds directly to Carlyle but moves beyond representative systems, arguing for "democracy in all public and private life." Parsons suggests that direct democracy is a key driver of social progress.

The power I call direct democracy is an empirical phenomenon, yet the literary representations of it are often masked. In chapter 3, I show how *The Confessions of Nat Turner* is a literary misdirection, leading readers mistakenly to understand what was the work of a group of people as the work of one person. Nat Turner the person and Nat Turner the symbol are both important, but the rebellion in which he participated was not the work of one person.

Through a reading of B. Traven's Mahogany Novels—six stories that show the rise and fall of the Mexican Revolution—in chapter 4, I examine direct democratic power as a collective and complex phenomenon. Traven shows at length how people acting alone, while possessing a certain kind of power, were insufficiently powerful to bring about substantive changes in their situations. When Traven's characters begin to cooperate, he represents them as a swarm; they show how direct democracy is multiplied in collective dynamics.

In chapter 5, I examine direct democracy as what Gilles Deleuze, following Spinoza, calls active power, and I do so through a reading of Marie Vieux Chauvet's novella *Love*. Dictatorships such as the one that Chauvet represents produce reactive powers: fear, suspicion, and silence. Yet they also repress active powers. In an overlooked part of the novella, Claire, the main character in *Love*, and her friend Dora show that even in the most difficult environments imaginable, two people can cooperate for mutually beneficial ends.

In the conclusion to this book, I return to what I called above the two paths for interpreting the etymology of democracy, sketching out further research about how direct democratic power might relate to political movements and to the forms of community organization that call themselves democratic, including traditional forms of representative democracy and more radical forms, such as what Spinoza calls absolute democracy.

"There Are 2,000 Leaders": The Swarm Metaphor and a Logic of Collective Action in C. L. R. James's *The Black Jacobins*

On July 1, 1802, Napoleon Bonaparte wrote to his brother-in-law, Charles Leclerc, the French officer tasked with quelling the Haitian Revolution, that he wanted him to deport "all the Black generals," because "without this [. . .] we will have done nothing, and an immense and beautiful colony will always remain a volcano, and will inspire no confidence in capitalists, colonists, or commerce."[1] During that summer and fall, the French colonial forces continued to fight the many insurgent groups in the various ways in which they encountered each other, but Bonaparte's letter conveys the overarching French strategy at this late stage of the Haitian Revolution. The largest achievements of this strategy were undoubtedly the capture and exile of Toussaint Louverture, who was the first among the revolutionary generals, and Leclerc's manipulation of the remaining black generals into fighting for the French, against the insurgents.[2] The strategy was built on the belief that to remove the leaders was to end the revolution. To this line of thinking, the groups of insurgents were merely "motley crowd[s]"[3] which would eventually collapse after their big leaders were removed.

Bonaparte and Leclerc's plan is a common, and often successful, counterrevolutionary strategy.[4] It may seem unbelievable, therefore, that the Haitian Revolution not only sustained itself when its leadership structure became unstable but adapted and grew to the point where Leclerc would write that it was not enough to have removed Toussaint, because 2,000 leaders had emerged to take his place.[5] Considering how stories and scholarship have traditionally portrayed such events, it is difficult to imagine the American Revolution at any moment without Washington, Jefferson, and Adams; the Mexican Revolution without Villa and Zapata; and the Cuban Revolution without Castro or Che, but *mutatis mutandis*, in Saint Domingue in 1802, their counterparts were captured, pacified, or killed. This is not to suggest such leadership is trivial—quite the contrary. The importance of Toussaint, Dessalines, Christophe, Moïse, and the other big leaders is considerable. The big leaders' contributions to the Haitian Revolution make the fact that the 2,000 could operate without them, if not in outright opposition to them, more remarkable, not less.

But although these events are remarkable, they are not inexplicable. As C. L. R. James emphasizes by quoting, twice, a letter from Leclerc written to the French minister of marine, the colonial powers had "a false idea of the country in which [they] fight and the men whom [they] fight against."[6] Put plainly, the insurgents were not irrational, but rather were well prepared for the task, and the fact that the revolution adapted and grew into a general insurrection at this point is proof of the matter. As Nick Nesbitt suggests, the Haitian Revolution was not unthinkable; rather, it shows that the colonial ideology failed to think through the simplest axioms of political philosophy: all people ought to be free, and that when they are made unfree, they will resist to the degree and in the ways available to them.[7] It is logical that the Haitian Revolution's 2,000 leaders emerged out of resistance to the domination of slavery, likewise to expect that the 2,000 would seek out a substantive alternative to that domination. As Carolyn Fick suggests, "every form of enslavement generates in one way or another an opposing struggle for liberation."[8] In this case, the decentralized, networked forms of resistance were quite precisely tailored to defeating the centralized, more hierarchical French colonial forces.

To say that the Haitian Revolution in 1802 was leaderless is not to say that it was being driven by accident or happenstance: it is, rather, to say that the multitude of efforts that sustained it came from the contributions of many people, not just a few people who directed those contributions from above. As Fick writes, the insurgents developed a "network of resistance, whose aim was to proselytize, to gather additional recruits and supporters, to call meetings and assemblies, and to devise plans of action. The whole burden of resistance now lay squarely upon their shoulders, and for resisting they would face firing squads, be hanged, drowned, even gassed to death."[9] It took coordinated efforts over time to build such a network, and when many of its main actors—Toussaint, especially—were removed, the network proved resilient enough to sustain itself and to grow. James's representation of this situation is multifaceted: clearly, the presence of Toussaint Louverture towers over *The Black Jacobins*, but even so, James could have judged that the 2,000 leaders were an anomaly in the Haitian Revolution, a mere ellipsis in the period between when Toussaint was captured and when Dessalines asserted his control over the revolution. He did not, however, and charting the reasons why he did not is one task for this chapter.

How groups like the 2,000 maintain their coherence, aggregate intelligence, and overcome cooperation problems are topics for this book's subsequent chapters and for further research.[10] After generations of experience with slavery and eleven years of coordinated resistance to it, the people who would soon become Haitian citizens did not need to be told to resist—their experiences with struggle gave them practice, and their hatred of slavery gave them motive. On the practice, Cedric D. Robinson writes that what he calls the Black Radical Tradition "was an accretion, over generations, of collective intelligence gathered from struggle. In the daily encounters and petty resistances to domination, slaves had acquired a sense of the calculus of oppression as well as its overt organization and instrumentation. These experiences lent themselves to a means of preparation for more epic resistance movements."[11] On the motive, Fick writes that "the uninstructed mass of slaves, and not their leaders,[. . .] saw so clearly what was at stake, regardless of the cost. And if the price they were ready to pay was high, it was no greater than the human suffering they had already endured."[12] Therefore, it was not an anomaly that the 2,000 could organize themselves into effective groups when their big leaders were removed; on the contrary, such forms of organization have logic that we can examine, although that logic is different from a hierarchy of leaders and led. One of the debts that contemporary scholars owe to James is that in *The Black Jacobins*, he recognized what was at issue—an alternative logic of collective action—and rather than dismissing it as an anomaly, he makes it one of the key aspects of his analysis. Even if, in 1938 and 1963, as he is writing and revising *The Black Jacobins*, or in 1971, as he is delivering his "Lectures on *The Black Jacobins*," he does not pursue the topic to as great a degree as he would like, that recognition is not insignificant, especially given the context in which he was writing, an intellectual environment that loudly condemned the Haitian Revolution. So in addition to this practice and motive the 2,000 possessed, as I noted above, it is evident that they possessed a sufficient amount of power to prevail against several of the Atlantic world's colonial states, supplanting a slavocracy with an independent nation. As I will show here, they also possessed a particular type of collective power, one that James would represent as a swarm, repeatedly and consistently in *The Black Jacobins*, and which I call direct democracy.

In the "Lectures on *The Black Jacobins*," which he gave to the Institute of the Black World in 1971, James stated that if he were to rewrite the book, he would focus to a greater degree on the 2,000 and the profound implications of their example.[13] Among James's concerns is that a rewritten book would, to a far greater degree, draw on primary sources written by the participants in the revolution, rather than sources with a colonial perspective found in the French archives.[14] There has been a range of responses to this call for further research—some, like Fick's book *The Making of Haiti: The Saint Domingue Revolution from Below*, Laurent Dubois's *Avengers of the New World: The Story of the Haitian Revolution*, and Jeremy Popkin's *Facing Racial Revolution: Eyewitness Accounts of the Haitian Revolution*, draw upon new archives, and some, like David Scott's *Conscripts of Modernity* and Nick Nesbitt's *Universal Emancipation*, use new critical perspectives. Much of the critical work on the problems presented by the 2,000 in particular has been framed by what Paul B. Miller, in his book *Elusive Origins: The Enlightenment in the Modern Caribbean Historical Imagination*, calls the "leader/masses dynamic."[15] This body of work is both substantial and insightful, and it builds from the idioms used by the socialist movements of James's era, which James both used and developed in his own ways in his writing.

I aim to build upon this work by tracing the trajectory of James's thinking about the logic of collective action that the 2,000 present and by proposing an alternative framework for understanding that logic. The scholarship on the "leader/masses dynamic" analyzes the situation as a problem with those two variables. This is useful, to a degree. I argue, however, that a framework with multiple variables—that is, a situation in which many people are seen to act, rather than one in which two groups are seen to act—is a better framework through which to view the logic of collective action in *The Black Jacobins*. From his earliest thinking about the 2,000 leaders, in his research and in the play *Toussaint Louverture: The Story of the Only Successful Slave Revolt in History*, which was first performed in 1936, through the 1938 edition and then the 1963 edition of *The Black Jacobins*, and to his 1971 "Lectures on *The Black Jacobins*," James comes to see 1802 and the logic of collective action the 2,000 display as the most important parts of the story. One question is: how is James able to recognize their importance? He could have seen the months of late 1802 as an anomaly, but he does not. Another question is, then, how does James represent the 2,000, the masses in revolt? I propose answers to both questions in this chapter.

The power that James shows the 2,000 possess and his use of the swarm metaphor in *The Black Jacobins* present the best set of examples of this book's two main claims: that direct democracy can be understood as a type of collective power, and that the swarm metaphor is like a signpost pointing to the presence of that direct democratic power. The moment the 2,000 emerged, and the lessons of the Haitian Revolution more generally, present indispensable material for analyzing the potential and problems of direct democracy.

Why the Haitian Revolution did not collapse in 1802 when its leadership structure became unstable has as much to do with who the insurgents were— a *demos*, even after generations of systematic attempts by the slave trade to dehumanize them—as it does with what they had—a *kratos* that was sufficiently powerful to end that domination.

In what follows, I will sketch a trajectory of James's thinking about the 2,000 and their logic of collective action through three sites—the play *Toussaint Louverture*, the text of *The Black Jacobins*, and James's 1971 lectures—to show the plot points in a trajectory of his thinking. His thinking on these topics continued to evolve over his career, as is evident in his writings on topics other than the Haitian Revolution. This body of work shows what I will call James's *ethos* of direct democracy—by which I mean a mind-set that prepared him to see why the 2,000 leaders in the Haitian Revolution were so significant. The trajectory I map in this chapter will provide a path to follow through additional examples in this book's subsequent chapters.

A Trajectory of Thinking about a Logic of Collective Action

From his earliest work on the Haitian Revolution, the 2,000 occupied a prominent place in James's imagination. In his play *Toussaint Louverture: The Story of the Only Successful Slave Revolt in History*, which was first performed in 1936 and which was the text that gave shape to *The Black Jacobins*, James takes the idea of the 2,000 from Leclerc and gives it to Toussaint. When Toussaint is in the French jail, moments away from death, his captors torment him with the idea of slavery reestablished in Saint Domingue. Toussaint replies:

> You can defeat an army, but you cannot defeat a people in arms. Do you think an army could drive those hundreds of thousands back into the fields? You have got rid of one leader. But there are two thousand leaders to be got rid of as well, and two thousand more when those are killed.[16]

In *The Black Jacobins*, James quotes Pamphile de Lacroix, who states that "no one observed that in the new insurrection of San Domingo, as in all insurrections which attack constituted authority, it was not the avowed chiefs who gave the signals for revolt but obscure creatures for the greater part personal enemies of the colored generals."[17] In his 1971 "Lectures on *The Black Jacobins*," James repeated this quote[18] and indicated that these are the ideas upon which he would expand if he had the opportunity to rewrite the book. He stated, "I am concerned with the two thousand leaders who were there. That is the book I would write. There are two thousand leaders to be taken away. If I were writing this book again, I would have something to say about those two thousand leaders."[19]

Yet James did not rewrite *The Black Jacobins* along the lines he speculates about in the "Lectures." That text, as it remained, as David Scott suggests in *Conscripts of Modernity*, "most of all is the political biography of this enlightened and inspiring leader, Toussaint L'Ouverture."[20] Among his many insightful points, therefore, Scott critiques the use of *The Black Jacobins* as a mere blueprint for political action in the present—James's problem space, to use Scott's terms, differs from ours in such a way to make a simple adoption of James's framework unwise.[21] Scott writes, "Many contemporary readers of C. L. R. James read *The Black Jacobins* as though it might provide them with answers to present problems, as though, for instance, it might tell them how to conduct oppositional politics today."[22] He suggests that such work should not search for new answers to the same questions James asked about colonialism, for example, but should ask new questions, based on the conditions of a given historical moment.[23] Scott suggests that James's work "directly challenges us to ask ourselves what kind of story might be best for the politicohistorical presents within which we now live and write. It is this that makes *The Black Jacobins* a work of unending critical value."[24] James's effort in *The Black Jacobins* was to look back to an earlier era in order to cull ideas that would be useful in the present: not a simple adoption of ideas and tools, but an adaptation of them fit for his political present.

The issue James faced when writing and rewriting, and then rethinking the Haitian Revolution, was how to construct a narrative about the situation that was both sufficiently complex and sufficiently coherent; his book's undiminished relevance speaks to the degree to which he was successful. The issue that we now face is how best to understand the logic of collective action that the 2,000 present—both as it is represented in James's writing and also in the light of the subsequent research about the Haitian Revolution. As I noted above, much of the scholarship on the 2,000 frames their dynamics as a binary between leaders and led. A multivariable framework is, I believe, more consistent with what we know about other similar groups, with what James suggests when he states that he sought to analyze the movement of forces, of masses, of individuals, and their influence on their environment at a fluid moment in history,[25] and also more in line with how he represents the actions of the 2,000.

In addition to Scott, who uses the example of the 2,000 in *Conscripts of Modernity* to reorient the ways in which researchers writing politically engaged scholarship interact with texts written by a previous generation,[26] several scholars, in writing about *The Black Jacobins* or the Haitian Revolution, have keyed in on Leclerc's comment about 2,000 leaders, and the points James makes about that comment. Carolyn Fick dedicates *The Making of Haiti* to "Haiti, her people, her obscure leaders, and her future";[27] and the book seeks, from start to finish, to tell the story of those obscure leaders, and does so in impressive detail. In *Avengers of the New World*, Laurent Dubois makes the 2,000 a key point;[28] Susan Buck-Morss refers to the idea in two separate moments in *Hegel, Haiti, and Universal History*.[29] Nick Nesbitt ends *Universal Emancipation* with a discussion of the 2,000.[30]

Seen all together, this work suggests that to understand the 2,000 one needs to understand them as people, with all the complexities of their personalities, as participants in groups, and how their interactions fuel the dynamics of those groups. One must also understand the material contexts in which they lived and acted and the ideas that motivated them. In other words, a fuller understanding of the 2,000 comes from archival history and from critical theory, from the content of primary sources and from the content of adequate conceptual frameworks. This is a considerable task, one I cannot answer fully here, but in what follows I hope to suggest a useful way for approaching it.

To address the specifics of the situation in the summer and fall of 1802, it is important to remember that the gist of the example the 2,000 present is that it is a situation where the revolutionary leaders are absent or actively fighting against the 2,000. Fick makes two points in *The Making of Haiti* that are worth quoting at length. First, she writes that the

> course of the struggle that [the blacks] began in 1791 had transformed them; they were no longer; nor could they ever again be, slaves. And so it was not merely the diverse insurrectionary bands that punctuated the countryside and the hills that Leclerc would have to crush. These he expected to be able to subdue, one by one, since there seemed to be no real cohesion to them, and no central leader. It was, as he would come to realize, the entire black population that would have to be annihilated in order to restore slavery and complete his mission. [. . . O]n their own initiative and with the meager means at their disposal for effective resistance, [the population] fought the French army by themselves, while Dessalines, Christophe, Laplume, and the other black generals were still cooperating with Leclerc, and whom Leclerc himself could not deport because he needed them to carry out the repression[.][31]

From spring 1802 through June 6, when Toussaint was taken, up to mid-October, when Dessalines asserted his control, the relationship between leaders and masses that had defined the revolution was severed and remade.

Second, the general insurrection lasted a considerable amount of time without the big leaders. In place of those big leaders, a decentralized network of resistance took up the fighting:

> These, then, were the black masses who, alone for the past eight months, had sustained the war against the French army in the south. The most significant feature of their efforts to organize and resist Bonaparte's expeditionary forces is that there was no single leader around whom the movement united, but literally hundreds of them throughout the department, and hundreds more throughout the county, for the most part, obscure individuals. In August, once the news that slavery had been restored in Guadalupe and French slave trade reopened, Leclerc remarked, and certainly did not exaggerate the case, that it was not enough to have removed Toussaint: "[F]or here there are two thousand leaders that must be removed."[32]

Yet the problem remains, as Paul B. Miller points out, that even with the importance that James places on the 2,000, *The Black Jacobins* is at difficulty to represent the individuals who constitute the 2,000 as distinct, fully actualized individuals. Miller writes that the "vital masses subsist beyond representation, as an elusive referent or signified."[33] To a significant degree, James is forthcoming in his retrospective comments about the reason for this in the "Lectures on *The Black Jacobins*": in 1936 and in 1963, archives did exist upon which he could have drawn in order to get a firsthand perspective on the views of the insurgents and other participants in the revolution.[34] Nevertheless, we must approach *The Black Jacobins* as the book that it is, not as the book that James wished that it could have been. It is a difficult problem: the 2,000 are not just the vital aspect of the events in 1802—they are the only driver of the revolution's forward dynamic. The task, then, is to conceptualize the 2,000 with the evidence available, some from James, some from the subsequent scholarship on the Haitian Revolution, and some from political theory that is relevant to groups like the 2,000. Ultimately, beyond "masses," there are two metaphors—the chorus and the swarm—that James uses to represent the insurgents. Both of these deserve scrutiny.

❦   ❦   ❦

The way James moves from narrating actions by principal characters such as Toussaint to narrating the actions of many people shows that he finds both the actions of important individuals *and* the dynamics of people cooperating vital to the story. He writes in the preface to the first edition of *The Black Jacobins* that he is "confident that the narrative will prove" that, perhaps with the exception of Bonaparte,

> no single figure appeared on the historical stage more greatly gifted than [Toussaint], a slave till he was 45. Yet Toussaint did not make the revolution. It was the revolution that made Toussaint. And even that is not the whole truth.[. . .] The writer has sought not only to analyse, but to demonstrate in their movement, the economic forces of the age; their moulding of society and politics, of men in the mass and individual men; the powerful reaction of these on their environment at one of those rare moments when society is at a boiling point and therefore fluid.[35]

The Black Jacobins negotiates between conversations about Toussaint and about the actions of the mass of people in an almost rhythmic fashion, keeping them together in a way that shows that James thinks that they are inextricable. Such movement is not formulaic, of course, but it happens consistently over the entire book. To give just one example among many, James writes of a moment in 1800, when Toussaint was solidifying his grip on power, but when independence was still four years away, that the actions of the people showed an "instinctive capacity of the masses for revolutionary organization." Two sentences later, James writes that this capacity "will display itself in all populations when deeply stirred and given a clear perspective by a strong and trusted leadership."[36] A more doctrinaire reading might see a contradiction here, but one of the strengths of *The Black Jacobins* is that it can hold two different thoughts together, namely, to show the importance of key protagonists in the drama, such as Toussaint, and simultaneously to urge the importance of the mass in revolt. What Miller calls the "leader/masses dynamic" is adequate for understanding this narrative movement, through most of the book, between scenes of Toussaint and scenes about the masses.

How to represent this complexity, however, is a difficult problem. As Miller writes,

> The question certainly bears asking how any historical account of a revolutionary epoch could be carried out without recourse to the leaders/masses dynamic. James, however, does not ask it. Rather than being considered as a mere aggregate of individuals, which, statistically speaking and demographically speaking, at least, is their only empirically verifiable status, the masses in James are homogenized into a single will or "spirit." This monolithic mass is then endowed with characteristics belonging to individuals only, such as goodness, etc.[37]

That James did not write the book he wished he had written is correct, of course. It may also be true that the 2,000 in *The Black Jacobins* as it is written are not much differentiated. But that such a differentiation does not happen in *The Black Jacobins* does not mean that the task has no possible path forward, as Miller seems to suggest in the first sentence of the quote above. An aggregate of individuals is not a group's only empirically verifiable status, and using a collective metaphor does not necessarily homogenize a group of people. As Aristotle suggested in the *Metaphysics*, there are situations where "the totality is not, as it were, a mere heap, but the whole is something besides the parts."[38] In other words, there are situations when a group becomes something more than the sum of its parts. The emergent characteristics of groups are difficult to assess, no doubt, but these emergent characteristics are not mere aggregation. Furthermore, there is no evidence in *The Black Jacobins* to suggest that James views the masses as homogeneous. Miller here perhaps comes a bit too close to the nineteenth-century popular psychology on crowds, a body of work that purposely sought to homogenize crowds in order to do political or physical harm to them. This is no doubt more than Miller meant to imply; nevertheless, that is the tradition such ideas participate in, whether Miller intended them to do so or not. He is correct, after all, to suggest that literary and historical scholarship about movements, crowds, groups, or mobs does often lapse into an easy dichotomy between, on the one hand, particular individuals who have been cut apart from the group for purposes of analysis and, on the other, the supposed detrimental effects of collective action. The first leads to simplistic notions of great men making history; the second can paralyze the solidarity necessary for any political movement.

If the "leaders/masses dynamic" necessarily leads to a conception of people as homogeneous, it has outlasted its analytical purchase. No group of 2,000 people, or even two people, is homogeneous, regardless of the degree to which they agree on issues or cooperate to achieve common goals. To state that people lose their individuality in groups is to discourage them from acting collectively, which is the only adequate strategy presenting a credible challenge to systematized injustices like the Atlantic slave trade.[39] Such homogenization is ultimately impossible: no one can give up his or her own thoughts and experiences, even when in tandem with others. To assume that people in groups are homogeneous is, at minimum, to do them a profound disservice; it may be more accurate to state that such homogenization perpetrates a type of representational violence against them.

An effective narrative about complex situations needs attention to both how particular protagonists in the drama—named or unnamed, playing large roles or small—react and make decisions. It also needs attention to the patterns and ideas that emerge from the millions of actions and decisions taken by the multiplicity of people who took part in that drama. To start to consider these problems differently, one might recognize that Miller's framework presents two variables: leaders and masses. A different approach, then, is to consider the situation as a problem with a multiplicity of variables. That approach is complex: individuals act, according to their abilities, limitations, and situations, and the aggregation of all those acts often reveals the emergence of insightful patterns, trends, and ideas.[40] Many intellectual problems can be analyzed usefully by reducing them to the dominant variables, to the exclusion of other, lesser variables, but the general insurrection in *The Black Jacobins* speaks to a situation that does not have only two variables, but rather thousands of variables.[41]

Multiple-variable problems, like the interactions of nodes in a network, traffic on highways, fish in schools, starlings in flocks, and bees and ants in swarms, are part of the body of research on complexity. As I note above, in the technical sense *complexity* is a synonym for *multiplicity*, not for *difficulty*—it is about how many different actors interact or cooperate, as distinct from structures of command and control.[42] A line of thinkers, as Warren Montag suggests, including Spinoza, Pierre Macherey, and others, see human beings not as atomistic, but rather as complex systems. They are assemblages each made of parts, themselves composed of parts ad infinitum.[43] The better framework, following these thinkers, is to treat the 2,000 as a problem with many variables—many people, in a group that is diverse unto itself, who have found ways to cooperate in pursuit of common goals and ideas. In *Elusive Origins*, Miller states that the "appropriate spatial metaphor to describe the dialectic of masses and leaders is the pyramid,"[44] which is correct. An alternative spatial metaphor is not simply a pyramid turned upside down—an appropriate alternative would operate on a substantially different logic. When Fick describes the 2,000, her metaphor is a network, which is an apt description. For his part, beyond "masses," James uses two metaphors to describe the insurgents as a group. The first is his famous phrase about the chorus: "not Shakespeare himself could have found such a dramatic embodiment of fate as Toussaint struggled against, Bonaparte himself; nor could the furthest imagination have envisaged the entry of the chorus, of the ex-slaves themselves, as the arbiters of their own fate."[45] It is a beautiful metaphor; even though it is isolated, it is further evidence that James was grappling with alternative ways to describe the collective dynamics of the 2,000. The metaphor of the ex-slaves as a chorus also reminds one of Aristotle's comment in the *Politics*: "There is a point at which a *polis* by advancing in unity will cease to be a *polis* . . . It is as if you were to turn harmony into mere unison, or to reduce a theme to a single beat.

The truth is that the *polis* is an aggregate of many members."[46] Superficially, a chorus, like any group, may seem homogeneous, but that is not the case; its harmony is the cooperation of diverse voices, its collective sound something more than just the sum of all its notes.

The other metaphor James uses to describe the insurgents is the swarm. Whereas the chorus metaphor appears once, James uses the metaphor of the swarm five times, each of which demonstrates not only a form of collective power, but also particular characteristics of that power. It is significant that James uses the swarm metaphor consistently over the course of the book, every time he represents the insurgents acting collectively. This consistency should be no surprise. As Frank Rosengarten and others have remarked,[47] James was a careful writer, dedicated to his literary craft. I am aware of no evidence to suggest that James used the swarm metaphor intentionally, so his use of it rises to the level of intuition, but that is not nothing: while he could not have known about the dynamics of actual swarms and networks—much of the research on them has come in the past several decades, after James's death—he intuits that the metaphor speaks to a logic of collective action that is an alternative to the pyramids of constituted power he sees in the organization of the French colonial forces.

When James wants to show the insurgents' actions, he repeatedly and consistently uses the language of swarms, and when he does, he uses it exclusively to represent insurgents in rebellion, acting for themselves, and in networks, never in a context that suggests that these masses are taking direction from Toussaint, Dessalines, or any of the other big leaders. Rather, he writes that if the insurgents "met with resistance they retired without exhausting themselves, but at the slightest hesitation in the defense they became extremely bold and, rushing up to the cannon, swarmed all over their opponents."[48] There is a method here: a conscious decision making about strategy, an affirmation of what Robinson noted above, about these insurgents knowing the calculus of domination, reasoning when to pull back and when to fight and win.[49] There is no leader present here: nowhere in the context of the passage does James suggest that this swarm has taken orders from anyone. It is collective: the insurgents move as a body. These movements are not explicable in terms of leaders and led—they are about many protagonists cooperating in pursuit of a common goal, each making sets of decisions in tandem with their peers.

The French colonial forces, organized into their pyramids and ranks, could imagine this organization only as a motley crowd.[50] But James views the groups differently. For him, swarming does not mean formlessness, a lack of organization. James writes that the insurgents "swarmed over guns and gunners, threw their arms around them and silenced them. Nothing could stop their devotion, and after six hours the troops of Port-au-Prince retired in disorder."[51] Here, swarming is not equivalent to mayhem: it is the French troops who retire in disorder, not the insurgents. This swarm is not disorganized—it *is* organized, albeit nonhierarchically. James and other scholars studying the methods used by the insurgents link the language of swarming to guerilla warfare. "In the north," James writes, "fired by Toussaint's audacious march, the blacks were now swarming out and reinforcing the regular army by guerilla methods."[52] In *Avengers of the New World*, Dubois uses a similar approach. Directly before he mentions Leclerc's letter about the 2,000 leaders, Dubois writes, "Many bands were led by 'fighting units of an army of liberation' composed of hardened veterans. Meanwhile there were hundreds of smaller bands who continually harassed the French."[53] Here one gets the sense that all of these diverse parts amount to something greater than the sum of those parts. The guerrilla bands and the regular army are not under the same control, yet they can operate in a cooperative manner. They are all working toward the goal of abolishing slavery, and therefore cooperating in a way that is both broad and profound, but also decentralized.

As if to underscore the importance of such swarms, James uses the metaphor in tandem with key moments in his history. He writes that "the road from the heights ran along the sea-shore, and the sailors who remained in [the French] ships in the harbour could see them hour after hour swarming down to Le Cap.[. . .] It was the end of white domination in San Domingo."[54] The paragraph before this includes Toussaint's name change from Breda to L'Ouverture.[55] This instance showcases two of the most important moments of the story: the narrative and symbolic importance of a former slave changing his name, and showing a swarm using guerrilla methods to end white domination.[56] James could have viewed these situations as anomalies, as if they were aberrations in an otherwise standard narrative about movements led by great leaders. He does not, however: he knows that there is something significant in the actions of the 2,000. Again, James could not have known about the dynamics of actual swarms, but he avoids the mistake that many others make, which is to assume that a different social order means disorder.[57]

This multivariable framework is more consistent with what James suggests when he states that he sought to analyze the movement of forces, of masses, of individuals, and their influence on their environment at a fluid moment in history.[58] Put another way, many intellectual problems can be analyzed usefully by reducing them to the dominant variables, to the exclusion of other, lesser variables, but this is not the best available framework for approaching the 2,000. James's comment about a fluid moment in history speaks to the fact that the situation he analyzes is not a two-variable problem, but rather one with thousands of variables. The example that the 2,000 in the Haitian Revolution presents is not fully explicable in the terms of a dichotomy between leaders and masses—it is an important start, but not an appropriate end. A collective logic—composed of both leaders and masses—does not cheapen or devalue the many vital contributions of its participants, but, rather, it depends on them. It does not hamper gifted people like Toussaint Louverture, but rather sets the conditions in which people like him can flourish. Such a collective logic also helps to explain why the Haitian Revolution as a whole was more than just the sum of its parts, why it was so successful, in part because of Toussaint and the other big leaders, and in part without them.

So when I write that *The Black Jacobins* is a biography of Toussaint, but not only a biography, I do so because the book is filled with James's analysis of Toussaint's actions, and also with commentary about the self-organized contributions by the mass of insurgents. In response to pervasive and multimodal forms of hierarchical domination, James repeatedly shows ordinary people as agents, but further, he signals that it is the mass, not the leaders, who is the revolutionary engine: when Toussaint steps away from the 2,000, he falls.[59] The book's nuance comes through because, in addition to what David Scott suggests, the book is a biography that also levels a critique of its hero and, tentatively but intuitively, begins to think about what a movement organized like a swarm might mean or be. James writes that the "slopes to treachery from the dizzy heights of revolutionary leadership are always so steep and slippery that leaders, however well-intentioned, can never build fences too high."[60] By the end of *The Black Jacobins*, James has noted that Toussaint had descended into authoritarian means, and that his successor, Dessalines, has authoritarian ends in mind.[61] Through all of this, James insists that "masses had shown greater political understanding than their leaders."[62]

James's *Ethos* of Direct Democracy

The thinking that James put into the logic of collective action in the Haitian Revolution would be developed and explored in various other contexts throughout his career. It is for that reason that I suggest that James had an *ethos* of direct democracy. As Cedric Robinson writes, James's work on the Haitian Revolution

> forced to the surface an unintended consideration.[. . .] For a decade after the appearance of *The Black Jacobins*, James would wrestle with the social and

ideological ambivalence of this "renegade" strata, eventually articulating the critique of it as the source of leadership of the revolutionary masses.[...] No revolutionary cadre, divorced from the masses, ensconced in state bureaucracy, and abrogating to itself the determination of the best interest of the masses, could sustain the revolution or itself. James could come to the theoretical position that "in the decisive hour" (as Marx and Engels were wont to say) it was only the consciousness and activity of the revolutionary masses that could preserve the revolution from compromise, betrayal, or that ill considered usurpation of revolutionary authority.[63]

This study, Robinson states, "would persuade him of the actual fact of Lenin's dictum 'Every cook can govern.'"[64] What I wish to suggest is that James could see the importance of the 2,000 because of this democratic ethos that he built and cultivated throughout his career. It is a point that many scholars have noted: Frank Rosengarten writes that the "unifying theme of James's conception of politics was his faith and confidence in the ability of ordinary people to run their own lives, and to do so collectively."[65] Similarly, Anna Grimshaw writes that James's politics was based on the "recognition of the creative energies of ordinary men and women and their critical place in modern history as the force for humanity," and Kara M. Rabbitt notes that the "arguments that James will later build against the concept of a vanguard party, against that of an educated elite leading a passive mass, are[...] already apparent [in *The Black Jacobins*]."[66]

This *ethos* is present in many of his texts, perhaps especially in his 1956 essay "Every Cook Can Govern: A Study of Democracy in Ancient Greece, Its Meaning for Today" and the 1958 text he wrote with Cornelius Castoriadis and Grace Lee Boggs, *Facing Reality*. In these texts, James examines the problems of direct democracy, by which he means a form of organization meant for constituent assemblies or labor cooperatives. To be clear, he uses the term *direct democracy* in a different way than I suggest in this book: he understands it in the common way, as a form of organization, whereas I wish to use that term to describe a type of power. Yet the ideas upon which James builds his conceptions of direct democracy are analogous to mine. What I call, therefore, James's ethos of direct democracy, he frequently calls "the creative power of freedom," which he links together with his understanding of autonomy and cooperation. So although James does not use the term in the same way, the two interpretations describe related concepts. As the scholars above note, these concepts were among the most important themes in his body of work.

The crucial resource for these ideas is James's particular strand of autonomist Marxism, a current that grew out of the antiauthoritarian, anti-Stalinist

Left. As Rosengarten writes, James applied Marxist theory "from an angle of vision that places heavier emphasis than was the case for many other Marxists on the human capacity for enterprise, for self-movement, in a word, for self-realization in all domains of creative activity."[67] That capacity, as noted above, like the Latin *potentia* or the French *puissance*, is intrinsic to the human experience, part of what I call the first mode of power. James's approach, Rosengarten writes, was a "Marxism grounded in a core concept of philosophical humanism, which subsumes the notion that creativity and individuality form part of every human's birthright."[68] This line of thinking stands in opposition to notions of vanguard parties, state bureaucracies, and representative forms of governance. James and other autonomous Marxists aim at one of the weak spots in capitalism's armor, namely, that without a version of the second mode of power, the power to command labor to work and to control that work, it is impossible to produce capital. But to disrupt the process at this point is only the first step: after this disruption, replacing one hierarchy with a different hierarchy may make the situation less miserable, but it does not solve the problem as such. That situation called for pushing against the boundaries of the critical tools that were available to him—as Rosengarten writes, James "wanted to stretch the limits of Marxist method and theory to make room for new forces, new movements, new ideas about how to achieve socialism. His ecumenical approach led him on occasion to blur some important distinctions, but it also saved him from the perils of ideological inflexibility."[69] Therefore, James searched for political models to provide substantive alternatives to the constituted powers he found unjust, and also to the critical tools he judged were lacking. He found considerable inspiration in the Haitian Revolution, of course, in the direct democracy of ancient Greece, and in the cooperative workers' movement in the Hungarian Revolution, as he describes in *Facing Reality*.

In the years between the publication of the first and second editions of *The Black Jacobins*, James was working with Grace Lee, Rava Dunyevskaya, and Cornelius Castoriadis. When he wrote "Every Cook Can Govern," James was reacting to the machinations of the Cold War, and also to the merger of the American Federation of Labor and the Congress of Industrial Organizations in 1955, a move that united the two largest labor union federations in the United States. In David Scott's phrase, James's problem space motivated him to argue for a direct democracy to counter the bureaucratic trends that he saw. Through Lee, James had a connection to Detroit, Michigan, one of the strongholds of organized labor at this time. Detroit had a militant labor movement, as well as the headquarters of the United Automobile Workers, one of the strongest and most successful unions in any industry. Detroit also had an established labor press and substantial working-class radical intellectuals, including James Boggs, Lee's future spouse.[70] This problem space was marked by an ever-increasing centralization of power, manifest in both the repression of leftist thinkers and groups during the Cold War and in the consolidated AFL-CIO.[71] Such centralization and bureaucratization, James correctly suggests, puts more distance between constituted power and the people who are subject to its decisions, further alienating their power from the institutions that govern their communities. He therefore argues that a study of ancient direct democracy is useful to counter this trend, and he also suggests that direct democracies offer particular benefits that other forms of political organization cannot.

In "Every Cook Can Govern," James sees the dangers of a gathering bureaucracy and writes that he believes "that the larger the modern community, the more imperative it is for it to govern itself by the principle of direct democracy (it need not be a mere copy of the Greek). Otherwise we face a vast and ever-growing bureaucracy. That is why a study, however brief, of the constitution and governmental procedures of Greek Democracy is so important for us today."[72] James quickly describes some of the institutions of ancient Greek direct democracy, including the Council of 500, which made decisions and administered justice; the selection of administrators by lot; the rotation of officeholders to facilitate wide participation of citizens in the governance of the community; and, perhaps most important for James, the procedure for the Festival of Dionysus, the festival of drama in which the general public, and later a group of judges who were chosen by lot, decided in democratic fashion who would win the competition. James's comment, bracketed for clarity, that a contemporary direct democracy need not be a "mere copy" of the older system, is a key point here. James looks back to an earlier era in order to cull ideas that might be remade into tools that would be useful during the era in which he was working.

James was keen to point out that a democracy where people actually rule could be an important change from the structures he saw gathering control around him, like a bureaucracy, where those at desks rule, or a plutocracy, where the rich rule. In James's use of the term, direct democracy implies that people in groups—unions, workplaces, associations, or communities govern those groups without others speaking for them. An ethos of direct democracy values autonomy and cooperation; indeed, for James, these values are the scaffolding upon which the form of direct democracy is built.

Compared to *The Black Jacobins*, however, which, in both its importance and size, continues to shake the ground with great force, the nineteen pages of "Every Cook Can Govern," which is perhaps James's most explicit analysis of direct democracy, seem like a mere tremor. It certainly does not have the power to knock over the structures of our understanding of representative democracy in the way that *The Black Jacobins* decimated the house of colonialism, but "Every Cook" displays the same emphasis on the collective power of human capacity that *The Black Jacobins* does and, in some ways, conveys that idea more clearly. Yet the essay has significant flaws: it treats the ancient Greek world's obvious injustices and citizenship exclusions dismissively, which is a curious omission when put together with his earlier and much more polished work on the Haitian Revolution. James does mention how women and slaves were excluded from the *polis*, and he notes the dangers of these exclusions,[73] but a further examination of these issues would have improved the essay considerably.

In those nineteen pages, however, James articulates his ethos of direct democracy quite clearly. "There is room for differences of opinion, and Greek democracy has always had and still has many enemies," James writes.

> But the position we take here is based not only on the soundest authorities, but on something far more important, our own belief in the creative power of freedom and the capacity of the ordinary man to govern. Unless you share that belief of the ancient Greeks, you cannot understand the civilization they built. History is a living thing. It is not a body of facts. We today who are faced with the inability of representative government and parliamentary democracy to handle effectively the urgent problems of the day, we can study and understand Greek democracy in a way that was impossible for a man who lived in 1900, when representative government and parliamentary democracy seemed securely established for all time.[74]

In this way "Every Cook Can Govern" ends with a call to study ancient Greek direct democracy in order to see what lessons it could teach the activists in James's problem space. As Scott notes in *Conscripts of Modernity*, James looks back to an earlier historical period to see what ideas, properly adapted, might make useful tools for imagining a more just and democratic future. The essay's brevity and its obvious errors, especially when compared to the rigor, depth, and elegance of *The Black Jacobins*, make it part of James's trajectory of thinking, but perhaps not the most significant part. Yet it is apparent that *The Black Jacobins*, like "Every Cook," is anchored on the foundation of his belief in the autonomy and creativity of women and men to conduct their own affairs. To extrapolate only slightly from James's "Lectures on *The Black Jacobins*," it is not just the "obscure leaders" in ancient Athens and Saint Domingue upon whom James bases his ethos: "They were obscure in Watts," he writes, "they were obscure in Detroit . . . in Newark . . . in San Francisco . . . Cleveland . . . Harlem."[75] The power that James suggests people have is the power inherent in human capacity multiplied by cooperation, what I call direct democracy.

James has no Pollyanna belief in some universal goodness of humanity—*The Black Jacobins*, to name but one text, is filled with too many examples of cruelty to see human relations in such a simplistic manner—but what he does see is that, given the right conditions and preparations, the power inherent in human capacity can be substantial enough to make dramatic changes. As Nick Nesbitt suggests, building an idea of universal inclusion in a political community from Spinoza, one might address human beings "both as they are (mired in violence and conflict) and as they can be: that is, capable of, but still lacking a fully reasonable or enlightened existence."[76] Given the right conditions and motivations, any person is most likely capable of both great kindness and great cruelty. It is just a short step from this to believe, as James believed, that under certain conditions, cooperative action was not only possible but could present a credible challenge even to entrenched injustices, and that it could be a key to understanding the events in the final years of the Haitian Revolution.

James's ethos of direct democracy prepared him to see that the Haitian Revolution led to such powerful outcomes because of the contributions of people, like Toussaint, who had seized the opportunity to develop themselves far beyond what would have ever been permitted to them in their former lives as slaves, and also because of the fact that such a radical equality sets the conditions for all people to develop their potential to the greatest degree possible. This is why James places such importance on Toussaint's accomplishments and also why he unequivocally states that it was not the big leaders who made the revolution possible; rather, it was the 2,000 leaders, acting collectively, who won their freedom.[77] If *The Black Jacobins* is the biography of an enlightened and inspiring leader, one whom James calls the "black Spartacus,"[78] it is not only that. It is also about that leader's limitations, and the contributions made by the mass of insurgents fighting for their freedom.

A Trajectory beyond the Haitian Revolution

Haiti's first constitutions declared that slavery is abolished forever; in the process of winning national independence, the revolution disproved the idea that some people need to be governed because they are incapable of governing themselves. Some would state that without leadership, no social or political organization is possible, but this belief is substantially no different than the colonial arguments that slaves need their masters to govern them, and it is disproven by the events in Saint Domingue in 1802, or at least shown to be a belief that needs further nuance. The story of the Haitian Revolution and James's emphasis on its 2,000 leaders show an alternative to the domination of the Atlantic world's colonial powers, an alternative that can still be seen in aspects of Haitian social and cultural structures.[79] Furthermore, the radically egalitarian ideas that emerged from the Haitian Revolution—universal emancipation, human rights without exception—came into being because of the interactions of many people, from both the exemplary contributions of people like Toussaint and the actions of many people determined to make those radically egalitarian ideas a material reality. For those reasons and more, the Haitian Revolution is a thunderclap in history, and a continually rich archive for studying the problems of democracy.

The collective logic of the 2,000 suggests that creativity, autonomy, and the ability to cooperate in pursuit of shared goals are not the sole purview of a special few, but are in all of us—even when dormant and unused, or suppressed by the enforced inequalities and injustices of constituted powers. The suggestion that the targets of dehumanization cannot rule themselves and therefore ought to be ruled by others has an opposite corollary: that while recognizing people and political conditions as they are—that is, often rewarding hostility and domination and penalizing generosity and solidarity—the collective power of human capacity, what I call direct democracy, is always present, if only like the energy waiting to be gathered together in a thunderclap. While James's work on the 2,000 in the Haitian Revolution presents perhaps the best set of examples for this book's main claims, it is not the only set of examples. His thinking does, however, present a trajectory that can be followed further. Direct democratic power is used and adapted by people according to their needs and situations; the next chapter shows how three of the most significant thinkers during the long nineteenth century understood and represented it.

CHAPTER TWO

Carlyle, Whitman, Parsons:
Three Perspectives on Direct Democracy

In the decades following the Haitian Revolution, through their words and actions, former slaves, women, and workers all displayed their direct democratic power, often in opposition to the constituted powers under which they lived. Their debates and struggles circulated throughout the Americas, the Atlantic world, and beyond: the story of the Haitian Revolution became a nearly ever-present specter to the Atlantic slavocracy.[1] During this era, as Sibylle Fischer writes, "radical anti-slavery was a shadowy, discontinuous formation with a risomatic, decentered structure."[2] Revolutions throughout Europe in 1848 and the Latin American wars of Independence grew from the cross-pollination of discontent. Part of this had to do with the nature of global capitalism in the long nineteenth century, Fischer continues: "the triangular trade and colonial commercial routes clearly produced circuits where cultural knowledge and political practices traveled back and forth across the Atlantic."[3] The Civil War in the United States was fueled by what W. E. B. Du Bois called a general strike of former slaves, who combined into a "swarming crowd of Negroes and white refugees" that had "no plan in this exodus, no Moses to lead it,"[4] but which was composed of people who knew to leave behind their chains as soon as they could break them. The Paris Commune in 1871 was perhaps the most famous democratic experiment of the era, what Marx called "a model [of] self-government of the producers."[5] The Commune was the inspiration for many movements, including the campaign in Britain and the United States to reduce the workday from twelve or more hours to eight. Increasingly by the end of the era, chattel slavery and wage slavery were discussed together in conversations about democratic alternatives to capitalism, and the women who learned how to agitate and organize in abolition movements became the backbone of first-wave feminism.[6]

The collective power that I call direct democracy is part of the human experience, and its representation can be found in these movements and struggles. Yet the manifestation of this power is not uniform: like the constituted powers it faces, direct democracy is, to some degree, adaptive, evolving in response to the environments in which people express it. Ideas about it develop out of such complex mixes, and they circulate in networks. From that circulation, we can see patterns and trends take shape. C. L. R. James states in *The Black Jacobins* that "phases of a revolution are not decided in parliaments, they are only registered there."[7] A similar comment can be made about direct democracy. My claims in this book are that direct democracy can be understood as a collective form of power, and that the metaphor of the swarm is like a signpost, pointing to the presence of this power. By this, I do not mean to suggest that direct democracy is the same in all times and in all places, but to argue that it has an adequate amount of common characteristics, such that it can be identified as a coherent phenomenon.

Writers during the era brought a variety of perspectives to bear on the analysis of, or critique of, what I call direct democratic power. In this chapter I show, in an echo of James's comment about how power is exercised outside of parliaments, a key debate about direct democratic power during the long nineteenth century between three of its most insightful commentators. These three voices provide the flashpoints of a debate: Thomas Carlyle, Walt Whitman, and Lucy Parsons each brought considerable analytical skills and political savvy to bear on the problems of democracy, labor, and slavery. All these writers define democracy not as the product of legislatures, but rather as a type of power produced in those cross-pollinated struggles, even though they use a diverse set of terms to enter the conversation. Whitman wrote *Democratic Vistas* in direct response to Carlyle's essay "Shooting Niagara"; Parsons writes in direct response to the ideas in these two texts, especially on the topics of slavery and the movement for the eight-hour workday, in which Parsons was a key participant. Yet while they speak to one another, their perspectives could not be more dissimilar. Carlyle writes about the "Swarmery" of such political movements, by which he means their irrationality. Whitman writes insightfully out of a profound ambivalence—*Democratic Vistas*, as is characteristic of much of Whitman's work, is valuable because he is able to see both the danger of cruel, vicious crowds and also the possibility that some future understanding of democracy may facilitate the best parts of human potential. Parsons lived a life excluded and dominated by the constituted powers under which she lived. In her speeches, especially those supporting the eight-hour workday movement, she was an unabashed promoter of the collective power to transform the world.

Direct democracy, in my understanding of that term, is not the sole possession of one people or group, but neither is it expressed in the same way in various contexts. For these reasons, it is useful to look at the concept in a comparative manner. My goal in this chapter, therefore, is to show this power from three diverse perspectives, each of which can contribute to a fuller understanding of the concept. I first sketch in brief Carlyle, Whitman, and Parsons's views on the topic, and then I analyze some of their key texts in greater depth. These debates provide a window to see how ideas about direct democracy developed and circulated; from specific debates we can track larger trends.

⑥　⑥　⑥

As Jacques Rancière says of Plato, Thomas Carlyle hated democracy, but in hating it, he was able to see aspects of it clearly.[8] By the middle of the nineteenth century, Carlyle's reputation as a commentator on literature and politics was considerable. His many books and his friendship with Ralph Waldo Emerson gave credence to James Anthony Froude's comment that in the 1860s Carlyle was "the fashion of the moment with the multitude."[9] That comment is probably polite hyperbole, but Carlyle's writings do provide insight about how reactionary writers of the era understood the threats to the constituted powers that they thought were just and worth protecting. Carlyle was, no doubt, a reactionary writer, but this is not to say that he was a caricature—his critical stance against unfettered capitalism, which he thought degraded the labor process through the production of useless, cheap materials, put him at odds with many of the other conservative writers of his era. In Carlyle's work, a reader does have to wade through no little amount of unabashed bigotry, yet in his candid writings about the democratic and anticolonial movements of his era, a reader can see quite clearly his belief in the power of those movements. It is a common thought that the censor believes most deeply in the power of literature; perhaps equally, reactionaries like Carlyle believe most deeply in the power of the political movements they oppose. Otherwise, such movements would not need to capture the attention of people like Carlyle, because those movements would pose no threat to the constituted powers that they wish to preserve. The situation is much like Hobbes writing against the political movements of his day in *Behemoth*: as Warren Montag notes, citing Spinoza's *Political Treatise*, Hobbes affirms Spinoza's maxim that the "multitude, if it is not afraid, inspires no little fear."[10] The same can be said for Carlyle.

Carlyle is perhaps most useful here for how he wields the concept of *Schwärmerei*, which, as noted above, is a common concept, one that Carl

Schmitt uses considerably in his book *Dictatorship*. "Swarmery" is Carlyle's term for political irrationality, especially when it leads to upheavals in political institutions, the result of which he predicted would be "unspeakable chaos."[11] In his defense of constituted power, the established institutions and cultural norms he wants to conserve, Carlyle clearly sees how the political movements of his era could be disruptive. Robert Leigh Davis writes that, for Carlyle,

> Swarmery threatens to wrest political control from Britain's "Real-Superiors."[. . .] True emancipation, Carlyle believed, comes from finding and fulfilling one's place in a social hierarchy and paying honorable allegiance to the cultural elite best suited by birth, training, precedent, and disposition to fulfill humankind's "instinctive desire of Guidance." Without that guidance, human society devolves into brutal and beastlike forms of existence, no better than cattle, beavers, and bees.[12]

It is true, of course, that this social hierarchy is code for hierarchies of race, class, and gender. Carlyle looks at the activism of emancipated slaves, workers, and women and sees disorder and chaos, but the reason for this is not simple: he sees the constituted powers that he defends as just—not perfect, certainly—but worth defending against an order that would be, in his judgment, less just than the one under which he lives.

In a memorable phrase in "Shooting Niagara," Carlyle writes that democracy is a "cutting asunder [of the] straps and ties . . . of old regulations, fetters, and restrictions."[13] Scholars have taken Carlyle's argument to be a critique of representative, parliamentary democracy, and it is. But the text actually spends very little time discussing what Carlyle calls "anarchic parliaments."[14] To put this point in high relief, Carlyle does none of the work that Schmitt would do a half century later, for example, in *Dictatorship* or *The Crisis of Parliamentary Democracy*, his detailed critiques of the parliamentary system. Rather, for Carlyle, aristocracy is the authority of the wise, which gives structure to a hierarchy of talent, backed by force. These systems are the straps and ties that keep people in place, but they are also what keep the world from coming undone. Democracy is the chaotic, disruptive power of people challenging that hierarchy and producing alternatives to it. Carlyle's picture of what democracy could be is made from images of people struggling against the exploitation of their labor: revolts of workers in Morant Bay, Jamaica, trade union strikes, and activists campaigning for the eight-hour workday. Carlyle's hatred of democracy, in other words, was produced on plantations, in factories, and in streets full of picketers.

Walt Whitman's *Democratic Vistas*, the text that Cornel West and Roberto Mangabeira Unger call "the secular bible of American democracy,"[15] was originally written as a response to "Shooting Niagara." For Whitman, "how to democratize" was a problem for "statesman, students, and men of any brains," regardless of what the "windy little gentlemen"—a reference to Carlyle—"who swarm in literature, in the magazines" might say.[16] Whitman steps quite close to advocating for a broad conception of direct democracy: he delayed the publication of *Democratic Vistas* until he could include a note on the recent news of the Paris Commune,[17] and in the text he calls for the democratization of schools, of workplaces, of the military, and of religious institutions.[18]

Yet as Ed Folsom points out, the metaphor of Whitman's title is more famous than the essay itself—perhaps justifiably so: *Democratic Vistas* shows the sharp limits of who he thought should be included and excluded from the nineteenth century body politic.[19] Whitman's imagination of democracy was made from the labors of soldiers, women, and workers but was tempered by his inability to see beyond Carlyle's basic assumptions about a need for hierarchy, even in a democracy, and about racial inequality—it is also notable for a nearly complete silence on the subject of slavery and Reconstruction, even though these topics often surface elsewhere in his texts, and even though *Democratic Vistas* clearly shows the resonances of the Reconstruction-era debates and institutional changes. That Whitman is silent on these matters does him no service. *Democratic Vistas* is a complicated text—certainly too complicated to be seen as an unambiguous celebration of democracy, either as a type of power or as a form of government. The text is, rather, a good example of what Kenneth Price calls Whitman's "signature phrase": "Be radical—be radical—be not too damned radical!"[20] One may wish for Whitman to be the unambiguous celebrator of democracy that many think him to be, but this is not borne out by the evidence in *Democratic Vistas*. Yet, as I will suggest, that ambiguity has value, too: Whitman has seen the collective power of people organized as race riot, and he has also seen the collective power of people undermine the system of racialized slavery. He has seen the constituted power of the state use the force at its disposal to perpetuate slavery, and also, later, use its force to abolish it.

In these ways, the debates in Carlyle and Whitman's essays are an insight into how two of the nineteenth century's most prominent writers understood the era's changing interpretations of democracy. But their conversation is also remarkable for what it leaves silent: the voices of the slaves, women, and workers who attract, respectively, their ire and their ambiguity. Whereas Carlyle mocked the movements hoping to secure an eight-hour workday,[21] Lucy Parsons was one of that movement's most important participants. Whitman

imagined the possibility of a democracy that moved beyond state governance, but Parsons was among the first who advocated for strike tactics that
she reasoned would win improvements in working conditions but would also
lead to an industrial democracy where workers would occupy their factories
and run them without managers. In these moments Parsons unmistakably
foreshadows the sit-down strikes in Flint, Michigan, during the 1930s, the
Hungarian Revolution that James would analyze in *Facing Reality*, and the
contemporary movements for *empresas recuperadas* in Argentina, worker-
run factories "recuperated" by those workers after the factories were shuttered by their previous owners. She writes, "My conception of the strike of
the future is not to strike and go out and starve, but to strike and remain in
and take possession of the necessary property of production."[22] Lucy Parsons
never adopted the position of looking from the perspective of constituted
power. She is not among the cadre of former radicals whose views mellow or
acquiesce as their careers grow longer. She provides a sharp contrast to both
Carlyle and Whitman, who both drifted further into reaction as their careers
went into their late stages.

Parsons writes that "there are actual, material barriers blockading the way"
to liberty, and they "must be removed."

> If we could hope they would melt away, or be voted or prayed into nothingness,
> we would be content to wait and vote and pray. But they are like great frowning
> rocks towering between us and a land of freedom, while the dark chasms of a
> hard-fought past yawn behind us. Crumbling they may be with their own weight
> and the decay of time, but to quietly stand under until they fall is to be buried in
> the crash. There is something to be done in a case like this—the rocks must be
> removed. Passivity while slavery is stealing over us is a crime.[23]

Parsons unequivocally believes in the power to remove those rocks, and what
she sketches here in metaphor, she would clarify in a life of writing and activism. In the 1870s and 1880s, Chicago was at the heart of the campaign to
reduce the workday from twelve or fourteen hours to eight, and Parsons was
one of that movement's most prominent participants. Relatively little scholarship on Parsons exists, however. This silence is due to several reasons: first, as
Carolyn Ashbaugh writes, "Lucy Parsons was black, a woman, and working
class—three reasons people are often excluded from history."[24] Second, the
day after Parsons died, the Chicago police raided her apartment and confiscated her library and writings.[25] Furthermore, Lucy Parsons was a radical,
even to other radicals, standing out in the anarchist and socialist movements
of her day. Parsons thought that representative democracy could be only a

sham—a tool for plutocrats to retain their power. Real self-government, she argued, is built from the direct action of people in their workplaces and communities, and is sustained by their cooperation.

The balance of this chapter delves into greater detail about these authors' work in order to show how they understood the power I call direct democracy. Whether they attack it, are ambivalent to it, or recommend it, none of the authors view democracy only as the embodiment of the institutional forms of representative, parliamentary systems, even though they lived under governments that could be described as such. To them it is people agitating for rights that have been denied them, the forces rising up to destabilize and change the forms and institutions of constituted power. As I wrote above, direct democracy has common characteristics—enough to recognize it as a coherent phenomenon—but it is not the same in every context. This is why it is useful to look at it in different lights, from different perspectives in a comparative analysis.

London, 1865–1867: *Vae Victis*, Woe to the Creed That Is Not Backed by Machine Guns

As far as Thomas Carlyle was concerned, democracy was a path to chaos and ruin. Thomas F. Haddox writes, "Although specifically a response to [Benjamin] Disraeli's Reform Bill, which was about to enfranchise much of the working class in Britain, [Carlyle's essay] 'Shooting Niagara' is more generally a condemnation of democratic government as such."[26] Haddox is correct, but there is more to the story. Carlyle was critical of democratic governance, to be sure, but his greater interest—and object of greater scorn—was what he called "the swarm": those people and political movements who were "cutting asunder [the] straps and ties . . . of old regulations, fetters, and restrictions."[27] Carlyle's examples of democratic excess never come from the inside of what he calls "anarchic parliaments,"[28] but rather are drawn from situations of workers in revolt, especially in Morant Bay, Jamaica; or from the "Trades Union, in quest of its '4 eights,' with assassin pistol in its hand,"[29] a grim reference to the labor movement's demand for "Eight hours to work, eight hours to play, / Eight hours to sleep, and eight shillings a day"; or from the needletrade workers on strike, "thirty thousand of [whom were] now on the pavements of London."[30] For Carlyle, democracy was like Peter Linebaugh and Marcus Rediker's many-headed hydra, a multiple and fearful representation of collective power, filled with hostility for the ideologies and institutions that dominate it and exploit it. Carlyle hated this democracy because he knew it could alter the constituted powers he believed in, and he could not see anything valuable in the new forms it would produce. Put another way, Carlyle was opposed to democracy as a form of government, but he was bitterly and vociferously opposed to the political movements and their direct democratic power.

⑥   ⑥   ⑥

"Shooting Niagara" appeared anonymously in *Macmillan's Magazine* in April 1867 and was edited and expanded soon thereafter into a pamphlet. James Anthony Froude, who was himself the author of *The English in the West Indies*, and who therefore not only was Carlyle's apologist but also responsible for circulating colonial ideologies, wrote that "Shooting Niagara"

> was Carlyle's last public utterance on English politics. He thought but little of it, and was aware how useless it would prove. In [Carlyle's] Journal, August 3 [1867], he says:—"An article for Masson and *Macmillan's Magazine* took up a good deal of time. It came out mostly from accident, little by volition, and is very fierce, exaggerative, ragged, unkempt, and defective. Nevertheless I am secretly rather glad than otherwise that it is out, that the howling doggeries (dead ditto and other) should have my last word on their affairs and them, since it was to be had."[31]

D. J. Trela, writing in *Victorian Periodicals Review*, argues that Froude and Carlyle may be a bit disingenuous here.[32] By showing the essay's publication history, Trela suggests that it was not hastily written, but rather was a carefully crafted document, containing ideas that Carlyle had held for some time. The essay's tone and content are harsh, which may lead to the assumption that it was something of a castoff piece, but in fact, the opposite is true: "Shooting Niagara" is haughty and bigoted—an apt representation of Carlyle's thought near the end of his career.

Nevertheless, Carlyle knew that his "last word" would be met with resistance. The appeal for electoral reform at the time was widespread, with support from the Reform League and Reform Union, as well as the British labor movement. In the same year that "Shooting Niagara" was published, the British parliament decriminalized labor unions and passed the Reform Act of 1867, known as the Second Reform Act, mostly in an effort to appease the demands of the political movements. The Second Reform Act was intended to enfranchise sober, skilled men, and it had the effect of enfranchising much of the male working class.[33]

The main argument of Carlyle's essay is a nineteenth-century update of what Michel Foucault calls "the aristocratic thesis" in *Fearless Speech*. Foucault suggests that the ancient arguments against democracy are rooted in the idea that certain people need to be led for their own good and for the good of the community as a whole: because in a democracy, the people are the most numerous and include the worst citizens, the best citizens are overruled.[34] Therefore, what is best for the *demos*, the people, cannot be what is best for the *polis*, the city. Carlyle wields the aristocratic thesis as a tool to maintain an established order that he sees as worth conserving. Like a modern Plato, Carlyle pins his hopes on the people he calls "heroes,"[35] who by their talent and merit ought to sit in positions of authority over others. Conversely, Carlyle is also concerned with the implications of the "worst citizens" having political power. The "And After?" of his title speaks volumes: if the democratic franchise were to be expanded too widely, Carlyle argues, everyone would suffer. As was apparent in arguments about the autonomy of former slaves in Haiti, the strongest arguments against democratic government concern the capacity of people to rule themselves. On this question, Carlyle's answer is unequivocal: the "Niagara leap of completed Democracy," taking too much, too soon, for too many, is a foolish way to commit suicide.[36]

The broader body of Carlyle's thought is more complicated than he displays in "Shooting Niagara": he did not view the political community in which he lived as ideal, as his critiques of the shabbiness and cheapness of capitalism make clear, but in comparison to the demands made by the anticolonial, suffrage, and labor movements of his time, demands he saw as folly, he viewed the constituted powers of his community as comparatively just, and he wrote to protect them. It is impossible, in my judgment, to separate Carlyle's bigotry from his defense of these constituted powers, because inequalities, especially inequalities of race and intellectual talent, are the most important characteristics of the constituted powers he defends.

He begins the essay by stating that he was waiting for

Democracy to complete itself; to go the full length of its course, towards the Bottomless or into it, no power now extant to prevent it or even considerably retard it,—till we have seen where it will lead us to, and whether there will *then* be any return possible, or none. Complete "liberty" to all persons; Count of Heads to be the Divine Court of Appeal on every question and interest of mankind; Count of Heads to choose a Parliament according to its own heart at last, and sit with Penny Newspapers zealously watching the same; said Parliament, so chosen and

> so watched, to do what trifle of legislating and administering may still be needed in such an England, with its hundred and fifty millions "free" more and more to follow each his own nose, by way of guide-post in this intricate world.[37]

In keeping with his nineteenth-century version of the aristocratic thesis, Carlyle argues that governing ought to be the purview of the educated and expert, who have the required skills for the task. Carlyle's preference is for a mix of aristocracy and meritocracy, where, in keeping with the lessons of Plato's *Republic*, those who govern are the best at governing:

> [The] Industrial hero, here and there recognisable and known to me, as developing himself, and as an opulent and dignified kind of man, is already almost an Aristocrat by class. . . . He cannot do better than unite with this naturally noble kind of Aristocrat by title; the Industrial noble and this one are brothers born; called and impelled to coöperate and go together. Their united result is what we want from both. And the Noble of the Future,—if there be any such, as I well discern there must,—will have grown out of both.[38]

He expresses the aristocratic wish for enlightened forms of authority: the problem he believes needs solving is to identify and train the people who would most skillfully hold the reins of power, regardless of whether these heroes are industrial workers or bluebloods.

Carlyle writes to defend hierarchical institutions like the "Aristocracy" because "[c]ertain it is, there is nothing but vulgarity in our People's expectations, resolutions or desires, in this Epoch. It is all a peaceable mouldering or tumbling down from mere rottenness and decay.[39] As Marx said of Napoleon, the despot always sees degraded people. What makes Carlyle worthy of attention here, then, is not just his insults, but his proposals for dealing with those he saw as degraded. Plato solved the problem of how to keep people in their place in a hierarchy by telling "noble lies" about how they were born with particular metals in their veins.[40] In the long nineteenth century, lies alone were insufficient, so Carlyle would solve the problem in a much more directly disciplinary fashion: "one often wishes the entire Population could be thoroughly drilled; into coöperative movement, into individual behaviour, correct, precise, and at once habitual and orderly as mathematics, in all or in very many points,—and ultimately in the point of actual *Military Service*, should such be required of it!"[41]

Thus far, there is little in "Shooting Niagara" that diverges from the ancient articulation of the aristocratic thesis, or from the conservative notion that a just order comes from finding one's place in a natural or meritocratic hierarchy. Race, gender, or class-based hierarchies, in Carlyle's vision, are not problematic; rather, they contribute to the overall stability of the community. As Catherine Hall writes in *Civilising Subjects*, "[f]or Carlyle, mastership and servantship were the only conceivable deliverance from what he saw as the really dangerous forms of tyranny and slavery, when the strong, the great, and the noble-minded were enslaved to the weak and the mean in the name of some foolish notion of rights."[42] But Carlyle is more than a cruel nineteenth-century Plato: he builds upon the aristocratic thesis and updates it to fit his time and situation. As I suggested, "Shooting Niagara" reveals several ideas about democracy that might be seen only by someone who hates it.

The hierarchy that Carlyle advocates is opposed to what he, like Carl Schmitt and others, calls "Swarmery,"[43] and he means it, like other writers in this tradition, to convey an insult that brings with it particular types of consequences: "enthusiasm" as excessive zeal, or uncritical, unreasonable advocacy. Therefore, "the gathering of men in swarms" is analogous, in Carlyle's view, to "perfection of unanimity and quasi-religious conviction" in which "the stupidest absurdities can be received as axioms of Euclid, nay as articles of faith."[44] Simply put, Carlyle suggests that while in groups, some people lose their abilities to think rationally; therefore, they become susceptible to proposals that would otherwise seem silly, such as "'Manhood Suffrage'—Horsehood, Doghood, ditto" or "universal 'glorious Liberty'" or even "the equality of men."[45] In Carlyle's definition, "swarmery" is when passions, not reason, lead groups to demand the rights that have been denied them. If such claims were based in reason, he suggests, people would give up what he sees as foolish notions of universal rights:

In our own country, too, *Swarmery* has played a great part for many years past; and especially is now playing, in these very days and months. . . . Ask yourself about "Liberty," for example; what you do really mean by it, what in any just and rational soul is that Divine quality of liberty? That a good man be "free," as we call it, be permitted to unfold himself in works of goodness and nobleness, is surely a blessing to him, immense and indispensable;—to him and to those about him. But that a bad man be "free,"—permitted to unfold himself in *his* particular way, is contrariwise the fatallest curse you could inflict on him; curse and nothing else, to him and all his neighbours. Him the very Heavens call upon you to persuade, to urge, induce, compel, into something of well-doing; if you absolutely cannot, if he will continue in ill-doing,—then for him (I can assure you, though you will be shocked to hear it), the one "blessing" left is the speediest gallows you can lead him to.[46]

This last flourish—Carlyle's advocating the death penalty for some unnamed crime—is like the first blow when someone is no longer playacting but is, rather, deadly serious. Two ideas become plain after a close inspection of "Shooting Niagara": the first is that Carlyle states openly what Plato could only imply, namely, that hierarchical institutions would have to be secured by a combination of ideology and force.[47] In this regard, George Orwell sums up Carlyle's view succinctly: it is "*vae victis*—woe to the creed that is not backed by machine guns!"[48] This is what Carlyle sees clearly: his addition to Foucault's aristocratic thesis, in short, is to apply the methods of control that were being used against the former slaves in the colonies to the population in the metropole as well. Carlyle sees what Carl Schmitt would see a half-century later in *Dictatorship*: a person cannot reason with another person who has no reason—the latter can be dealt with only by using force. This is, of course, a cynical definition of "reason": to be "reasonable" in such a case is to operate within the logic of constituted power, taking the structures and ideologies of that constituted power as given and beyond critique. The question of whether constituted powers can themselves be irrational is not one that Carlyle finds worth asking—he has harsh words for the "cheap and nasty" capitalists of his day, but he never calls for killing them.

Carlyle here shows with plain language, furthermore, what Schmitt could only state circumspectly, even though their logic is parallel and their metaphor identical. *Schwärmerei* and its uses here are plain: what Carlyle sees as illogical and unexplicable, others see as rights; what he sees as animalistic behavior, others see as an expression of their collective power to protest, to act directly against the institutions that oppress them. Schmitt's writing is far more judicious, both in his tone and his examples, than Carlyle's writing is. Even in *Dictatorship*, where his example questions whether a constituted power could legally use poison gas against people in the name of protecting those people, Schmitt is serious about state terrorism, whereas Carlyle's tone suggests that he is glib and untroubled. But to suggest a distinction between them would be to mistake tone for content; their logic is analogous, even if the gallows is not poison gas. The effects of being found guilty of *Schwärmerei* are the same. Carlyle says plainly what Schmitt only implies: the alternative logic that opposes a constituted power is not logic at all but is, rather, illogic, and one cannot negotiate with illogic; one can only command it. Reason dictates, says Schmitt.

The content of what Carlyle calls "liberty" is what is in contention here: more precisely, who would be fit for it. This is evident when he asks, in the quote above, what his audience really means by liberty—he raises this question because he assumes his audience cannot answer it. The answer to it, of course, is in the streets, striking for an eight-hour workday, and on the plantations where the unhealed wounds of forced labor still sting, but these answers express a logic that Carlyle would not understand.

What Carlyle could understand, and wrote about insightfully, was a view of democracy as a struggle between the hydra-like power of direct democracy and the institutions and ideologies of the constituted powers that he holds dear. Carlyle's position in this debate could not be any clearer: the power of aristocracy, to him, with its stability and tradition, needs protection against the power of people agitating to demand their rights. To perhaps a greater degree than any other example he mentions in "Shooting Niagara," the rebellion in Morant Bay, Jamaica, in 1865 provides Carlyle with his ideas about democracy, at home or abroad. "Jamaica is an angry subject," Carlyle writes, "and I am shy to speak of it."[49] This is a bit coy: Carlyle knew more about the history of forced labor in the Caribbean than many of his contemporaries—a fact he shows through references to the Haitian Revolution in his history of the French Revolution.[50] Carlyle knew how the power of revolutionary slaves could topple the Atlantic slavocracy, so when he saw open, massive rebellion of exploited workers in Jamaica, he knew where the implications of that struggle could lead: Jamaica could be a second Haiti.

The British Emancipation Act had taken force in 1838, ostensibly freeing the former slaves in Jamaica, but in the decades after, high poll taxes and widespread unemployment, together with hard conditions, including a severe drought in 1863–1865, made the situation for many black Jamaicans intolerable. As Sarah Winter observes, "political instability [was] caused by economic hardship," together with long-simmering racial tensions.[51] On October 7, 1865, after months of "Underhill Meetings," named after Edward Underhill, the Secretary of the Baptist Missionary Society, to discuss these problems, a black man was sentenced for trespassing on a plantation that had long sat vacant. This was the match set to dry tinder. Four days later, two hundred to three hundred people marched to Morant Bay, in the eastern part of Jamaica, where they were met by a small, inexperienced militia. In the confrontation, the crowd threw rocks at the militia, which returned fire. The crowd then attacked the militia. Seven people from the crowd and eighteen militia members were killed.[52]

Like Carlyle, Jamaica's colonial governor, John Eyre, knew that such rebellions could lead to a replay of the dynamics in Haiti.[53] Eyre sent military troops to check the rebellion, and the reprisal was fierce. Eyre declared martial law and instructed the military to repress all who had taken part in the rebellion. Such an order led to indiscriminate domination of the black population: in the following days, hundreds of people were killed outright, or were arrested, flogged, then executed.[54] Eyre passed sedition laws in order to squelch unrest further. "One moment's hesitation," Eyre said, "one single reverse might have lit the torch which would have blazed in rebellion from one end of the island to the other; and who can say how many of us would have lived to see it extinguished."[55]

News of the Morant Bay Rebellion reached London in late October 1865 and became a major event for press attention and public debate. The Jamaica Committee, to which Carlyle mockingly refers in "Shooting Niagara,"[56] was set up to urge Eyre's prosecution; the committee included John Stuart Mill, Charles Darwin, Thomas Huxley, and Herbert Spencer.[57] In contrast, a committee was established to defend Eyre, and Carlyle was elected its chair.[58] So while Carlyle is coy in "Shooting Niagara," his material support for Eyre tells a different story. Carlyle was willing to reinforce his positions in his essay with deeds. He saw Eyre's repression as necessary and proper for the maintenance of hierarchy, and thought that such remedies were as applicable to the colonies as they were to the metropole.

None of the details about Carlyle's work to defend Eyre appear in the text of "Shooting Niagara." Instead, what Carlyle delivers there is a bigoted colonial fantasy, which is worth quoting at length:

> I have sometimes thought what a thing it would be, could a Queen . . . pick out some gallant-minded, stout, well-gifted cadet;—younger son of a Duke, of an Earl, of a Queen herself . . . and say to him, 'Young fellow, if there do lie in you potentialities of governing, of gradually guiding, leading and coercing to a noble goal, how sad is it that they should be all lost! They are the grandest gifts a mortal can have; and they are, of all, the most necessary to other mortals in this world. See, I have scores on scores of 'Colonies,' all ungoverned, and nine-tenths of them full of jungles, boa-constrictors, rattlesnakes, Parliamentary Eloquences, and Emancipated Niggers ripening towards nothing but destruction: one of these *you* shall have, you as Vice-King; on rational conditions, and *ad vitam aut culpam* it shall be yours (and perhaps your posterity's if worthy): go you and buckle with it, in the name of Heaven; and let us see what you will build it to! To something how much better than the Parliamentary Eloquences are doing,—thinks the reader? Good Heavens, these West-India Islands, some of them, appear to be the richest and most favoured spots on the Planet Earth.[59]

Veiled but unmistakable, considering the time and context: Carlyle's text is a response to the Morant Bay Rebellion. In the next sentence, Carlyle mentions Jamaica by name, only to switch topics quickly.[60] But context makes plain what Carlyle only represents vaguely. The lesson Carlyle takes from the Morant Bay Rebellion is that repression is the remedy for these situations, whether the rebellions are in the colonies or on the London streets. Carlyle observed all around him that members of the working-class movements sympathized with the murdered Jamaicans.[61] He saw that rebellion in Jamaica was cross-pollinated with the movements in London, and he wanted them repressed in similar fashion.

Carlyle's hatred of democracy, therefore, was rooted in a wish to put some check on it; "Parliamentary eloquences" are just one in a larger list of the characteristics of that power. He hates it because in it he sees real threats to the political order: he sees an uncontrollable swarm remaking the world around him. He correctly sees that these political movements may refigure the dynamics of political power, and he reacts to conserve the order that he believes to be worth protecting. Carlyle's arguments are usually read as a condemnation of the burgeoning parliamentary democracy, and they are. But while parliamentary democracy was problematic for Carlyle, the root of his concern does not come from parliament—it comes from plantations, factories, and from streets full of strikers. So from Morant Bay to the streets of London, and then from Carlyle's pen, ideas circulate in networks, informing democratic struggle. After Walt Whitman read "Shooting Niagara," he used that text as a springboard for his own evolving ideas.

Washington, D.C., 1865–1871: The Democratization of All Public and Private Life

"Democracy," Walt Whitman writes, "is a word the real gist of which still sleeps."[62] In response to Carlyle, Whitman argues that to think of what democracy could be was to think of the future, both for good and for ill. This suited his era: he was living in a moment of what he considered to be rapid and considerable change to the institutions of representative democracy and of new experiments with alternative forms of democratization. In the years he composed the essays that would become *Democratic Vistas*, Whitman was living in Washington, D.C., where many early struggles for black suffrage took place, well before the Fifteenth Amendment to the US Constitution was ratified.[63] In 1871 he stopped *Democratic Vistas* on its way to the printer because he received news of the Paris Commune, which he recognized as precisely the type of experiment with the new forms of democracy that his essay imagined.[64] Whitman drew both from the Commune's example and from Carlyle's hostility in order to look into democracy's future.

To his credit, Whitman had a far greater tolerance for innovations in democracy than many people in his era. "[A]ll appears impracticable," Whitman writes, referring to Carlyle, "among these windy little gentlemen that swarm in literature, in the magazines."[65] But while Whitman "presume[d] to write, as it were, upon things that exist not, and travel by maps yet unmade,"[66] his views are both radical and reactionary. His examination of democracy in America after the Civil War led him to imagine a form of democracy in workplaces and schools, a democracy that is far less alienated than anything that a government exercises. Try though he does, however, Whitman cannot make a clean break with Carlyle: in substance, Whitman, like Carlyle, also subscribes to what Foucault calls the aristocratic thesis. Rather than solving the problem of what Whitman calls "the people's crudeness, vice, [and] caprices"[67] with military drill or repressive force, as Carlyle does, Whitman advocates for a class of what he calls "divine literatuses"[68] to prepare the people for the tasks of democratic citizenship. For Whitman, democracy could be a political system fit for free people, but only if poets did the job of training them properly.

Whitman sees ambivalence in the masses of people—he has seen mobs in race riots and masses of people organized to overthrow racial slavery; he has seen vicious crowds and emancipation movements. That he nevertheless advocates for a wider commitment to democratic principles—although with caveats, as we will see—is to his credit, but *Democratic Vistas* is not simply a celebration of democracy's forward march. The text is a touchstone in a particularly transitory moment, when most people considered the idea of democracy dangerous, part of the logic of what Schmitt and others call constituent power, but also in a moment when democracy is coming to be seen as a part of the logic of constituted power. As he asks in the essay, "Who bridle Leviathan?" Whitman recognizes that people have power, enough so that they may need to be bridled, but he also sees democratic innovations and institutional changes that he supported, to some degree.

As was also true for Carlyle, Whitman spends surprisingly little time in *Democratic Vistas* on the problems of representation and parliaments, and sees democracy in the actions of wide swaths of people, not in anything he observes in Congress. He is concerned with the expansion of the voting franchise, but his preferred set of examples is about issues far removed from congresses: Whitman's antislavery views are well known; for good or ill, his ideas about including women in the body politic, for example, are rooted in their labor. Likewise, in early versions of the text, he highlights "the labor question" and its bearing on how democracy might evolve beyond questions of governing and elections, even though in later editions of the text, he removes that reference.[69] In short, Carlyle thought that little of value could ever come from the people, with few exceptions; democracy was chaotic and irrationally dangerous. Whitman thought that every person had the capacity for autonomy—they only needed the proper training for democratic participation. They agree on the need for hierarchy, one aristocratic and the other democratic; and equally important, both authors see the problems of slavery and labor as problems of democracy, not of representative democracy, but rather a more direct manifestation of people expressing their power.

⑥ ⑥ ⑥

Whitman was fairly frequently concerned with Carlyle's writing. In 1846 Whitman wrote in his *Brooklyn Daily Eagle* review of Carlyle's book *On Heroes, Hero-Worship, and the Heroic in History* that Carlyle is a "Democrat" in an "enlarged sense," meaning that "he is quick to champion the downtrodden, and earnest in his wrath at tyranny."[70] But by the time Whitman read "Shooting Niagara," his critique had crystallized. In *Specimen Days*, published in 1882, Whitman's views on Carlyle were apparent. In the essay "Carlyle from American Points of View," for example, Whitman writes that "Carlyle's grim fate was cast to live and dwell in, and largely embody, the parturition agony and qualms of the old order, amid crowded accumulations of ghastly morbidity, giving birth to the new."[71] Whitman recognized in Carlyle something quite useful: a voice for this "old order," an articulation of the key ideas about aristocracy against which Whitman could imagine a more democratic future.

Betsy Erkkila writes that while *Democratic Vistas* "originated in an effort to 'counterblast' Carlyle's attack,[. . .] Whitman quickly realized that he shared Carlyle's diagnosis of the diseases of democracy."[72] "I was at first roused to much anger and abuse by this essay from Mr. Carlyle, so insulting to the theory of America," Whitman writes,

> but happening to think afterwards how I had more than once been in the like
> mood, during which his essay was evidently cast, and seen persons and things
> in the same light, (indeed some might say there are signs of the same feeling in
> these Vistas)—I have since read it again, not only as a study, expressing as it does
> certain judgments from the highest feudal point of view, but have read it with
> respect as coming from an earnest soul, and as contributing certain sharp-cutting
> metallic grains, which, if not gold or silver, may be good hard, honest iron.[73]

Whitman first was stung by the argument Carlyle makes in "Shooting Niagara" but, after further reflection, saw in Carlyle's essay a problem Whitman thought democracy would have to confront, namely, as he writes in *Democratic Vistas*, "who [would] bridle Leviathan."[74] In other words, how to find the class of people who would train the rest of the population so they would be fit for democratic participation? Whitman writes that Carlyle "sneeringly asks whether we expect to elevate and improve a nation's politics by absorbing such morbid collections and qualities therein. The point is a formidable one, and there will doubtless always be numbers of solid and reflective citizens who will never get over it."[75] In short, Carlyle's views on common people are final—with few exceptions, nothing is ever to come from the vast majority of the "rubbish heap."[76] Whitman sees "the people's crudeness," but he thinks that poets can train this crudeness out of them, and therefore, this crudeness is not a sufficient basis for their continued disenfranchisement.[77] Whitman's comments about idiocracy—which he spells "idiocrasy"[78]—most clearly separate his point of view from Carlyle's. Idiocracy, which literally means personal rule or government, is a loose synonym for autonomy. Many have missed the connection between idiocracy and autonomy, a connection which is underscored by the reference Whitman makes to "John Stuart Mill's profound essay on Liberty in the future."[79] The point is important to Carlyle and Whitman because they reason that the metric used to determine if the people could rule in a democracy is whether or not the capacity for self-government could be cultivated in the people. Carlyle sees no intrinsic capacity, no *potentia* or *puissance* in most people; Whitman sees this capacity in people but thinks it needs to be cultivated by a particular class, by a priestly vanguard that goes by the name of divine literatuses.

⑥ ⑥ ⑥

Whitman had a greater tolerance for innovation and change than Carlyle did, but ultimately Whitman cannot separate himself fully from Carlyle's views on the aristocratic thesis, and therefore, he translates the aristocratic thesis into the language of democracy. It is difficult to overstate the importance of this move. Carlyle's understanding of democracy had long been dominant: most people saw democracy as little more than mob rule, anarchic, and akin to disorder. To recast the aristocratic thesis into democratic language is less to separate democracy from aristocracy and more to remake democracy so it looks more like an elected aristocracy.[80] It is a move to place the interpretation of democracy in the realm of governance: because in the generations previous to Whitman's, democracy was seen as little more than mayhem, to reinterpret it in a way that makes it palatable to the rulers is to remove much of its radical potential. Over the course of the long nineteenth century, this interpretive move would come to have wide purchase: representative democracy became the default definition of democracy, thus removing the need for its adjective. As is frequently pointed out, the architects of representative governance in the United States, with notable exceptions, perhaps,[81] had skepticism about democracy as such and therefore designed a system that would check popular participation in representative governance.

Whitman was well aware of these facts and, to his credit, tried to imagine a more expansive democracy, both within and outside of those parameters. But the gist of *Democratic Vistas* is about a debate with Carlyle over the people's capacity. Stephen John Mack writes that "Whitman had always understood that democracy could only be justified by a faith that every human being possessed a natural capacity for self-governance."[82] But unlike James in the "Lectures on *The Black Jacobins*," in *Democratic Vistas*, Whitman gets lost in a fog of a conversation about capacity: the problem is that, for Whitman, having a faith that every human being has the capacity for self-governance is entirely compatible with the position that a certain segment of the population might be ready for self-government someday, but not today. Whitman's disagreement with Carlyle therefore is not about the need for a hierarchy of people, but about the substance of that hierarchy. They agree that some type of hierarchy will be necessary, if only, in Whitman's case, for a limited time. What kind and for what duration, Whitman does not specify. One gets no sense from *Democratic Vistas* of the kind of vicious domination Carlyle recommends, of course—Whitman's approach is more like literary paternalism than Carlyle's proposed military drill. But questions of capacity are the way for Whitman to maintain his ambivalence between the failings of actual people and the hopes for a more democratic future. Put plainly, Whitman does not rebut the aristocratic thesis in any sense: rather, he recasts the aristocratic thesis in democratic language.

Whitman's position is apparent, for example, when he shows his nascent support for women's equality. As Whitman was writing, many women were putting the skills they learned in abolition movements to use to advance their own rights. On this topic, Whitman is tentative but hopeful:

Democracy, in silence, biding its time, ponders its own ideals, not of literature and art only—not of men only, but of women. The idea of the women of America, (extricated from this daze, this fossil and unhealthy air which hangs about the word *lady*,) develop'd, raised to become the robust equals, workers, and, it may be, even practical and political deciders with the men.[. . .] Then there are mutterings, (we will not now stop to heed them here, but they must be heeded,) of something more revolutionary. The day is coming when the deep questions of woman's entrance amid the arenas of practical life, politics, the suffrage, &c., will not only be argued all around us, but may be put to decision, and real experiment.[83]

Whitman anchors his support for women's equality on the basis of their labor.[84] He spends a rather significant section of *Democratic Vistas* justifying equal rights along gender lines by showing the dignity of women's work: as domestic workers, but also as mechanics, farmers, and "Peacemakers."[85] Ed Folsom notes that many women in the suffrage movement noted Whitman's support, and that they in turn admired Whitman's writing.[86] One can imagine that these activists would have preferred Whitman to write in more definitive terms, would have preferred him to stop and heed his "mutterings" at greater length, but tentative support is better than none, or outright opposition, which was frequent during the era in which Whitman was writing. Nevertheless, of all the groups making demands for a more inclusive and better democracy in the era in which Whitman was writing, he pays the greatest attention to women.[87]

Women in particular fare better than the working class does in *Democratic Vistas*. Whitman valued equality and the "great word Solidarity," and, as Andrew Lawson suggests in *Walt Whitman and the Class Struggle*, Whitman wanted to represent himself as "one of the roughs," but Whitman relegates "The Labor Question" to a footnote in the original edition of *Democratic Vistas* and deletes even that in subsequent editions.[88] This hesitance to discuss labor as such—even though the essay is filled with images of work and workers—is of a piece with Whitman's express refusal to discuss the problems of slavery's legacy directly. The latter is a fog in which Whitman gets lost completely.

Struggles over slavery are, as W. E. B. Du Bois writes in *Black Reconstruction*, struggles over "a real and new democracy in America": its nature, its scope, who would be included and excluded, and its virtues and vices.[89] Considering that the Civil War and its ramifications provide the occasion to write *Democratic Vistas*, its silence on the questions of Reconstruction tolls like a bell. As Folsom notes, for "Whitman, as for many white Americans in the Civil War era, it was possible to be opposed to slavery but also to be against equal rights for African Americans."[90] Whitman refuses to deliver a defense of the people formerly enslaved, let alone to advocate for any reparations, but he also refuses to relent in his defense of what democracy could be.

What Plato needed from noble lies and Carlyle needed from military drill, Whitman gets from his concept of "divine literatuses."[91] He left the concept of divine literatuses in each subsequent republication of *Democratic Vistas*, but the clearest definition appears only in the original edition:

> I say my eyes are fain to behold, though with straining sight[. . .] that Order,
> Class, superber, far more efficient than any hitherto arising. I say we must enlarge

and entirely recast the theory of noble authorship, and conceive and put up as our model, a Literatus—groups, series of Literatuses—not only consistent with modern science, practical, political full of the arts, of highest erudition—not only possessed by, and possessors of, Democracy even—but with the equal of the burning fire and extasy of Conscience.[92]

This is not so harsh as Carlyle's formulation, but it is a nevertheless apparent way to discipline a population for civic participation. Whitman rejects Carlyle's aristocracy or, as Whitman terms it, "feudalism," but the thing, the idea remains: a specialized few, Whitman argues, must lead an unprepared many. Whitman takes the idea of the aristocratic thesis and reworks it into a democratic frame. It is a concession to Carlyle that even democratic communities need a hierarchy of leaders and led. Whitman looked about him and saw a nation of people with promise, but who could be trusted to rule only at some future date.

Amid these weaknesses, there are suggestions in *Democratic Vistas* of a much more radical view of democracy. Perhaps put more sympathetically, it is consistent that Whitman, a writer who delighted in contradictions, would be inconsistent: *Democratic Vistas* contains material that fits within a broad democratic framework, one that sees democracy as the power to rule, and also as a direct expression of a people's power. Although he admits that his "mood" had been much like Carlyle's, it is "[t]o him or her within whose thought rages the battle, advancing, retreating, between democracy's convictions, aspirations, and the people's crudeness, vice, caprices, I mainly write this essay."[93] Whitman writes, "Anything worthy to be call'd statesmanship in the Old World, I should say, among the advanced students, adepts, or men of any brains, does not debate to-day whether to hold on, attempting to lean back and monarchize, or to look forward and democratize—but *how*, and in what degree and part, most prudently to democratize."[94]

It is a paradox: the vaguer Whitman gets, the more useful *Democratic Vistas* becomes. His comments on specific questions of his day, like women's suffrage and labor, are tepid, timid. His comments about Manifest Destiny make him out to be the policy's most poetic booster. One could speculate about the institutional form that a body of divine literatuses might take, but such speculation seems more comic than serious. The most interesting moments of *Democratic* Vistas, therefore, are those where he is vague, perhaps purposely. His concrete proposals tend toward hierarchy and reaction, but his principles and abstractions tend toward radical ideological and institutional change.

The radical abstractions, Whitman seems to suggest, are opportunities for subsequent generations to make material what his generation could only dream.[95] Whitman glimpses, somewhere in the future, what a better democratic government could be, but there is more. In response to "Shooting Niagara," Whitman suggests a full reinterpretation of democracy that would expand it beyond issues of governing and elections. Whitman's approach has less to do with being outside mainstream political opinion, and has more to do with getting to the roots that sustain political, educational, economic, and military institutions. Whitman's proposal in *Democratic Vistas* is for the radical democratization of civil society—of literature, churches, schools, and even the armed forces:

> Did you, too, O friend, suppose democracy was only for elections, for politics, and for a party name? I say democracy is only of use there that it may pass on and come to its flower and fruits in manners, in the highest forms of interaction between men, and their beliefs—in religion, literature, colleges, and schools—democracy in all public and private life, and in the army and navy.[96]

The radicalism of Whitman's proposal is palpable: he wants to democratize even the armed forces, the institutions that one might think would be most hostile to democratic organization. Whitman's radical idea is to democratize "all public and private life," an idea that is far-reaching in its implications, and has not been satisfactorily explored. To put it another way, Whitman was dissatisfied with an interpretation of democracy that limited its practices to periodic elections. Such a shallow concept restricts democracy to governance only and keeps its practices away from the institutions and situations where most people spend the majority of their time. A democracy limited to periodic elections would leave those practices outside the workplace, for example, and therefore condemn all labor to be at the command of capital.

Whitman underscores the proposal to democratize even institutions like "the army and the navy." He chooses this example purposefully, and confronts it directly:

> The whole present system of the officering and personnel of the army and navy of these States, and the spirit and letter of their trebly-aristocratic rules and regulations, is a monstrous exotic, a nuisance and revolt, and belong here just as much as orders of nobility, or the Pope's council of cardinals. I say if the present theory of our army and navy is sensible and true, then the rest of America is an unmitigated fraud.[97]

Why would Whitman place such an emphasis on democratizing the military? One possible answer is that it is difficult to find a set of organizations that is more rigidly hierarchical, and Whitman wants to present this specific challenge. Whitman also no doubt remembered that the military is Carlyle's model for the broader society, one where his heroes hold a high rank and where the people march in precise formation. It is no accident, then, that Whitman places such an emphasis on democratizing the armed services: to use his language, they are feudal organizations founded on the idea that authority ought to flow from the top of the hierarchy down. Whitman also looks at schools, churches, and literature and observes that they are all operating on similarly feudal foundations.

What concerns Whitman most about this future democracy is its principles. The problem Whitman sees is that the ideological foundations of the institutions he names are antagonistic to democratic ideals. Both the "spirit and letter" of the rules that govern the military, like other institutions in American civil society, are "aristocratic," and are therefore "exotic": they are not autochthonic, not rooted in America's grass, so to speak, but rather are borrowed from a country with "feudal" foundations.[98] Whitman's proposal to democratize "all public and private life" would seem to Carlyle as *Schwärmerei*: beyond the logic of constituted power, and therefore illogical, unwise, impractical, or impossible, but this is consistent: Carlyle writes to conserve the constituted power he believes to be just. While Whitman retains the gist of the aristocratic thesis, his translation of that idea into the language of democracy is not just to put the wolf of aristocracy into the sheep's clothing of democracy: Whitman feels that a democratic frame of reference and a democratic ideology are needed to reinterpret all aspects of American civil society, and that this democratization is a test to America itself: either democracy would take root in "all public and private life" or America would be "an unmitigated fraud."[99]

So in a certain sense, Whitman is proposing a type of deconstruction with this project: he is critiquing not just "public and private life" as they are but also their ideological foundations. Those "interior and vital principles" are the theoretical scaffolding for democracy; if those foundations were antithetical to democracy, then, like the army and the navy, American democracy would be an "unmitigated fraud." A democratic community, in Whitman's mind, cannot remain divided for long between a democratic ideal and a reality of a civil society and an economy operating with nondemocratic foundations. Yet while Carlyle is consistent in his defense of hierarchy, Whitman oscillates between advocating for the creativity of democracy and calling for the hierarchy of divine literatuses to guide people in more prudent directions. In a way, the problem of autonomy is simpler for Carlyle: because he thinks that the majority of people could never have it, he sees no reason even to begin thinking about altering political and cultural institutions accordingly, but rather he thinks about how best to conserve them as they are. Whitman, on the other hand, has the more complicated problems of both training people for this future democracy and sketching out what the principles of that future democracy would be.

But perhaps because of the conflict between his inability to move beyond the basic assumption of the aristocratic thesis and his hope for a future democracy, Whitman is honest about the difficulties of his suggestions. He writes,

> For America, type of progress, and of essential faith in man, above all his errors and wickedness—few suspect how deep, how deep it really strikes. The world evidently supposes, and we have evidently supposed so too, that the States are merely to achieve the equal franchise, an elective government—to inaugurate the respectability of labor, and become a nation of practical operatives, law-abiding, orderly and well off. Yes, those are indeed parts of the task of America; but they not only do not exhaust the progressive conception, but rather arise, teeming with it, as the mediums of deeper, higher progress. Daughter of a physical revolution—mother of the true revolutions, which are of the interior life, and of the arts.[100]

Much of Whitman's vision is in line with the constituted powers in the United States during the latter part of the nineteenth century. As Reconstruction was starting to fray, much of the rest of Whitman's political vision became more conservative, for example, his race, gender, and class analysis; his explicit support for Manifest Destiny; his phrases that have a dark nationalistic overtone; and his tendency to suggest that his ideas have divine origins. The notion of the "progressive conception," on the other hand, the power that arises, teeming, fits squarely with a conception of direct democracy. How might the power I call direct democracy find institutional form in the project that Whitman calls the democratization of "all public and private life," exactly? Whitman does not specify what he means by "all public and private life," other than mentioning religion, literature, colleges, schools, the army, and the navy; neither does he provide much practical detail. How might a democratic military operate? What would a democratic workplace look like? He does not sketch what, exactly, the institutions of this future democracy would look like, and rightly so: he knows that it is possible to look at trends and patterns in the dynamics of democracy, and from those, to look into its vistas, but also that any tangible prediction of the future is likely to be false, given the fact that human capacity evolves and adapts according to various dynamics. The vagueness of Whitman's ideas about the possible forms of democracy is like moldable clay: the material is there to make something with them, but the shape they will take is yet to be determined. It is an irony, then, that Whitman's vagaries suggest his most promising ideas about what democracy could be. This is part of the circulation of ideas: it would be left to others to make what Whitman suggests vaguely into more tangible forms, but vagueness provides that opportunity.

Chicago, 1871–1887: The Adaptation of Old Words to New Uses

Carlyle and Whitman had, in varying degrees, deference for authority, whether aristocratic or democratic. Lucy Parsons had none. She had seen too much of the violent repression that Carlyle advocated for, and had seen it from the opposite perspective that he did, to believe that a class of heroes or divine literatuses could ever advocate for her best interests. Unlike Whitman, Parsons could not wait for a future democracy: the repression she endured and observed made it clear to her that the work of making a better world is always something that continues in the present and never ceases. These experiences shaped her politics and proved to her that to look for salvation from above was a fool's errand. Real self-government means control over one's life and labor in cooperation with others, all of whom have those same rights. Parsons saw the collective direct democratic power of political movements through experience in those movements, and she saw that cooperation, not control, could be the basis for the organization of workplaces and communities.

In contrast to Carlyle and Whitman, Parsons rejected the aristocratic thesis completely, and like C. L. R. James, she viewed people's intrinsic power, not later, but in the present, as the key to their liberation. "The disinherited," Parsons wrote, "must work out their own salvation in their own way."[101] If democracy could only be a system where a person transferred her power to a representative, Lucy Parsons wanted none of it—that act is too similar to the ways in which capitalism transfers the wealth generated by a person's labor into the pockets of the bosses and owners.

However, much as Carlyle took from Plato, and Whitman from Carlyle, Parsons also picks up ideas and reworks them to meet her goals and her situation. She writes,

The introduction of new ideas into a man's mind is not accompanied by the use of a specially coined word, but by the adaptation of old words to broader uses. Even the word self-government would not convey our meaning in its broadest generalization. This word has been understood since its introduction into general use to mean a system of representative government—the delegation of personal rights to be represented by another person [is] deemed to be the highest approach of liberty possible in a state.[. . .] In every instance in which Americans use the word "self-government" it carries with it the idea of representation as well as administration."[102]

Therefore, to understand what democracy could be requires using this old word in new ways. To produce this thought, she mixed several intellectual traditions, most notably Marxism and anarchism.[103] The labor community in Chicago held celebrations marking the anniversaries of the Paris Commune; on the lecture circuit, Parsons would routinely give talks about the Commune and its lessons. What is known of her biography suggests that she was born into slavery; it is certain that she knew what life as a low-wage worker meant. She linked those two forms of labor together, arguing that the "overseer's whip is now fully supplanted by the lash of hunger."[104]

Lucy Parsons's ideas and activism in radical labor movements were dedicated to dismantling the systems and institutions she thought were unjust and to building better alternatives. Parsons rejected the basic premise of the aristocratic thesis, stating that the type of hierarchy was not the question, but rather the problem was hierarchy itself. Instead of an order based on authority, she suggested, cooperation, not control, could be the basis for a just community. In the same manner that Carlyle and Whitman do, but to vastly different purpose, Parsons mentions representative institutions, but only to transition away from them. Her understanding of democracy was rooted in places other than government:

> The old bottles answered to hold the old wine of politics. Economic questions, not being solvable by political methods,[105] demand new bottles for the new ideas time evolves. Government is stationary, social growth progressive; consequently we find ourselves arrived at a point where governments become a barrier to economic progress. True, this position is a reversal of the common accepted belief, which is that government is a help to progress. But a close study of the origin, tendency and operations of all governments will show that they *never* lead to progress. Governments always stand for the "established order of things."[106]

Parsons here develops further the ideas William Lloyd Garrison would say as he burned copies of the United States Constitution at abolitionist meetings: human capacity wants to grow; the established order of things wants to conserve itself and to maintain the power it has in relation to others. Both will adapt as necessary to continue their logical paths. Parsons's context and terminology are different from Garrison's but the gists of their ideas are analogous.

Perhaps to the same degree that Carlyle hated democracy, Parsons hated the constituted powers under which she lived, which she called "the established order of things." She knew, however, that the force for which Carlyle advocated had been deeply engrained in peoples' minds:

> So used have we become to "organized authority" in every department of life that ordinarily we cannot conceive of the most commonplace avocations being carried on without their interference or "protection."[. . .] People have become so used to seeing the evidences of authority on every hand that most of them honestly believe that they would go utterly to the bad if it were not for the policeman's club or the soldier's bayonet.[107]

It may be true that Parsons believed a bit too readily in something like an innate goodness to human nature, but she knew that the "policeman's club and the soldier's bayonet" were overwhelmingly used to make people submit to institutions that sacrificed the lives and labor of the poor, of slaves and ex-slaves, and of women, to serve the greed of a privileged few. If she hoped that, when uncoerced by illegitimate forms of authority, the better characteristics of humanity would present themselves more fully, she knew certainly that the institutions that are the objects of her critique not only permit but also perpetuate some of the worst characteristics of humanity: domination, exploitation, and bigotry. Therefore, to challenge the constituted powers—in her phrase, established order of things—requires a critical analysis of injustice, a proposal—even a tentative one—for what a better alternative could be, and a clear understanding that any real threats to that injustice would be met, just as Carlyle suggested and Parsons saw firsthand, with "the policeman's club and the soldier's bayonet."

⑥   ⑥   ⑥

Parsons's analysis of the established order of things was forged through a lifetime of writing and activism. Little scholarship on her writing exists, and details of her biography are often ambiguous, including her maiden name: on official documents over her lifetime, she listed it variously as Gaithings, Carter, Hull, Diaz, and Gonzales.[108] Yet what is known suggests that constituted power gave her little else but pain: she had plenty of reasons to want to find an alternative to it. She was born in Waco, Texas, sometime around 1853. Because of when and where she was born, and because she later lived with a man named Oliver Gaithings, a former slave, it is probable that she was born into slavery. She had a *mestizo* identity: she claimed that she had Mexican and

Native American ancestry, but most biographers, and even some of her family members, suggest that she also had African ancestry. Carolyn Ashbaugh writes that Parsons denied the African part of her heritage due to intense violence at the hands of the Ku Klux Klan, "a terrible indictment of the racist society which made her feel compelled to do so."[109] At approximately the same time Whitman was drafting *Democratic Vistas* and the world was reading news about the Paris Commune, she met Albert Parsons, a white former Confederate soldier turned Radical Republican. They married and moved to Chicago sometime before 1874, mainly to avoid the hostility they felt as an interracial couple in the postbellum southern United States.

In Chicago, Lucy and Albert Parsons wove themselves into the city's radical fabric. They were both active organizers, Lucy with the Working Women's Union and Albert with the Socialistic Labor Party, and then both in the Knights of Labor and the International Working Persons' Association.[110] As Robin D. G. Kelley writes in *Freedom Dreams: The Black Radical Imagination*, Lucy Parsons was "one of the brightest lights in the history of revolutionary socialism."[111] Kelley is an exception, but much of the writing on Lucy Parsons frames her rather simply as Albert's spouse.[112] They both were deeply involved in the campaign for the eight-hour workday, but Albert gained notoriety from the events at Haymarket Square on May 4, 1886. The day before, during a strike demanding the eight-hour day at the McCormick Harvesting Machine Company, police fired into a crowd of strikers, killing two of them. The Parsons were outraged and helped to plan a series of sympathy strikes and demonstrations in response, one of which was in Haymarket Square. At that meeting an unidentified person threw a bomb, killing a policeman and wounding six people. Albert Parsons, together with seven others, were tried and convicted, not of detonating the bomb, but of advocating violence in their writings and therefore, in the logic of the state, of being accomplices to the bombing. On the eleventh of November 1887, Albert, together with August Spies, George Engel, and Adolph Fischer, was hanged.[113]

After Albert's death, Lucy was often mischaracterized as little more than a grieving widow. Recent scholarship on her life and writings is presenting a more complicated picture, however. As Gale Ahrens writes,

> that Lucy was a force to be reckoned with is beyond all doubt: the Chicago cops didn't call her "more dangerous than a thousand rioters" for nothing. A commanding presence, she was also a powerful speaker. In her youth as in her old age, people *loved* to hear Lucy Parsons speak; she had a musical voice, tremendous delivery, and no need of oratorical pretensions.[114]

Lucy lived for fifty-five years after Albert's death and traveled frequently on the lecture circuit, speaking about the Paris Commune, various aspects of the labor movement, especially the campaign for the eight-hour day, the problems of child labor, and the meaning of anarchism.[115] Lucy published Albert's writings, including his autobiography, and continued to work as a journalist, editor, and publisher. She was a delegate at the convention that founded the Industrial Workers of the World in 1905[116] and continued to play an active role in radical politics until she died in an apartment fire on March 7, 1942. Many of Parsons's books and papers survived the fire, but all except for the most badly damaged were confiscated by the Chicago police; they have never been released.[117] In short, the "established order of things" excluded Lucy Parsons from participation in the civic life of representative democracy, it was organized in a way so she was born into a life of slavery, it sent policemen and hired Pinkerton guards to repress her when she went on strike, and it hanged her spouse, not for throwing a bomb, but rather for writing newspaper articles that defended labor rights in militant language. Parsons had, therefore, ample motive to oppose the constituted powers around her and to build an intellectual and activist strategy on direct democratic power.

⑥　⑥　⑥

Parsons's writing is filled with proposals for radical change, but her contributions to the labor movement and to the campaign for the eight-hour workday stand out. Parsons often ties slave labor to wage labor, noting how the former was able to evolve into the latter. Parsons lived in the historical moment, and both in the southern and northern United States, that gave her unfortunate experience with both forms of exploitation. She wrote that the "overseer's whip is now fully supplanted by the lash of hunger! And the auction block by the chain-gang and convict cell."[118] When the proposal was first made to join the movement coalition to achieve the eight-hour workday, Parsons saw it as a half measure, a concession to the so-called right of capital to decide the conditions of labor.[119] But the idea circulated around the labor movement in Chicago, and in other cities and countries, and grew to the point where its realization became a mass movement. When she joined, Parsons gave those efforts her full support. The twelve- or fourteen-hour workday was pernicious and back-breaking, but it was a potent tool for maintaining constituted power. It was an idea that John Locke, who provided inspiration to many of the founders of the American Revolution, thought was an elegant solution to what he saw as one of the fundamental problems of democracy, and which Carl Schmitt notes as one of the key problems of political representation: when people work so hard and so long, they cannot engage in political affairs.[120]

In a discussion of Locke's idea, Staughton Lynd points out in *The Intellectual Origins of American Radicalism* that the property-owning revolutionaries who drafted the Declaration of Independence of the United States and its subsequent Constitution exploited the excessive working hours of the poor in order to avoid getting too much democratic participation from the people they governed.[121] How to remove the vast majority of the population, and nearly all of the poor, from participation in the political process, whether from representative democracy or from other avenues of civic and community participation? Legal disenfranchisement—denying the right to vote, assessing poll taxes, these are known methods. One not commonly considered, however, is to work people to exhaustion. With a twelve- or fourteen-hour workday, a person has little time left to attend to human needs like food and sleep, let alone time for political activity like voting or union organizing. If a person has other responsibilities, say, to family, or has the hope to do something pleasurable in her or his off hours, like hearing a lecture or a concert, the hours of the day grow even more precious.

Yet such exploitation breeds resistance, in this case, a mass movement to reduce the workday to eight hours with no reduction in total wages. The movement explicitly aimed to strike at the exploitation of labor, but it had implications for other aspects of constituted power. With "eight hours for work, eight hours for rest, eight hours for what we will," people had greater time outside of work to develop their lives in ways of their choosing, rather than having their bosses direct the vast majority of their waking hours. Parsons writes that "to be really free is to allow each one to live their lives in their own way so long as each allows all to do the same."[122] Parsons never suggests that an eight-hour workday is the *telos* of a free community, but she did argue that it—and later, a four-hour workday—is an important material step to improve a working person's life.

The movement for an eight-hour day is one of the most successful efforts at curtailing constituted power in United States history: the proposal grew from the imagination of people who wanted their lives to be a little less miserable. Laws were passed in legislatures to mandate the eight-hour day, but those laws were simply ignored by the corporations—they knew that the police, the state militias, and hired Pinkerton mercenaries would protect their interests, not the flimsy legal rights of workers.[123] It took mass action of people who went on strike, endured hunger and blacklisting, and even death, in the case of the McCormick strikers and Haymarket martyrs, to secure their rights. The eight-hour-day campaign would be a success that Parsons would build upon for the rest of her career. "Forty-four years from now," she wrote, "and a long time before that, four hours and even less they will demand, until there isn't one man or woman in the world who wants to work who cannot get it. That is the kind of movement of the future."[124] Lucy Parsons saw the need for organization, not organization to maintain a hierarchy, but rather to facilitate the ideas she saw as just: liberty, cooperation, equality.

Her experiences proved to Lucy Parsons that the existing order was not worth keeping, and that changes to it do not come from governments, aristocrats, or from divine literatuses: any change in the form of constituted power would come from the efforts of people who think and act to demand alternatives to the injustices they face. The aristocratic thesis is premised on the idea that people like Carlyle's heroes or Whitman's divine literatuses will act to improve the lives of the people they govern. But Parsons's writing and experience suggest that the premise of the aristocratic thesis can provide little evidence for proof: its advocates fought Lucy Parsons and the movements in which she took part at every turn. "I came to understand," she wrote,

> how organized governments used their concentrated power to retard progress by their ever-ready means of silencing the voice of discontent if raised in vigorous protest against the machinations of the scheming few, who always did, always will, and always must rule in the councils of nations where majority rule is recognized as the only means of adjusting the affairs of the people. I came to understand that such concentrated power can be always wielded in the interest of the few and at the expense of the many. Government in its last analysis is this power reduced to a science. Governments never lead; they follow progress. When the prison, stake, or scaffold can no longer silence the voice of the protesting minority, progress moves on a step, but not until then.[125]

So Parsons saw clearly not only the relationship between direct democracy and constituted power, but also the only effective tactics that people could use against an established order that deserves to be overthrown, namely, the building of movements large enough and strong enough to challenge that order, making it adapt accordingly if possible, or overthrowing it if necessary.

The Circulation of Democratic Ideas

People like Parsons are the motors of democratic innovation; people like Carlyle write to protect the established order of things. The Whitmans are caught in the middle, seeing virtues and vices in both positions. The three writers in this chapter show flashpoints in the era's debates about direct democracy. What democracy could be is defined by the collective, cross-pollinated struggles of people who imagine alternatives to the existing order and work to make those visions material realities. The "swarmery" of direct democracy is not mayhem, as Carlyle assumed, but rather presents alternative ideas, often quite different from the institutional structures of representative, parliamentary democracy. Its innovations are difficult for the Carlyles of the world to see, because people like him have an incentive to mischaracterize democratic innovations as disorder—they write to protect the constituted powers they hold dear. But this democracy is in the Underhill Meetings in Jamaica that led to the Morant Bay Rebellion, as well as in the rebellion itself, and in the way working-class activists in London built from the struggles of those black workers. It is in the Paris Commune, and in the democratic schools and workplaces that Whitman imagined after reading news about those events, and it is in the way Parsons weaves Marxism and anarchism together to theorize how a reduction in the workday could reduce the misery of what she called capitalist slavery.

Out of these diverse cross-pollinated movements, patterns and trends take shape. In the long nineteenth century, ex-slaves, women, and workers all asked what democracy could be and attempted, even in tentative ways, to use its power to shape their worlds. Their answers were complex, drawing from and building upon one another, each pushing the idea of what democracy could be in new directions. What is clear, however, is that the material for an answer to what democracy could be is not born from parliaments and congresses, but rather emerges from the ideas and interactions of the people upon whom Carlyle, Whitman, and Parsons focus their attention: the ex-slaves, women, and workers who struggled to find alternatives to the existing order.

As these three writers, perhaps especially Parsons, saw, direct democracy is creative, productive. In efforts to avoid domination and exploitation, people like Parsons imagine alternatives and do their best to put those alternatives into place—such is clearly the case with the campaign to reduce the workday to eight hours. What Parsons calls "the established order of things" is conservative in the strict sense of that word: it acts, as Carlyle's arguments show, to protect and maintain current norms or institutions. The task the Whitmans of the world set for themselves is to sketch out what this alternative might mean or be, oscillating between direct democratic power and the reactive tendencies of the established order. People like Lucy Parsons also take up the task of finding alternatives, but due to the domination and exploitation they face and the injustices that demand their responses, their thinking and their actions take on an immediate urgency.

People like Lucy Parsons are the engines of direct democracy: they are the ones outside what are considered the acceptable parameters of debate, too radical to be acknowledged by the Carlyles and Whitmans of their day. But through the ways they exercise their direct democratic power and struggle to make their visions material realities, they make the Carlyles take notice and the Whitmans pause to think. As is the case with the struggles for the eight-hour workday, sometimes people like Parsons use their power to drag the Carlyles and Whitmans of the world—against their wishes—a bit closer to a more just order of things.

⑥　⑥　⑥

Throughout the literatures of the Americas during the long nineteenth century, there are examples of people like Lucy Parsons, struggling against different types of constituted powers. The problems and possibilities of direct democracy, evidenced by the creativity, autonomy, and cooperation inherent in human capacity, and frequently described as a swarm, are pressing concerns for these characters. In the next chapters, slave revolt, labor activism, and resistance to gender domination and neocolonialism are the remaining pieces to form a literary history of direct democracy, providing both the theories that undergird it and models for further study.

These models raise difficult historical and theoretical problems. For example, groups such as the 2,000—like any group of people—will not be homogeneous; therefore, what gives them coherence? As I ask in the chapter below on Nat Turner, why are narratives about movements often recast as narratives about particular leaders? When people act collectively, as they do in B. Traven's Mahogany Novels, what is the nature of their intelligence, and how does that intelligence compare to the intelligence of more hierarchical forms of organization? The formation of such groups presents cooperation problems, especially when they grow into credible threats. Many of the examples in this book appear in moments of spectacular violence, a fact that is perhaps unsurprising—the examples set by an independent Haiti or a Nat Turner in rebellion are explosive, and it is no wonder that they attract such loud hostility from people who would like to see them suppressed. But as I show in the book's final chapter, on Marie Vieux Chauvet's *Love*, direct democracy is not always spectacular; it can also be seen in acts of kindness and caring, examples that are no less powerful because of their subtlety.

Nearly One Hundred Nat Turners: Collective Power in the 1831 Southampton Slave Rebellion

The thunderclap of the Haitian Revolution echoed throughout the Atlantic world, but perhaps nowhere louder than in southeast Virginia. In 1793, once news of the revolution had reached Petersburg and Richmond, the mayors of those cities ordered every slave in the vicinity searched, and they mobilized militia patrols to detect any sign of rebellion.[1] It would take nearly four decades for the rebellion these mayors suspected to begin, but when it inevitably did begin, it made material for stories that were both shocking and spectacular. From August 21 to 23, 1831, a group of up to seventy enslaved people carried out an insurgency in Southampton County, Virginia, that killed approximately sixty whites—men, women, and children. Militia and regular military troops put the rebellion down after less than two days, overpowering the black population with a disproportionate and indiscriminate violence.

One participant in the rebellion, Nat Turner, evaded capture for nearly nine and a half weeks, a fact that raised his reputation considerably, to both the surviving slaves and free blacks in the area, and to the slaveholders.[2] In the time that Turner remained free, stories circulated and ultimately fixated on his role in these events. John Hampden Pleasants wrote in the September 3, 1831, edition of the *Richmond Whig* that the "origin of the conspiracy, its prime agents, its extent, and ulterior direction, is a matter of conjecture. The universal opinion in that part of the country, is that Nat, a slave, a preacher and a pretended prophet, was the first contriver, the actual leader, and the most remorseless of the executioners."[3] By the late fall, Nat Turner's name was a symbol for the whole rebellion, and depending on who was telling the story, the symbol meant either murder or militant resistance.

The fact that Turner successfully hid for such a considerable time meant that others told his story while he was in hiding. When he was captured, this problem grew worse, not better, for him. As he was in jail awaiting trial, Turner was interviewed by Thomas R. Gray on the first through the third of November 1831.[4] Then, on November 5, Turner was tried; on November 9, he was hanged. On November 10, Gray registered the copyright for a text that was titled, and claimed to be, *The Confessions of Nat Turner*. The text was published in that same month. In the text, Gray poses as a stenographer, stating that he presents Turner's words verbatim.[5] There is much doubt about that claim. For example, the document is called a "confession," but Turner never makes such an admission. Rather, as Gray writes, Turner pled not guilty at trial, "saying to his counsel, that he did not feel [guilty]."[6] To make the text, Gray adds editorial notes and colors the content in ways that are provable and, one can suspect, are now unprovable.[7] In terms of the text's dissemination, Gray was certainly successful: it sold approximately fifty thousand copies in the following months.[8] Such numbers show why *The Confessions* became, and continues to be, the text that has shaped the understanding of the uprising in Southampton County to a greater degree than any other.

Like Pleasants, Gray admits in his prefatory remarks that the details of the uprising are in dispute, but he states plainly, on the title page and in the text, that Turner was the "leader of the late insurrection."[9] Two initial aspects of these narratives are noticeable: first, although both writers state that many facts are uncertain, they are both certain that Turner was the leader and the key to reaching an understanding of the situation, yet second, both authors state that Turner's motives are beyond any understanding. It is a pattern observable in writers whose interests block them from seeing contradictory lines of thought: Gray, like other authors who defend constituted power, blames Turner's "enthusiasm" and fanaticism.[10] Gray, therefore, like Carl Schmitt, Thomas Carlyle, and others we have seen in this study, participates in the tradition of writers who, in their defense of constituted power, deny that others who critique or act against that power have any rationality. Here, in the material fact of rebellion, was a counterpoint to the mythology of racial capitalism, but this is not the conclusion that Gray reaches. None of this is to suggest that *The Confessions* lacks thought, although it does bear the marks of a hastily written text, as David Allmendinger and others have noted.[11] Rather, it is to say that the fullness of Gray's hostility to Turner is not most usefully measured by the handful of substantive but seemingly casual insults about Turner's intellect and motive. Gray calls Turner a "gloomy fanatic," for example, which, considering the range of what a bigoted vocabulary could be, is fairly mild.[12] Put another way, that Gray is comparatively temperate, not vitriolic, in the language he uses to critique Turner goes a good distance to establish Gray's wish to be viewed as impartial, as someone who only conveys

Turner's words. Instead, the better measure of how Gray manipulated Turner's story is in the framework of *The Confessions* itself, the way Gray's facade as a stenographer misdirects away from a fuller comprehension of the events in Southampton County. Proving that Gray was unreliable and hostile to Turner is comparatively simple; my goal here is to analyze the significant repercussions of how Gray framed his narrative.

At stake here is what gets lost when a story about a collective act of rebellion is rendered as the story of a single person. Slavery in the Atlantic world in the long nineteenth century was systematized and institutionalized: it was a braid of economies, laws, cultural norms, and racial ideologies, what Robin Blackburn, in *The Overthrow of Colonial Slavery*, calls the "structures of empire."[13] Against such powerfully woven structures, individual resistance will always be inadequate. Individual resistance to slavery was not futile—it was often the only way to survive—but the only effective challenge to such a system of domination is collective resistance. In the Southampton Rebellion, a group of slaves fought for their liberty in an act of collective liberation—this fact gets lost when the story is focused on a single leader. Put differently, systematic injustices demand collective responses; that is what happened in Southampton County in 1831, but it would be difficult to arrive at that observation if one takes at face value the dominant narratives about the rebellion.

Considered in that way, *The Confessions* presents a master-level class on narrative and the nature of power, about whose stories are told and whose stories are not told, as well as what gets clarified and obscured in the telling. The degree to which Turner told his own story is a matter of some debate. Many scholars—and I am among them—would state that Turner's voice does come through in *The Confessions*, even considering Gray's manipulations, and even if the degree to which his voice comes through is ultimately impossible to say with much certainty. David Allmendinger, for example, carves out the section of *The Confessions* that he calls Turner's "memoir," which may not be quite precise but which may still pass muster.[14] Elsewhere, he writes that this section is a "narrative cast in the voice of Nat Turner," which provides more nuance.[15] In any case, it is clear that Turner did not control the writing and publication of his story. In speaking for Turner, Gray had a relatively free field to tell a story in the way he wanted to tell it, and he told it in such a way as to create an irrational and exceptional main character. Yet hidden in plain sight at the end of *The Confessions* is a list of the participants in the rebellion—forty-eight names in total, including Henry, Hark, Nelson, and Sam, who are also briefly mentioned in Gray's text.[16] The highest speculation puts the number of participants between sixty and eighty.[17] These participants are little more than an afterthought to Gray, as well as to others who have written about the rebellion, for an interesting set of reasons, to which I will return below.

The so-called *Confessions* of Nat Turner, therefore—a text controlled and published by Thomas R. Gray—is a literary misdirection, one that obscures an understanding of the Southampton Rebellion as a collective act against the constituted power of slavery and instead focuses attention on the part played by one of its participants. To paraphrase John Plotz, *The Confessions* does not show the power to shut someone up, but rather to put words in that person's mouth.[18] From that perspective *The Confessions* is a very advanced text, and it is no wonder that it has set the trajectory in which the Southampton Rebellion would be understood. Gray does not silence Turner's actions—in many ways, he publicizes them—but *The Confessions* publicizes the Southampton Rebellion in a way that serves the interests of the constituted power of the slavocracy by obscuring the insurgents' collective direct democratic power.

There is also a paradox at the heart of this problem: the major part of Gray's work was to represent Turner as irrational but also as an exceptional individual, which is significant here because an exception can be more easily marginalized as an anomaly. Promoting an exceptional Nat Turner isolates him from his peers and isolates their actions from what caused those actions, the consequences of which are to minimize the power that the group possessed, yet—here is the paradox—also to elevate Turner's stature. Even though I wish to suggest a more complicated reading of the Southampton Rebellion, one that is not entirely explicable by telling the story of its leader, what Nat Turner the person has come to symbolize is substantial. *The Confessions* remarks on Turner's intelligence, charisma, and influence in order to separate him from other slaves, but these characteristics nevertheless stand, even if the motive behind the comparison is faulty. There is tremendous power in these abilities. Many observers have believed Gray's representation of Turner as an irrational religious zealot acting out of enthusiasm, not reason, but other writers and activists have looked to Turner's example as an inspiration. John Brown, the nineteenth-century abolitionist, points to Turner as evidence of slavery's injustice; Malcolm X attaches profound significance to Turner in his autobiography. Kyle Baker's recent graphic novel *Nat Turner* shows its main character as "a hero with superhuman abilities."[19] Assata Shakur writes in her autobiography that

> Harriet Tubman had always been my heroine, and she had symbolized everything that was Black resistance for me. But it had never occurred to me that hundreds of Black people had got together to fight for their freedom. The day i found out about Nat Turner i was affected so strongly it was physical.[. . .] I tore

through every book my mother had. Nowhere could i find the name Nat Turner. I had grown up believing the slaves hadn't fought back.[. . .] Many of us have misconceptions about Black history in amerika.[. . .] Belief in these myths can cause us to make serious mistakes in analyzing our current situation and in planning future action.[20]

Like John Brown and Malcolm X, Shakur finds a particular value in Turner's story. She finds here one more flaw in a racial mythology, and it helps her, at an early moment in her political development, to think beyond that mythology and therefore to plot better activist strategy. But another idea, to which Shakur alludes, deserves to be stated forthrightly: it is not only that some stories go untold—the ways in which stories are told can also lead to markedly different implications. Individual acts of rebellion can be inspiring—this is one important lesson Shakur learns from discovering that Nat Turner existed at all—but, as she also recognizes, the Southampton Rebellion was not an individual act.

Accordingly, this chapter is about the narrative that emerged after the rebellion ended. This narrative needs to be questioned from several perspectives, starting with the relevant facts of the case, including the nature and name of the event, which will in turn provide a firmer foundation for a critique of the narrative structure of Gray's *Confessions*. Any scholarship on *The Confessions* must negotiate the recognition of two difficult facts: that the text's claims of complete truthfulness should be doubted, but also that it is the best primary source document about the rebellion. A complicated set of interests led to the decisions to tell the story in the way it would be told: both the surviving slaves and free blacks in the area, as well as the supporters of the slavocracy, helped to shape how people would remember these events. There are many iterations of the story, but the narrative is usually told as if its main character is its only relevant variable. Even in this framework, there are many Nat Turners: the Nat Turner of the juridical documentation, the General Nat of the oral tradition, the specter of gothic horror stories, the rebel of the Black Radical Tradition. Also literally, Turner was one of many who participated in the Southampton Rebellion, making it, to borrow Shakur's phrase, like those in which "hundreds of Black people had got together to fight for their freedom." Turner and his peers pooled their power in order to resist the structures of empire, even though the main texts and much of the subsequent scholarship have focused on the role played by one participant. My purpose here is to trouble these comparatively simple narratives. The story of the Southampton Rebellion is not just about one Nat Turner—it is about nearly one hundred Nat Turners.

"We Again Divided"

In the first decades of the nineteenth century, southeast Virginia, like much of the region, experienced an economic depression that drove down the prices for cotton and other commodities, as well as the price for slaves.[21] This region of Virginia trafficked enslaved people to much of the South, so when the depression slowed down this trafficking, the black population in the area rose. As census data show, from 1800 to 1830 the white population in Southeast Virginia rose marginally, but the black population rose to a far more significant degree.[22] The area's population therefore was influenced by the movement and circulation of people, and also of ideas. Cedric Robinson writes that "in the late eighteenth and early nineteenth century, Franco-Haitian slave owners fled to Louisiana, Virginia, and the Carolinas with as many slaves as they could transport, thereby also transporting the Haitian Revolution."[23] It was a dangerous mix: anxiety over the economy, a growing black population, and reports of slave rebellion throughout the South, the Caribbean, and Latin America combined to make the life of a slave, which was brutal to begin with, even worse. Nat Turner's body bore the marks of what this life must have been: descriptions of him state that he had scars on one of his temples and the back of his neck, as well as a large knot on the bone above his right wrist, the result, most likely, of that bone breaking and then healing without having been set properly.[24]

Such repression breeds resistance, and a growing black population in proximity to a population of whites growing increasingly frustrated yet comparatively smaller provides a good explanation of why such a rebellion occurred where and when it did. Turner and his peers must have noticed this shifting terrain and sensed an opening. There may have also been a more immediate effect of the economic situation: Allmendinger speculates that the whites' debt may have prompted talks of a sale of slaves, an act that always split families and laid bare the cruel characteristics of the slavocracy's racial capitalism; predicting the impending sale may have prompted the plotters to carry out plans that had been long in the making.[25]

One is tempted to speculate about what success may have meant in practical terms to Turner and his peers. The most likely goal seems to have been a life of marronage in the Dismal Swamp, about forty miles from Jerusalem, now Cortland, where the rebellion started. One could also take *The Confessions* literally on this point and believe that the rebellion's goal was to spread fear throughout the region.[26] At minimum, it needs to be recognized that given the right set of circumstances, rebelling against an unjust system is itself an endeavor worth undertaking. This is not a blind lashing out, but rather merely to suggest that there are times when passive resistance becomes insufficient or intolerable and active resistance seems to be the only logical option, regardless of the consequences that may follow. In any case, the Southampton Rebellion is another piece of evidence to support C. L. R. James's comment that slaves rebel because they want to be free, and that this is a fact that no ruling class wants to admit.

It has been written, correctly in my judgment, that the Southampton Rebellion was like the drop that overflows the cup.[27] In the early morning of August 22, 1831, the fortieth anniversary of Haiti's Night of Fire,[28] a group of people, including Turner, began entering the houses of their enslavers, intending to kill everyone they found, and thus secure their liberty. As the rebellion moved from house to house, the number of participants swelled. While the rebellion may have been planned earlier by Turner and six others, or it may have been planned a year in advance by fifteen slaves, not including Turner, once it began, it grew into something of a general insurrection, involving up to seventy insurgents, in at least two groups. Because the rebellion divided into groups and spread like a swarm as its participants multiplied, it is difficult to say with any certainty that the rebellion was directed by any single person or, if Turner did provide its direction—in oral histories of the event, ex-slaves and free blacks call him "General Turner"—at a certain point the events built beyond his control. The evidence from *The Confessions* supports both of these interpretations: the text shows Turner debating plans with his peers, "still forming new schemes and rejecting them," and drilling the insurgents as if they were the counterpart to the slavocracy's militias.[29] If these statements were Turner's, not Gray's, they are evidence of Turner's participation in the advance planning for the event. But also, after the rebellion was under way, different groups fanned out for various purposes: in a sort of shorthand, *The Confessions* has Turner state, late in the event, "We again divided."[30]

That the rebels fanned out in groups is supported by both *The Confessions* and the available historical record.[31] Yet as Mary Kemp Davis writes, the "event invites and resists interpretations at every turn."[32] Facts, of course, matter, even when it is the nature of the story at issue, so it is fortunate that several pieces of recent scholarship have established much of what we now know to be factual about the rebellion. Daniel S. Fabricant compares *The Confessions* to the trial record, to judicial conventions of the era, and to Henry Irving Tragle's book *The Southampton Slave Revolt of 1831: A Compilation of Source Material* and finds that Gray's version of the story includes many significant differences from those records.[33] It is no surprise that Fabricant also finds many details that would shock a sense of judicial fairness, including the fact that one of the justices hearing Turner's case, James Trezvant, provided testimony against Turner.[34] David Allmendinger notes that both Trezvant and Gray were part of the first militia response to the rebellion.[35] Allmendinger, in his book *Nat Turner and the Rising in Southampton County*, brings to the investigation of the historical record an antiquarian's archival exhaustiveness and is therefore able to represent as credible many ideas that were previously speculation. For example, he posits that Turner had much of the rebellion's plan worked out in advance but shared his plans with the rest of the group only as the rebellion unfolded.[36] Coming at the material from a different direction, in his book *The Rebellious Slave: Nat Turner in American Memory*, Scot French examines trial evidence and early newspaper accounts and concludes that Turner played a key role in the rebellion but probably was much less of a mastermind than Gray portrays him to be. French cites early reports from "civil and military authorities," who early on represented the rebellion "as a brief, spontaneous act, with little planning and no clear motive behind it,"[37] and he also culls trial evidence from a female slave named Beck who told a story of fifteen slaves, not including Turner, who plotted a rebellion for a year. She gave names and dates, and French notes, "Accurate or not, her story posed a direct challenge to the emerging master narrative of 'Nat Turner's Rebellion.' Not once in the trial record did Beck mention Turner by name or indicate that the 'fanatical preacher' described by . . . others had any involvement in the plot she described."[38] French culls court records, newspaper accounts, and local legend—in his phrase, relying on both memory and history[39]—in order to show that Turner has come to symbolize a great deal to a great many different people, both positively and negatively, but to say that he was the singular mastermind of the rebellion overstates the case.

But as I noted above, the issue here is not leadership, exactly. The issue is that—whether or not Turner was the rebellion's leader in the way *The Confessions* makes him out to be—a focus on the leader alone, rather than on the many participants, obscures the collective power of the rebellion. It is not difficult to imagine Nat Turner and his peers dreaming of escape or revenge or to see Beck's version of fifteen plotters. These dreams are plans by another name. If one assumes that resistance is present wherever slavery is present, there must have been many of these plans and dreams, either whispered quickly or talked out fully. It is certainly reasonable to assume that if a group of slaves had the time to sketch a plan and the opportunity to put it into action, they would. As William C. Parker, one of the magistrates at the trials of the slaves after the rebellion, wrote, "I have no doubt, however, that the subject [of a rebellion] has been pretty generally discussed among [the slaves], and the minds of many [are] prepared to cooperate in the design."[40] What can be said with some confidence with the available facts, then, is that the Southampton

Rebellion began with some level of planning and then evolved to have a fairly high degree of spontaneity. Especially late in the rebellion, when the rebel groups were starting to fracture and Turner wished to proceed to Jerusalem, previous plans gave way to spontaneous improvisation.[41] But spontaneity is not the creation of something from nothing—it is rather the bursting forth of something whole and coherent from complex elements that have just coalesced. As mentioned above, in Southampton County the ingredients that made the cup overflow were systematized injustice, multiplied over generations; economic pressures, the brunt of which were born mostly by the enslaved; and a growing black population, both slave and free, that must have felt the power of its increasing numbers. In this case, therefore, the distinctions between calling the event a planned rebellion or a spontaneous eruption may not matter much. Both descriptions fit the Southampton Rebellion to some degree, and without one or the other, a full understanding of the event is lacking. The Southampton Rebellion did not spring fully formed from the earth; its constituting elements are plain to see. There were repression, power, and organization; when these elements burst forward in the form of a slave rebellion, some people must have thought that it came from nowhere. But anyone willing to pay attention knows that a cup can hold only so much.

⑥　⑥　⑥

The Southampton Rebellion and *The Confessions* raise many more questions than a book chapter can examine, but two questions deserve discussion, even if briefly, before moving on to an analysis of the text, because they put this chapter's primary concerns into a proper context. First, the Southampton Rebellion raises considerable questions about the ethics of decolonial violence, questions that are silent in *The Confessions*. Second, in 1831 there was a diverse set of motives to give Turner all the credit or blame for the rebellion. Turner wanted to tell his story; both the surviving slaves and free blacks in the area and the supporters of the slavocracy benefited from characterizing the rebellion as the act of a single person. Gray also had motives for wanting to tell the story of an isolated individual. It is notable that the vast majority of the scholarship on the Southampton Rebellion has retained Gray's focus on Turner as an individual, obscuring the fact that he did not act alone, but rather as part of a larger group. For these reasons the event is most commonly called "Nat Turner's Slave Rebellion," rather than the name I use for the event, the Southampton Rebellion. I will discuss these two questions here and then return to the way the scholarship has framed the rebellion after the analysis of *The Confessions*.

The stories told after the rebellion promoted the idea that Turner and his peers targeted people indiscriminately, including men, women, and children; less has been said about the disproportionate violence that ended the rebellion. Both aspects raise important questions about the ethics of decolonial violence. Tragle, in his anthology of primary sources, provides a map of the nonlinear path the rebels took. Building from this material, Allmendinger analyzes what he calls "the zigzag course" and finds that the attack "would move neither randomly nor door to door.[42] The first four attacks—and six of the first nine—would follow a route through farms and plantations where at least one of the insurgents had been enslaved in the past, or remained so on that day."[43] Allmendinger shows that Turner and his peers killed only whites who owned slaves in 1830–1831.[44] Perhaps most important, however, is that the whites killed were the enslavers of all of the participants who are suspected to have been part of Turner's inner circle of plotters, but also whites who were the enslavers of others not included in the plotting or the rebellion—this leads Allmendinger to the conclusion that Turner and his peers did not merely have personal revenge in mind, but a larger strike against the institution of slavery as such.[45] Had the rebels stolen goods useful for purposes other than a rebellion, Allmendinger reasons, or had they killed whites who did not directly benefit from slavery, a reader may have justification for questioning the rebels' motives, but to date no such evidence exists.

If the fact that Turner and his peers also killed the children of their enslavers is offensive, that must be considered together with the fact that one of the children killed was Nat Turner's legal owner, the six-year-old boy Putnam Moore. The legal documentation at the beginning of *The Confessions* states that Turner was the "late property of Putnam Moore,"[46] yet in the text Turner states that at the time of the rebellion, he was living with Joseph Travis, "who was to [Turner] a kind master."[47] This has led to some confusion. Putnam Moore's father, Thomas Moore, died in 1827; his mother, Sally Moore, became the court-appointed executrix of Thomas's estate, but Putnam, as heir, inherited six slaves, including Nat Turner. When Sally Moore later married Joseph Travis, Travis assumed Turner's practical management, but the boy Putnam retained legal ownership.[48] Furthermore, this was not the first time Turner was owned by a child—the first was Polly Turner.[49] Ownership of one human being by another is no more objectionable when the owner is a child than when the owner is an adult, but the situation shows the absurdity of the legal framework of the era's racial capitalism. Putnam's age is not mentioned in *The Confessions*, nor, of course, is a description of how slaves' children were routinely sold from their parents. Such omissions obscure the agonizingly violent system against which Turner and his peers fought. That Gray left this violence silent is a sure sign of how his framework, what was told and what was not told, helped to shape the understanding of the event.

The Confessions is equally silent on the scale and nature of the military and militia violence that followed the rebellion, and was used to end it. All Gray writes in *The Confessions* is that "the hand of retributive justice has overtaken [the rebels]."[50] As Thomas Wentworth Higginson wrote in the aftermath of this suppression, "[i]n shuddering at the horrors of the insurrection, we have forgotten far greater horrors of its suppression."[51] Although a count of the tax rolls and census, which provide the most accurate number of slaves and free blacks in Southampton County before and after the rebellion, suggests that the number killed in the repression may have been less than what it was thought to be,[52] it is nonetheless telling that the rebellion was met with a disproportionate and indiscriminate response. Additionally, the total number of deaths in reprisal for the rebellion cannot tell the story of the many different ways the survivors must have encountered their enslavers' retributions, no doubt ranging from whippings and beatings, to more tightly enforced oversight of their daily activities, to the millions of petty and not-so-petty indignities of a life in slavery.

An estimated three thousand troops, made up of both militia and regular military forces, marched to Southampton County in response to the rebellion.[53] In "1831, Virginia was an armed and garrisoned state," Tragle writes; the military and militia

> was a "paper army" in some ways, in that the country regiments were not fully armed and equipped, but it is still an astonishing commentary on the state of the public mind of the time. During a period when neither the state nor the nation faced any sort of exterior threat, we find that Virginia felt the need to maintain a security force roughly ten per cent of the total number of its inhabitants.[54]

This is the material structure that sustains a system of forced labor, without which such a system could not survive for long. It is telling: if the rebellion really could only be understood as the work of one person, why would a force of approximately three thousand armed men be required to suppress it? That these numbers were so uneven ought not to surprise—the material and ideological structures that support slavery may not always be the same in every situation, but one of its most common characteristics is that it presents an overwhelming force against the enslaved. Without that force, the structures of empire are tenuous. Such responses have material, physical components, but also spectacular components. They are meant both to repress and to send messages about subsequent possible repression.[55]

In 1831 there was a complex set of interests at play in shaping how the story of the Southampton Rebellion would be told. In his book *Nat Turner's Slave Rebellion*, which for many years was the most credible scholarly contribution to the topic, Herbert Aptheker writes that it "may at once be said that there are features of the Turner Revolt that are still uncertain and probably will remain so.[. . .] [T]here is unanimity on two things and only on two things. First, all agree it took place, or, at least started[. . .] in Southampton County and, second, that the leader was Nat Turner."[56] This is perhaps understandable. Aptheker was not alone in holding the position that Turner was the sole leader and mastermind of the event—as Aptheker points out, nearly everyone who spoke or wrote about the rebellion held this position. Yet, as French has shown, it may not be substantially truthful. It does seem to be the case, however, that almost everyone involved wanted it to be true, and therefore, this unanimity of wishes came to be seen as truthful. First, and perhaps most importantly, Turner wanted his story to be told.[57] Even given his situation—in jail, waiting for a trial that he must have known would lead to his execution—Turner told his story to Gray. This telling, Gray states in *The Confessions*, is evidence of Turner's character: the reason Turner did not fight when he was captured was so he could tell his story.[58] It seems a reasonable speculation that Turner must have known that Gray was not his ally, but that because of his own interests—clearly different from Turner's interests—Gray could be used as a vehicle to disseminate his story.

It is also apparent why the surviving slaves and free blacks in the area would want to give the responsibility to Turner—doing so could keep them alive, and besides, for more than nine weeks after the rebellion, Turner was nowhere to be found. French looks at early oral legend and newspaper accounts and finds that most people believed that Turner had escaped.[59] In the nine weeks when he could not be found, at least, Turner could have been given responsibility without facing the burden for that responsibility. As noted above, the repression after the event was severe, so the surviving slaves and free blacks in the area had a motive to limit any further retribution. The surviving slaves and free blacks also had motive to mythologize another hero in the struggle against slavery, another name to mention along with Toussaint Louverture and Gabriel Prosser, whose rebellion in Richmond in 1800 still lingered in recent memory.

Though his are different, Gray also had his motives to tell a story about a single leader. Gray wanted to tell a story that would sell, as well as one that could both thrill and placate a white audience. Gray had material and ideological ties to the slavocracy and was part of the early militia efforts to suppress the rebellion.[60] He and his family were all enslavers, at various points throughout their lives, and the depression in southeast Virginia had hit Gray's family particularly hard.[61] Gray thus had motive to sell a captivating story—even after Turner's death, his name would be used as a profit mechanism for the slavocracy. But if Gray profited from sales of *The Confessions* (fifty thousand copies sold at twenty-five cents would have netted $12,500), it was insufficient; Gray appeared in court in 1835 as an insolvent debtor.[62] More importantly, however, after the Haitian Revolution, the slavocracy saw abolitionist conspiracies in every shadow. In *The Confessions*, Gray asks Turner whether he has knowledge about a contemporary rebellion in North Carolina and shows Turner denying any such knowledge.[63] This denial may have been truthful, but regardless, this moment presents in a concise way what the most substantial practical effect of the text would come to be. Due to a multiplicity of interests, but most importantly Gray's framing, *The Confessions* tamps down fears of slave rebellion by redirecting them into something smaller and thus more manageable for the slavocracy.

Stories Told and Not Told

The opening section of *The Confessions of Nat Turner* is a two-paragraph narration of the process by which Gray secured the copyright for the text—this section is written, signed, with seal affixed by the clerk of the District of Columbia, where Gray obtained that copyright.[64] Even given the standards of the time, this documentation draws extraordinary attention to Gray's ownership of the text (such is the function of copyright) and to the veracity of the statements.[65] One gets a feeling of the lawyer doth protest too much here; an author's overinsistence on truthfulness can lead to skepticism, justified in this case. Regardless, the conclusion that ought to be apparent from the first words of the text is that the narrative it contains has an actual stamp of approval from the slavocracy. From the perspective of the constituted powers in Southampton County, Gray has permission to speak for Turner; they codify that the text is the official truth.

But the juridical codification of the text's truth is more easily dismissible than the more advanced elements of Gray's framework. *The Confessions* set a trajectory that conversations about the Southampton Rebellion have followed with very little variation. In his first paragraph, Gray states that the insurgent slaves had all been destroyed, or apprehended, tried, and executed (with the exception of the leader,) without revealing any thing at all satisfactory, as to the motives which governed them, or the means by which they expected to accomplish their object. Every thing connected with the affair was wrapt in mystery, until Nat Turner, the leader of this ferocious band, whose name has resounded throughout our widely extended empire, was captured.[66]

Leadership is the only lens, Gray states, through which the rebellion can be understood; without the testimony of its leader and the framework that testimony can give to the story, the story itself is inexplicable. None of the other participants—all of whom, like Turner, pled not guilty at their trials and provided substantial testimony[67]—provided any information Gray sees as worthy in analyzing their motives or means. The quote above is placed directly after the copyright notice and before a statement from the court magistrates further codifying the veracity of the text.[68] This comment is therefore the opening and framing idea, designed to orient an understanding of the text as a whole.

On this idea, regardless of the text's other inconsistencies and flaws, Gray is single-minded and certain throughout. Consider the title as further evidence: *The Confessions of Nat Turner, the Leader of the Late Insurrection in Southampton, VA, as Fully and Voluntarily Made to Thomas R. Gray* represents Turner as a "black Spartacus,"[69] elevating him to the level of a substantial historical myth. As opposed to many aspects of the Southhampton Rebellion that may always be speculation, it is a fact that Gray focused on a single person, attributing to him complete credit for organizing and carrying out the rebellion. It is also a fact that the rebellion was a collective event; this Gray hides in plain sight by appending a list of the other rebels' names, together with the punishments they received, at the end of the text.[70] By forcing the story into an ill-fitting frame, he codifies the leader he assumes must be present, but he conceals the more complex story of a general insurrection against slavery as such. Gray set a trajectory for the conversation so that it would be about one person rather than a group of people, and with very little variation, the conversation has been on this trajectory ever since. It is in this sense that I write that *The Confessions* is a successful misdirection, an effort to frame the story so that it focuses on one person and directs readers away from an understanding of the Southampton Rebellion as a collective event.

The evidence for the durability of Gray's trajectory is that while subsequent scholarship has questioned his credibility and has more sharply focused on Turner's obvious motives to be free, the vast majority of the writing on the event has left one of Gray's biggest assumptions unchallenged: that leadership is the lens through which the rebellion ought to be understood. Even though there is a range of ways the subsequent scholarship has discussed the event and the narrative, to a considerable degree much of that scholarship has continued to view the material through the lens that Gray first constructed—this is the case even for scholarship that is more sympathetic to the rebellion, like Aptheker's, mentioned above. The vast majority of the best work—by people like Eric Foner, Kenneth Greenberg, and Steven B. Oates, for example—follows this trajectory begun by Gray, and continued by Aptheker, and, whether explicitly or implicitly, perpetuates the idea that Turner himself is the only participant worth mentioning to any significant degree. The conversation developed an inertia along the trajectory Gray set, and the idea that Turner had nearly complete responsibility for the rebellion came to acquire the status of an unchallenged truth.

The main repercussion of this trajectory is to reduce the collective power of the rebellion, through a variety of means. The story of a single hero or villain, depending on one's perspective, obscures more than it reveals. Crucially, it obscures the labors and efforts of Turner's peers. This move illustrates what is in my judgment the most comprehensive way to view how Gray approached his task, that is, to move in any way possible from multiplicity to singularity, from complexity to simplicity. *The Confessions* turns the story of a collective rebellion into a story of a single person; a story with many contributing factors and repercussions into a tidy summation. As French writes in *The Rebellious Slave,* Gray's effort was "the making of a master narrative designed to tranquilize an agitated public and facilitate the restoration of order throughout the region."[71] In the aftermath of the rebellion, a thousand different stories seemed to come out of Southampton County, many of which were about Turner, some about the rebellion spreading out of Virginia into neighboring states, and others that did not mention Turner at all.[72] The rebellion must have seemed to many in the slavocracy like an omnipresent, hydra-like threat, sustained by sensational newspaper accounts and hearsay. In *The Confessions,* Gray notes that the rebellion "led to a thousand idle, exaggerated and mischievous reports"[73] and therefore wanted to give the story coherence with what French calls "a single definitive account of the conspiracy."[74] This coherence, however, comes at the price of simplifying and reducing a matter that is much more complicated than would seem from the text. Gray "put Turner on record as saying that he alone conceived of the plan, sharing it only with a few close confidants, and that he knew nothing of any wider conspiracy involving slaves from neighboring counties and states."[75] Like this one, the moves Gray makes are always to simplify, to turn a story with many variables into a story with only one variable.

There are three aspects, at least, of the way Gray framed *The Confessions* and thus misdirected an understanding of the rebellion: first and perhaps most importantly, in controlling the writing and publication of the text, Gray speaks *for* Turner. As seen above, Gray's copyright is more than a legal claim: it is the assertion that even though Turner's voice emerges, Gray owns the text. Second, Gray limits the narrative by attempting to shorten the focus to the days of the rebellion only and to Turner's participation. Third, after isolating the rebellion to Turner's actions, it then becomes comparatively simple to marginalize this one participant, and therefore the rebellion as a whole. All of this work, of course, serves the purpose of minimizing the collective power of the rebellion. In the balance of this section, I will treat each of these aspects in turn.

⬧ ⬧ ⬧

Much of storytelling is retelling, at a certain level—one thinks here of the many ways Turner's story has been kept alive through a black oral tradition—so the fact that others have told Turner's story is not necessarily objectionable. Likewise, there are situations where someone could give their consent, for a specific and limited purpose, for someone to speak for them—for advocacy, as one example, or because the speaker possesses technical knowledge or skills in a particular context. Yet in this precise circumstance, Gray's act of speaking for Turner is difficult to see as anything other than a form of literary manipulation, at best, and literary violence, at worst. What is most relevant is that the content of the text did belong to Turner, to some ambiguously small or large degree, but also that control over that text ultimately belonged to Gray, who transcribed the interview, perhaps, then wrote and edited it, including both emphasis and interjections where he saw fit.

Claiming consent is the first step in the misdirection. The opening of the text repeats the same phrase from the title: that Turner's statement was "fully and voluntarily made," and that it "is a faithful record of [Turner's] confessions," which Gray published "with little or no variation, from his own words."[76] As noted above, it is certainly likely that Turner would have wanted to tell his story, but if a reader does not consider the context carefully, it may seem that Gray was, to some degree, Turner's ally.

The Confessions is not unique, of course, in presenting the problem of the amanuensis, a situation where someone speaks for another. This situation is quite common in slave narratives, usually where a more literate white person speaks for a black person who is less literate or who does not have the leisure to write. Such is the case, to name just two examples, in *The History of Mary*

Prince and in Solomon Northup's *Twelve Years a Slave*. In these cases, there are issues inherent for an ally writing on behalf of an ex-slave.[77] Neither of these is the case for Nat Turner. One can see why Turner would speak to Gray in the first place—Turner knew that he would be hanged, and soon. There was no possible way, given the situation, that Turner could have been released after trial, in this era, in this particular context, so it is reasonable to expect that he wanted to tell his story, even if he was also aware of the probability that Gray would, at minimum, misrepresent aspects of the story, tell a slant truth, or lie outright. But even if Gray ought not to be considered Turner's ally—he should not—there remains the issue of consent. At minimum, the differing levels of power that Gray and Turner had, one enfranchised and white, one a rebellious slave, each on opposite sides of a jail cell's bars, would complicate the claim that Turner gave Gray his consent to publish the story: in such a situation, it is difficult to believe that consent could be given freely.

ⓖ ⓖ ⓖ

In what Allmendinger calls the "memoir" portion of the text, that is, the section in which Turner is speaking, Turner immediately acts to complicate Gray's moves: Turner does not answer Gray's prompt to begin with the rebellion, exactly, but rather begins with a discussion of his early childhood.[78] The place Gray wishes to begin is a substantial part of his framework for the text: starting with the rebellion would have provided no evidence of Turner's life and labor, no picture of the causes and injustices that led to the rebellion. That framework would have severed the causes of the rebellion from its effects, providing the reader—especially a contemporary reader—with no evidence of the rebels' motives.[79] One of Gray's first public writings on the Southampton Rebellion states that Turner's "object was freedom."[80] In *The Confessions*, Gray changes tack, writing that the slaves' motives were not comprehensible. This could show a change in Gray's thinking or different representational tactic; in either case, the change obscures and minimizes the nature of the rebellion.

Having established the facade of consent and that Turner was the only participant worth considering, it becomes a comparatively simple task to marginalize this one participant and therefore the rebellion as a whole. Gray is not impartial, contrary to his self-representation as a stenographer. He had material and ideological ties to the slavocracy,[81] and the text paints Turner in a negative light: Gray describes Turner as "a gloomy fanatic [with] a dark, bewildered, and overwrought mind,"[82] a religious and bloody zealot pulled from gothic horror fiction, a monstrous main character leading the others.[83]

Put another way, it takes Gray two moves to dismiss the rebellion as an anomaly, rather than a substantial and powerful collective act of resistance against the system of slavery: first, he isolates the rebellion to a single person, and second, he defames that person's character.

But as noted above, there is also a paradox here: in order to represent Turner as an exception in comparison to other slaves, Gray also elevates Turner's stature, writing that "for natural intelligence and quickness of apprehension, [he] is surpassed by few men I have ever seen."[84] Yet two sentences later Gray writes that Turner "is a complete fanatic or plays his part most admirably."[85] This seeming contradiction is no surprise. "At the heart of the nineteenth-century culture of slavery," Sibylle Fischer writes, "in the aftermath of the Haitian Revolution, is the act of disavowal: the slave is and is not a social being; she or he is at once submissive and a deadly threat; at once unthinking and forever plotting."[86] Thus, whether in Gray's view Turner was uncommonly intelligent or gripped by "enthusiasm,"[87] the effect is the same: to separate Turner from his peers as an exception, who can then be marginalized and explained away as an anomaly.

As readers will remember from earlier chapter discussions of Carl Schmitt's and Thomas Carlyle's writing, "enthusiasm" and "zealotry" are the most common translations for the concept *Schwärmerei*, the term often used by constituted powers to characterize challenges to those powers as based in emotion, not reason, and therefore as baseless. It should come as no surprise, therefore, to see these words used to describe Turner in many texts, including, of course, *The Confessions*. Consider, for example, a letter published in the Richmond *Whig*:

> I have heard many express their fears of a general insurrection, they are ignorant who believe in the possibility of such a thing.[. . .] Is it possible for men, debased and degraded as they are, ever to concert effective measures? Would the slaves alone in St. Domingo ever have attempted insurrection? I humbly apprehend not.[. . .] Our insurrection, general, or not, was the work of fanaticism—General Nat was no preacher, but in his immediate neighborhood, he had acquired the character of a prophet [. . . and therefore . . .] he acquired an immense influence, over such persons as he took into his confidence.[88]

The representation of Turner as "a dangerously irrational rebel" reappears throughout the writings on the topic.[89] Gray's contribution to this understanding in *The Confessions* shows that he participates in the tradition of writers who, in their defense of constituted power, deny that others who critique or act against that power have any rationality. For his part, Gray uses both the language of enthusiasm and fanaticism; *The Confessions* has Turner say, at the very start of his speech, that his childhood "laid the ground work of that enthusiasm, which has terminated so fatally to many, both black and white."[90] Near the end of the text, as Gray is summing up Turner's words, Gray writes that Turner is "a complete fanatic, or plays his part most admirably," and describes "the expression of [Turner's] fiend-like face when excited by enthusiasm, still bearing the stains of the blood of helpless innocence about him."[91] As Marx critiqued and Schmitt affirmed, this logic outlines how, if people operate outside the bounds of what constituted powers consider to be rational, they can only be dealt with using force. The repression with which the rebels in Southampton County were met shows the outcome of this logic once more.

But as in this book's earlier chapters and other examples, it bears repeating that the wish to be free is not tantamount to illogic, but rather a call upon an alternative logic. As Eugene Genovese asks, "what judgments should be rendered on a society the evils of which reach such proportions that only mad men are sane enough to challenge them?"[92] Putting it a bit differently, Aptheker writes that "Nat Turner was one who refused to 'be reasonable,' and it is believed that as the present–day stirrings of the American Negro people grow, the significance of the Turner revolt as a tradition of progressive struggle will increase."[93]

⑥   ⑥   ⑥

Before concluding, I wish to clarify one possible assumption about Gray's work: I know of no evidence to suggest that Gray intentionally made the moves that I suggest here. Rather, the better explanation for why Gray framed *The Confessions* in the way that he did is simpler to explain, but that explanation brings with it larger consequences. It is most likely that Gray had merely internalized the values of a hierarchical, slaveholding ideology and wrote the text in keeping with those values. Whether Gray did this on purpose or not is beside the point—the most likely explanation is that he told the story in the way that he did because that was the way it made sense to him. Gray is skillful, but he is not particularly inventive—in many ways, Gray merely repeats slavocracy's common claims. He told the story of one exceptional leader, for example, because that was the best way he could understand any act against the institution of slavery. This makes his version of the narrative more complicated, not less: if he would have manipulated the narrative on purpose, that would make him a savvy political commentator, which is not nothing, of course, but simply telling the story of the rebellion as the story of one exception to the rule of otherwise "content" slaves reveals the thorough degree to which the proslavery ideology structured his understanding of the events. He either had no alternative framework upon which to call or, what is likely, had some grasp of the antislavery argument and rejected it. Either way, for Gray, the story is comprehensible only as the story of a leader—Turner's leadership is the only variable that is relevant to Gray.

Gray's stamp on *The Confessions* is part of an ideological apparatus designed and deployed to repress slave rebellions, to protect and extend the slavocracy's constituted power. Framing Turner as he does is rather smart, from Gray's perspective, but not unexpected: a narrative about leaders and led allows Gray to isolate Turner from his fellow insurgents, to show him as both exceptionally gifted and zealous—either way, clearly not, in the eyes of someone who thinks that forced servitude is morally permissible, representative of the "normal" slave who, in Gray's mind, must be content with her or his condition. To be exceptionally gifted, signified by his literacy, is to separate Turner from his peers, an outlier who is able to lead others, but who is not "normal," not representative of the average slave who, Gray would believe, would not have the capacity to take such actions. But paradoxically Gray also represents Turner as a "gloomy fanatic" with a "mind[. . .] endeavoring to grapple with things beyond its reach."[94] There is no logic to make these two characteristics cohere in Gray's narrative, but oppressive structures are often held together by force, not logic. Yet both of these characterizations have the same purpose. They are tools in the slavocracy's ideological toolbox, used to separate and therefore isolate Turner in order to minimize the power of the rebellion.

What is really quite cunning, however, is that Gray's framing of the story as one about leaders and led reinforces the hierarchical worldview that Gray sought to protect. Again, I make no claim to know whether Gray intended to make this move—but whether through intent, through an expression of his internalized values, or simply because he knew no other way, Gray tells a story about leaders and led, both the content of which and the narrative framework of which reinforce the slavocracy's hierarchical ideology. In short, for people who believe in a racial hierarchy, where there are people fit for liberty and others fit only to take direction, this narrative framework is not just the most appropriate framework; it is the only framework that could accurately represent the events in Southampton County, or any event that takes place in the world he inhabits.

Although incorrect, this framework is thoroughly effective, for two reasons. First, Gray's content fits this framework: if only the presence of an exceptional leader can explain such events, then only a narrative of one main character and other, mostly nameless, supporting characters could be the frame that fits this content. Second, representing the story as such suggests the validation of individual acts of rebellion that, although often admirable, have insufficient power to do real damage to a system as densely woven as slavery was into the material and cultural institutions in the Americas.

Gray, of course, is not the only person to have internalized the values of a hierarchical society. The court transcript of Turner's sentence, appended at the end of *The Confessions*, also promotes the idea that Turner manipulated unwilling others into following him; these "poor misguided wretches" were his "bosom associates," yet in the view of the court, Turner was the "author of their misfortune," and "forced them unprepared from Time to Eternity."[95] These statements reveal that in the court's opinion, Turner must have coerced the cooperation of all the other participants—to think otherwise would be to admit that a multiplicity of enslaved people had the motive and willingness to rebel, a far larger thing than one rebel. Some contemporary scholarship likewise perpetuates these ideas. Although he correctly sees the rebellion as a larger strike against the institution of slavery, not as a smaller, localized event, Bryan Rommel-Ruiz writes that the other participants "were merely pawns in Turner's rebellion."[96] Perhaps less is better said about this conclusion, as it requires us to take *The Confessions* at face value and reinforces the assumption that the other participants had no direct democratic power of their own to express. While we admittedly know less about the other participants than would be preferred, the archival record does provide some information. Of this material, one image stands out. The archive names a female participant in the rebellion, Lucy Baron; the detail that it gives is that after she was sentenced for her participation, she rode to the gallows on her coffin, providing a spectacle of defiance.[97]

Multiplying the Rebellious Slave

Gray writes from the perspective of the constituted power of the slavocracy, and in his hands, the story has only one relevant variable—the rebellion's leader. Gray's version of the story hinders the collective praxis that could be built from it by making the vast majority of the participants irrelevant, relegated to obscurity by an overemphasis on a single person in command. The alternative version of the Southampton Rebellion is about a multiplicity of people striking out against an unjust system. It is about Nat Turner, Lucy Baron, Henry, Hark, Nelson, Sam, and perhaps up to seventy more people. It is about both particular people acting in hostile situations and logic of collective action expressed by many; it is about the power of an inspirational example and about the collective power of people to resist the injustices they face.

From a reactionary perspective, Gray's narrative is a masterwork, telling the story of a mass movement as the story of a single leader. It places a tale with revolutionary content into a reactionary framework.[98] In representing the rebellion as the act of one person, Gray is able to isolate the rebellion, to contain it and make it seem lesser than it actually was. To Gray, Nat Turner, this one person, could be explained away by replacing his reason with "enthusiasm" and dismissing his acts as an anomaly. What Nat Turner has come to represent in the imagination of subsequent generations of activists is considerable, but there is no necessary choice in deciding between acknowledging Turner's humanity and symbolism and also acknowledging that he was part of something larger than any one person. Both positions have a claim on the truth: to paraphrase C. L. R. James, in the Southampton Rebellion we can see both individual people, masses of people, and their dynamics when they interact at a fluid moment in history. However, these two elements need not be, and in fact cannot be, split apart. To separate Nat Turner from his cooperation with others is to suggest an interpretation that will always be less complete than it could be. Put another way, to say that the Southampton Rebellion was the work of nearly one hundred Nat Turners is not to devalue the one Nat Turner, but rather to multiply his significance and his symbolism, and to bring his peers out of obscurity and silence.

Greenberg writes that to call the event, as contemporary newspaper accounts did, "the Southampton Tragedy," had the effect of "shifting attention away from the agency of the man who was at the heart of the rebellion—turning it into a kind of uncaused disaster."[99] This is undoubtedly correct. Yet calling it "Nat Turner's Rebellion," as Greenberg does, emphasizes that one participant and obscures the fact that up to seventy people participated in the rebellion. Tragle writes, "In Virginia, the terms most generally used are 'insurrection,' or 'servile insurrection.'"[100] Tragle uses the term 'revolt,' following from a reading of Virginia law and federal law.[101] In doing so, he takes issue with Aptheker's term, "rebellion," because, as Aptheker writes, "the aim of an insurrection is not revolutionary; the aim of a rebellion is. A revolt is of less magnitude than rebellion."[102] In my judgment, Aptheker is correct on this point; as noted above, Turner and his peers struck at the braid that was the slavocracy, an institution woven together by law, economics, and culture. To strike at that braid in the way they did was revolutionary.

This leaves only the question of whence the direct democratic power of the rebellion was derived, and what its name ought to imply. Calling the event

"Nat Turner's Rebellion" locates the power of the event in its main protagonist and obscures its other participants. In contrast, calling the event "the Southampton Rebellion," as I choose to do, no more devalues Nat Turner's power than the name "the Haitian Revolution" devalues Toussaint Louverture's power. To the contrary, such names multiply the power of these key participants by acknowledging the fact that they were part of collective efforts. There is much to be gained by making that choice. Individuality matters, but so does solidarity, and the only way to threaten a systematized injustice credibly is to present a collective challenge to it. As troubling as "Nat Turner's Slave Rebellion" would have been to Gray's proslavery readers, they would have been far more troubled by the possibility of hundreds of Nat Turners. Stories like the one about the Southampton Rebellion include the astonishing actions of people like Nat Turner, but they also include the collective actions of many people who play roles both small and large. A fuller narrative of events would require attention to the multiplicity of these people and the dynamics of how they interact. Nat Turner's name deserves to be remembered, but a story of a single heroic leader gives that leader nearly all of the power to act, when the fact of the matter is that large-scale rebellions, especially ones that are spontaneous to some degree, rely on the collective power of all their participants. It should also be noted that in this debate, the Southampton Rebellion is one example of many. Stories about collective movements are often mistakenly represented as narratives of leaders and led.[103] In an alternative story, every enslaved person is potentially a rebel. A single "black Spartacus" is a potent threat; but that threat is present wherever slavery is present.

Although evidence from participants like Lucy Baron is scant, it is reasonable to expect that among all the participants in the Southampton Rebellion, each had diverse ideas about what liberty meant to them, varying opinions of what the outcome of their rebellion might be, and various suggestions about the most effective tactics. Some of the participants may have joined knowing that it would be among the last choices they would make. Some may have fought out of rage, some to repay particular grievances, some because they thought the rebellion was a path to freedom for themselves or for their families. Some participants may have acted out of an altruism that hoped that their rebellion would be a step toward universal emancipation. Yet the people who chose to participate found ways to cooperate even in the face of great difficulties, and they struck a blow that left a lasting mark on the slavocracy. They did not need to define liberty in exactly the same way; what they needed was to find ways to cooperate in order to make an effective challenge to the systematized injustices they faced. They were successful in forging that cooperation, and that fact deserves recognition. No group of nearly one hundred people will be homogeneous, but even large and diverse groups can find shared ideas that allow them to act in collective and coherent ways. In the Southampton Rebellion, those shared ideas facilitated a comparatively brief but nevertheless substantial type of cooperative power; in B. Traven's Mahogany Novels, to which I now turn, those shared ideas, built over a longer amount of time, facilitate the production of the collective power I call direct democracy on a larger scale.

CHAPTER FOUR

The Emergence of the Swarm
in B. Traven's Mahogany Novels

B. Traven's six Mahogany Novels—*The Carreta, Government, March to the Montería, Trozas, The Rebellion of the Hanged,* and *The General from the Jungle*—track the causes, rise, and end of the Mexican Revolution of 1910–19. The novels' collective title is a reference to the commodity that occupied a place in the economy and culture of Chiapas, Mexico, where the novels take place, that was analogous to sugar in the Caribbean and cotton in the southern United States. Mahogany—the rich red wood that darkens with time—grows in Chiapas, and the workers who process it labor on *monterías*, debt slavery plantations. Over the course of the novels, the *monterías* produce tons of this lumber, and they also produce a revolution. Like the rough wood that is made into beautiful furniture, over the course of the novels the raw material of disorganized discontent is shaped into organized rebellion.

In some ways, what Traven produces in these novels is the reverse of what Thomas R. Gray presents in *The Confessions of Nat Turner*: whereas Gray writes to misdirect and obscure the power of the Southampton Rebellion, Traven puts the collective power I call direct democracy on display. In contrast to Gray, who moves from complexity to simplicity, Traven shows the complexities of systems and collective dynamics. Part of this is the difference in the lengths of the respective texts, of course, but most of it is in the manner of approaching the material. Altogether, the Mahogany Novels total over a thousand pages—as compared to the twenty-five pages of *The Confessions*—so it is too great a scope to cover all of their content in a book chapter, but these novels nevertheless present a long-form exploration of the Riot Act situation, which is, as I noted in this book's introduction, a situation where direct democracy and constituted power come into comparatively clear relief. Jonah Raskin writes that the books "are among the very finest novels in any language to describe the genesis, growth, and triumph of a revolution."[1] As we will see, the novels are not without their flaws, but Raskin is correct: in terms of their scale and their effort to help a reader see the material experience of oppression and the painstaking labors that are required to build a movement to challenge that oppression, the Mahogany Novels present few comparisons.

Over the course of the novels, many isolated characters find that their individual power is overmatched by the constituted powers that dominate them. In contrast to the slavery and dictatorship they hope to abolish, a diverse group of escaped slaves, *campesinos*, military deserters, and one blacklisted college professor begins to form in the novels, and when it does, Traven explicitly represents this group as a swarm. The ways that Traven uses the swarm metaphor are perhaps unique to this study: Traven goes to great lengths to show that the rebellion in the novels is no mere *Schwärmerei*. The rebels have a logic and a vocabulary in their struggle that point to an alternative. Perhaps more importantly, however, Traven uses the swarm metaphor in tactical ways, the first instance of which is in *The Rebellion of the Hanged*, the penultimate, fifth novel, and he uses it at the precise moment when the rebels have, at long last, built a method of cooperation that allows them to challenge the system of debt slavery under which they work. From that point forward, Traven continues to use the metaphor, in ways not unlike how James does in *The Black Jacobins*, exclusively to show these rebels acting in concert, using their collective power. When the rebels attack a *finca*, a large farm that holds their fellow workers in a form of brutal servitude, the narrator writes that "the muchachos swarmed through the rooms in the buildings."[2] Likewise, when they began their assault on Achlumal, the town that holds their debt records, "the muchachos were swarming[. . .] from all directions."[3] Other characters in the novels also describe the rebels as a swarm, as when Gabino Villalava remarks about the "bandit gangs that are swarming about here reducing all the *finqueros* to desperation."[4] In each of these instances, Traven uses the language of the swarm to show the power in the rebels' cooperation.

The rebels have both successes and failures as they set out to overthrow a dictatorship. That dictatorship is ultimately overthrown, but not by them—an outcome that presents difficult questions for an understanding of the relation between the power I call direct democracy and constituted power. "It is not just the dictator who ruled," Traven writes. In these novels, that statement is all too true for the rebels. In the novels, readers see how this swarm emerges out of resistance to a debt slavery that is enforced by economic, cultural, and military hierarchies. Through experimentation, failure, and setbacks, the rebels forge a method of cooperation to challenge the constituted powers they face.

What I show here is that for Traven, the rebels express a power that is characterized not just by strength, but also by intelligence. Readers may be drawn to the conflicts of force that play out across the novels, and for good reason: in painstaking ways Traven's novels narrate the brutal repression of Mexican society under the dictatorship and the "crescendo of violence and brutality" that completes the novels.[5] But, I will argue, this is to miss the striking comment the novels make about the characteristics that define the rebels' intelligence. Martín Trinidad, the rebel nicknamed "Professor," who had been driven from several positions for teaching and agitating against the dictatorship, states that individuals who resist are simply drowned in blood, but

> when we work together in a mass, things are different. Then a thousand heads and two thousand vigorous arms make up a superior force. That is why I've been telling you that freedom can evade us easily if we don't form a large mass and if we don't all arrive at the same time. The strongest lion is helpless in the face of ten thousand ants, who can force him to abandon his prey. We are the ants, and the owners are the lions.[6]

The second metaphor in the passage, about ants and lions, a swarm of smaller force against a singularity of concentrated force, gets the rhetorical weight here, but the first metaphor, about a thousand heads and two thousand vigorous arms, merits a reader's attention. Force is important here, but so is intelligence. This power comes from ability, skill, and cooperation, and the rebels put these together in the service of ending the exploitation and domination they face. It is a situation that echoes the Southampton Rebellion and an idea from Spinoza's *Political Treatise*: "Individuals alone do not possess sufficient power to preserve themselves and thus of necessity unite with others to survive," Spinoza writes. "[I]f two jointly come together and unite their strength, they have jointly more power and consequently more right over nature than both of them separately, and the more there are that have so joined in an alliance, the more right they all collectively possess."[7] This situation plays out in Traven's novels quite explicitly. As Warren Montag writes, glossing this idea from Spinoza, "collective existence, far from limiting or curbing the power of individuals, only increases it."[8] Such is a crucial fact for Traven's characters, both concerning the power of their arms and of their heads, and it has much consequence: when one considers that the Mahogany Novels are works of historical fiction, and that conditions and characters—such as Porfirio Díaz, the dictator that the Mexican Revolution deposed—are represented with all the brutality that hierarchy can bring, it may be easy to focus on the "two thousand vigorous arms" and therefore miss the complicated suggestion that Traven's narrator makes about this swarm's "thousand heads."

The rebel victories are ambiguous, as we will see, but that the swarm of rebels in the Mahogany Novels possesses "a superior force" is not in question. In addition to being strong, however, the swarm is also smart, and as it emerges, it comes to be more than just a sum of its parts. The narrator writes, "No one had taught [the rebels] self-discipline, how to work without being told and supervised.[. . .] No one had taught them how to organize their work, in order to be able to form themselves into a cooperative society."[9] Nevertheless, this rebel swarm organizes itself and completes tasks that require high levels of cooperation—not the least of which is the defeat of the better-trained, better-equipped federal troops. The rebels in the novels are "common people" who "had been so long whipped and hanged, so long humiliated and robbed of free speech," yet they form an impressively complex organization.[10]

The goals of this chapter are twofold: first, to give a sense of the complexity Traven brings to an extended representation of the Riot Act situation, as theorized by Benjamin and Schmitt. Second, to track Traven's use of the swarm metaphor, showing that the rebels' collective power is both strong and smart. This swarm possesses not just the force of numbers, but also the power of intelligence. To meet these goals, some prior context is necessary. Traven's novels are attracting some attention because they take place in Chiapas, Mexico, the home to the contemporary Zapatista movement,[11] yet Traven's name is nearly unknown to English-language readers and scholars. Therefore, this chapter briefly makes a case for why Traven's work ought to garner more attention, especially in scholarly conversations about transnational studies. This chapter then provides a reading of the novels, especially the last two, *Rebellion of the Hanged* and *The General from the Jungle*, in order to show the complexity of their relation between direct democracy and constituted power, and to illustrate Traven's use of the swarm metaphor.

Traven's Place in Transnational Studies

At various points in his life, B. Traven also used the names Ret Marut, Hal Croves, and Traven Torsvan, among others. All of these names were part of a lifelong effort to keep his biography mysterious. Traven wrote fifteen novels, many short stories, and one work of nonfiction about Chiapas, Mexico, *Land des Frülings* (*Land of Springtime*). Traven wrote his books in German, most often, but also some in English; the vast majority of his books were published first in German, and then translated.[12] Scholars assume that Traven was born in Chicago in 1890, emigrated to Germany, participated in the 1918–1919 Bavarian revolution and, after the Bavarian republic was suppressed, escaped from a death sentence for treason. Traven then lived in Mexico until his death in 1969. Traven's legendary secrecy, however, means that no detail of his biography is beyond debate. As the editor of the German journal *Der Ziegelbrenner* (*The Brick Burner*—one who makes material to build a new world), he delivered public readings from behind a darkened lectern. Traven misled journalists and aspiring biographers, and argued that his writing, not his biography, should get attention. Readers interested in a good mystery and the relation between an author and that author's work might consult the two articles about Traven written by Judy Stone in *Ramparts*, and her subsequent book, *The Mystery of B. Traven*. At present, the definitive biography is Karl S. Guthke's *B. Traven: Biographie eines Rätsels*, the English translation of which is *B. Traven: The Life Behind the Legends*. Regarding the many tall tales about Traven, often seeded by the author himself, Guthke states that for much of the writing on Traven's biography, "a good mystery proves more enticing than the banal truth."[13] But the story of his biography, whether factual or peppered with fictions, is not usually banal.

Traven's life and work, Guthke writes, was "born of the spirit of the Mexican present and the trauma of the European past."[14] Traven had an ethos of direct democracy that was like C. L. R. James's in many ways, and which makes the dominant theme of much of his work. Traven wrote, "Workers should not respect any figures of authority, neither kings nor generals, nor presidents, artists, nor transatlantic fliers. Everyone has the duty to serve mankind according to the best of his powers and abilities, to make life easier for others, to bring them joy and direct their thoughts to great goals."[15] In the early and mid-stages of his career, his major publisher was the Büchergilde Gutenberg in Berlin, which "vocally promoted the interests of German workers in Social Democratic trade unions during the Weimar Republic."[16] The Büchergilde was a membership organization, and most of its members, and thus the first readers of Traven's books, were working class.[17] But Traven also had and has an audience beyond the working class; Guthke notes that German readers and critics generally do not refer to Traven's work as "*Unterhaltungsliteratur*:" "light reading."[18] While his works consistently resonate with working-class themes and are almost always populated with working-class characters, he maintained that he wanted his texts to have a broad appeal, saying, "I wish to do my share so that authority figures and authority worship vanish, so that every man strengthens his own awareness that he is just as important and indispensable for mankind as everyone else, regardless of what he does, and regardless of what he has done."[19] Traven wrote that his work gave an insight into the conditions of workers in Central America and Mexico that would certainly be of particular interest to German workers.[20]

Traven's books, including *The White Rose*, "were embraced by readers with unusual vigor in those turbulent final years of the Weimar Republic."[21] Of particular note along these lines is that *The White Rose* was an inspiration for the prominent German antifascist group The White Rose Society.[22] After the Nazi takeover, two of the Mahogany Novels, *The Carreta* and *Government*, appeared on the new regime's first list of banned books.[23] At this point Traven switched his publisher to the Zurich Büchergilde, because of its opposition to the new regime.[24]

Traven is perhaps best known to English-language readers and scholars as the author of *The Treasure of the Sierra Madre*, which was made into a film directed by John Huston and starring Humphrey Bogart.[25] His other works include *The Death Ship*, which is the story of a sailor who loses his identification papers and is then treated by the various states through which he travels with the particular form of brutality reserved for people who do not have state identification papers and are therefore treated as less than human. *The Death Ship* is rumored to have been one of Albert Einstein's favorite novels.[26] Like much of his work, that novel presents the case for Traven's greater inclusion in transnational studies scholarship.

Traven's place in transnational literary studies might be justified not only on the fact that he lived in and wrote about many different places, but also on the fact that he had a hostility to the concept of nations and the constituted powers they can house. Traven's content is likewise international: his characters are American drifters, European workers, and Mexican *campesinos*. German, Mexican, and American scholars all claim Traven for their national literatures. He was a US-born, German-raised and then-deported author, living the balance of his life in Mexico writing about the struggles of indigenous and working-class people, mostly in Mexico. Perhaps more importantly, however, expressing his indignation, Traven wrote, "A human being qualifies as a person, a citizen, a valid member of society only when he has the proper papers, which the government alone may issue and deny."[27] Most of his books problematize the state; the critique of nationalism and its relation to capitalism is perhaps his most dominant theme. His books have been translated into dozens of languages. Traven's work, in other words, is transnational in its themes, and in its production and distribution.

But at present his writings have received less attention than has been devoted to assembling the details of his enigmatic biography. Richard E. Mezo, in one of the few book-length works to treat Traven's fiction, writes that "an enormous amount of effort has been expended upon the biographical questions concerning Traven, but surprisingly little has been devoted to his work."[28] Unfortunately, at this point, Mezo's words are still correct, with perhaps one exception: there is a growing number of oblique references to Traven, and to the Mahogany Novels in particular, because they are set in Chiapas, Mexico, the location of the contemporary Zapatista movement, and because the novels strike a resonant note with that movement.[29]

On that point Traven is certainly an ancestor to the contemporary Zapatistas, and, as I hope to imply in the next section of this chapter, his work presents a counterpoint to many of the literary representations of the 1910–1917 Mexican Revolution. The ambiguity of the end of the revolution is perhaps its most dominant theme—much of the literature of the Mexican Revolution laments that the revolution overthrew a dictator but led to the establishment of a party-state system, what some have called "the perfect dictatorship," that governed Mexico for nearly seventy years after the revolution and which was, in the judgment of many, more objectionable than the previous dictatorship or, at minimum, objectionable in a different way.[30] Certainly this ambiguity also looms large at the end of the Mahogany Novels, as we will see, but what separates these works from many of the others is that the Mahogany Novels focus to a far greater degree on the injustices overthrown than on the regressiveness of the new constituted power.

Multiplicities of Power

Perhaps to a greater degree than any other text in this study, with the possible exception of *The Black Jacobins*, the Mahogany Novels represent the relations between the power I call direct democracy and constituted power as multifaceted and complex phenomena, greater than the sum of their distinct parts. It is difficult to give a sense of the scale necessary to show such complexity, and Traven is not always successful in going beyond an easy binary of workers and rebels who are to be praised and governments and capitalists who are to be condemned, but what the Mahogany Novels show (especially in the end of the series, painfully so) is that both modes of power are complex, in the technical sense of that word: they are not singular, but multiple and overlapping.

This approach does have consequences. Richard Mezo writes that "perhaps the most obvious flaw in the Jungle Novels [as they are sometimes called] is the absence of some central point of focus, particularly significant locale, or strong central character who might be a reference point for the dramatic action of the work."[31] This is not necessarily incorrect. The six Mahogany Novels are a coherent cycle in terms of their place and in terms of the building of events that propel the story, and some characters do recur, but in comparison to stories with comparable scopes and themes, the Mahogany Novels do differ. In Traven's books there is no Pierre, Prince Andrey, or Natasha for a reader to follow from start to finish, as in Tolstoy's *War and Peace*. The narration in Traven's books does not connect its characters through direct relations, as the child Cosette connects Fantine to Jean Valjean in *Les Misérables*. The organizing principle of Traven's Mahogany Novels is multiplicity: they present characters in in a particular place, caught up in a fluid moment in history. The characters in the novels are all caught up in the same tide of events, and part of Traven's task in the early novels is to show how disparate and isolated they are, and how relatively ineffectual their separate struggles. This is, in part, in order to show a distinction to the nature and success of their collective struggles in the later novels. Instead of a narrative with the usual characteristics of historical fiction—a main character or a set of main characters, a single narrating voice, or a linear thread that moves the story through time, what the Mahogany Novels show is complexity, in the technical sense of that term. The story in the novels is a machine with many parts, some of which mesh and cohere, some of which grind and break. It is true that the novels present a bit too stark a picture of rebels who are almost always praiseworthy and oppressors who are almost always objectionable, but neither group is singular. The constituted powers are a braid, and the rebels are an intersectional mix of agricultural and urban workers, professionals, and regular soldiers who have defected. In this section, I will give a sense of this complexity.

⑥ ⑥ ⑥

In painstaking detail over the course of more than a thousand pages, the Mahogany Novels narrate the conditions that agitate the Mexican Revolution—the domination of a dictator, pervasive debt slavery, military repression of strikes, rigid racial, gender, and class hierarchies—and the subsequent revolt. In the Mexico that Traven describes, elections were held, but the outcome was certain; business flourished, but conditions for workers were reprehensible; slavery was outlawed, but a system of debt slavery cropped up in its place.[32] To the outside world, however, Mexico was a model of democratic peace and prosperity: with heavy irony, Traven writes that Porfirio Díaz, the dictator whom the revolution will eventually overthrow, "had astonished the world by showing in a brief space of time that the bankrupt Republic of Mexico was so flourishing that other countries could only envy its bursting treasury. It was proved by the statistics, which proved also that a great statesman had brought the Mexican people to a level of civilization and prosperity which no one would have thought possible."[33] This miracle of economics is mystical, of course. As the "treasury grew richer and richer, the national debt, on paper, smaller and smaller; the poverty of the people, ignorance, corruption, and shameless injustice were, on the other hand, more and more widely diffused.[34] This is a facade, of course, benefiting those who prosper under the dictatorship and horrifying the rest. Traven's narrator points out, "Where there is a dictator at the top of the ladder, you find nothing but dictators on every other rung. The only difference is that some are higher up and others lower down."[35]

But that these large and small dictators share the same ladder does not mean that they are homogeneous. In fact, the opposite is true: the economic, juridical, and cultural systems are diffuse but overlapping. The narrator suggests that, at first, the rebels do not fully grasp the systems that dominate them, but they certainly know that they want to dismantle them. Because the hierarchical systems of power here are so complex, it is worth quoting Traven at length to get a sense of them. "The power which determined the fate of [the workers] was invisible and intangible," Traven writes. The workers'

> fate was determined not by the agents or the *contratistas* of the *monterías* but by
> the dictator, whose actions, in turn, were influenced by the idea that the welfare
> of the Republic was guaranteed only if native and foreign capital was granted
> unlimited freedom and if the peon had no other object in this world than to obey
> and to believe that which he was ordered to believe by the authorities of the State
> and Church.[36]

The workers see constituted powers close up, in the agents who trick them into debts they cannot pay, and who then provide a "solution" for them to work off those debts in the lumber camps. But the agents are not the root of that power—that power has no singular root but is rather rhizomatic, growing from many different places: from capital, from the government, from the church. It is an "anonymous power," Traven writes, and it

> was intrinsically interwoven with all other powers in existence. The import-
> export companies in New York were not sovereign in their might or influence.
> Their power, in turn, depended upon the good will of the hardwood import
> companies in London, in Liverpool, in Le Havre, in Hamburg, in Rotterdam,
> in Genoa, in Barcelona, in Amsterdam and in Copenhagen. And the power of
> all these companies again depended upon the good will of the thousands of
> hardwood-consuming companies and individuals which in their ramifications
> and branches could, in hundreds of instances, be followed to village carpenters in
> the smallest countries.[. . .] [F]undamental power was so dispersed, so ramified,

so branched out and so interlaced with all the activities of human production and human consumption.[37]

Therefore, this domination takes on a mystical quality: with so many moving and interlocking parts, it becomes difficult for those oppressed by such forces to see how they are systematic. It is a hierarchy, where the benefits of the system flow from the labor of those below to the accounts of those above, but it is not a simple machine: a dictator ruled the government, in collusion with business owners, intellectuals like Díaz's *científicos*, and foreign backers, but there is no single chain of command.[38] As elsewhere, this constituted power is a braid composed of different kinds of threads. It is strong because it is woven so tightly, and it therefore makes resistance to such domination seem useless. The government proxies defend the system of debt slavery, because in doing so, they also defend their interests; the beneficiaries of debt slavery are among the most patriotic citizens. For all who benefit from the system, the amount of money it generates is more than sufficient to trump any fidelity to human rights: "You cannot have cheap mahogany and at the same time save all those innocent Indians who perish by the thousands in the jungle to get it for you," Traven's narrator writes. "It must be either one or the other. Either cheap mahogany or respect for the humanity of the Indian."[39] In this competition between profit and concern for the workers, profit wins.

The *montería* owners find reasons to justify their actions, and these reasons are directly linked to the ways that the dictatorship operates in order to maintain its constituted power. "It was[. . .] a highly patriotic activity to supply the coffee plantations and the *monterías* with labor and to keep the supply constant; it was just as important as dying gloriously and miserably for the honor of your country."[40] Whenever the *montería* owners were questioned about the reasons for their domination, they "had only one line of defense—patriotism: nothing they did was done for business reasons, still less from greed, but simply from genuine and unalloyed patriotism."[41] This patriotism has a strong allure, and it suggests that deception and pathetic manipulation contribute to the attempts to dominate the workers.

Furthermore, the people in positions of authority are not homogeneous, and there is no single hierarchy that unites them. The situation does not have only two variables, but rather a multiplicity of variables. "It was not only the dictator who ruled," Traven writes. "The big industrialists, the bankers, the feudal lords, and landowners had the well-defined duty of assuring the dictator's domination."[42] Their interests are at times indistinguishable from state interests. By "[d]ictating to the dictator what he should decree," the constituted powers use juridical decree in the service of capital, and thus mystify the mechanisms at work. When financial interests become indistinguishable from the "public interest," this becomes a potent weapon for deception and domination. This hierarchy is aimed at keeping profits unchecked, but it is also aimed at keeping the population in its subordinate position.

The constituted powers in the novels cope with this complexity by enforcing hierarchies wherever possible. The authorities in the Mahogany Novels believe that organization requires hierarchy, and they justify their rule on the grounds that it is in the best interests of the whole nation. The dictator Porfirio Díaz, the Federal Army General, and the *montería* owners, for example, see themselves on the top of a hierarchy that is, they believe, beneficial to all involved. Furthermore, they believe that they have found themselves in their high positions because of what they see as innately superior characteristics: light skin, Spanish heritage, wealth, gender privilege, or military cunning. They see this society as worth defending, a profitable and prosperous order that is fundamentally good. The *jefes* in the Mahogany Novels believe that the governance of nations, corporations, or communities must be left to those who have the intelligence and technical skill for such tasks. Thus, hierarchy based on authority is believed to be in the best interests of the community.

The dictator in the Mahogany Novels appeals to hierarchy explicitly: "the dictator thought himself the best Mexican alive and the only Mexican whose life was of consequence."[43] The General of the Federal troops holds a similar idea: through his "training he was gradually set apart from the common race of men and had climbed a fair number of steps nearer to the gods."[44] The General cannot see that people resist oppression because they want to be free; he suggests that if the rebels "had been reasoning men they would never have rebelled. Uprisings, mutinies, revolutions, are always irrational in themselves, because they come to disturb the agreeable somnolence that goes by the names of peace and order."[45] These "louse-infested, filthy Indians," the Federal General says, "could not think for themselves, and that was why they needed dictators and tyrants to relieve them of the burden of thinking."[46] As Marx wrote, the despot always sees degraded people.

The general's language belies the extent to which he will go to reinforce "peace and order"—a goal in the name of which he would unleash near total destruction. This "peace and order" requires a high degree of paternalism— this ideology brings with it a noblesse oblige that requires the authorities to direct the lives of those beneath them, but not in a way that gives much consideration to their best interests. Paternal domination leads to degradation of the population, a state that deprives them of their liberty. This situation of mental, physical, and economic poverty becomes another reason the authorities use to justify their paternalism. Thus the workers find themselves in a vicious cycle.

The owners of the *monterías*, the debt slavery mahogany plantations, express this idea most clearly, and in doing so, call on the now-familiar language of *Schwärmerei*, the idea that obedience to constituted power is logical, and thus disobedience is illogical:

> It is all so clear, so simple, so logical, so reasonable, that one has only to wonder why the proletariat won't understand it when they are dictated to. Once they understand for the first time and fully accept that everything done is done only for their good, that no dictator, no shareholder, thinks or has ever thought of impinging on the value of the worker or making him into a beast of burden, once they begin to see that people only want their good, even their best, then the time will at last be ripe when they may be counted among the reasonable, and every single proletarian will have the prospect of actually becoming a factory manager and chairman of a board of directors.[47]

The assumption made by these authorities is that any deviation from this system is a sign of irrationality and chaos. They hope to persuade the workers to work to climb the ladder of hierarchy rather than seeking to dismantle it. As with the other authors we have seen, these constituted powers mistake a different social order for disorder. These cultural myths about a climbable social ladder are told in order to conceal exactly how rigid hierarchies are in prerevolutionary Mexico. Traven's narrator presents a complex mix of racial, class, and gender domination, but the thread that unites all these systems of domination is hierarchy itself. The people on the top of the hierarchies in the Mahogany Novels like to think of themselves as benevolent fathers, not as masters, but these "fathers [would be] transformed into monsters as soon as their paternal domination and the authority that went with it were threatened."[48] They justify that monstrousness because any challenge to hierarchy or authority, no matter how small, is considered to be a challenge to "peace and order." Thus any such challenge is treated as a capital offense. Traven's narrator writes that "the death penalty is inflicted on anyone endangering the life of any person representing authority. That includes not only *El Caudillo* [the dictator], but all officers, soldiers, and police forces. Even an attempt on the life of a man in authority, be it no more than a threat, is punishable with shooting or hanging."[49] The notion of hierarchy itself is jeopardized when authority is resisted, and this is why punishment is so severe.

The Emergence of the Swarm

In that way, distinct from many other novels about the Mexican Revolution, the Mahogany Novels are as much about domination and submission as they are about resistance to that domination; they provide many examples of methods of domination, which range from subtle ideological coercion to overt violence. Few children go to school in the Mahogany Novels, but when they do, they find that the curriculum is designed to reinforce racial, class, and gender hierarchies.[50] The military is used to keep the population pacified. Torture is used as a means to make sure that the workers submit to the orders of their overseers. But a particular form of economic coercion is the backbone of this structure of empire. While "slavery was strictly forbidden and severely punished, debt was not slavery.[. . .] If the debtor could not pay in money he had to pay with whatever else he had. If he had nothing but his labor he had to pay with his labor.[51] At best, workers took on debt for the necessities of life, and when a parent would die, their debts were passed on to their children; at worst, workers would be tricked and cheated into debt.[52] Wages were far below a workers' expenses in the *monterías*: the "hard workers, the fellers and *boyeros*, earned[. . .] four or five *reales* a day, but for that they also had higher advances and debts, and moreover higher deductions for inadequate production and higher payment to the kitchen. It was all so fair, every one of them needed between six thousand and ten thousand years to be absolved of his debts through his work."[53] In large and small ways, the constituted powers in the Mahogany Novels repress the power of the various characters, and in the early novels the characters resist to the degree and in the ways they are able. Individual resistance is nearly always ineffectual, but over the course of the novels, the characters slowly build links of mutual cooperation, and when they do, they find that their resistance grows more successful. As mentioned above, once the characters' cooperation becomes refined and coherent, Traven explicitly represents them as a swarm. In this section, I provide a reading of these conflicts, and an examination of Traven's use of the swarm metaphor.

⁙　⁙　⁙

The novels' narrator frequently hints at how far the dictator and the *montería* owners will go to dominate the public. When workers would rebel or strike, the dictator, in collusion with the *montería* owners, would not hesitate to send in federal troops or the *rurales* to put the strike down. The *rurales* "were the instrument of terror, by which [the dictator] mercilessly and ruthlessly repressed the slightest resistance or criticism of his authority."[54] The *rurales* are a specter, always present in the minds of the workers, and always ready to be called up by the dictator. Juan Méndez, the *montería* worker who would become the rebel general, confirms this, saying that when he was a sergeant in the federal army, he "saw [the *rurales*] take part in suppressing strikes and punishing runaway peons."[55]

In a prominent moment at the start of *General from the Jungle*, the last novel in the series, Traven fictionalizes the story of the Río Blanco textile strike, which is one of the largest triggering events of the Mexican Revolution. The strike took place at Río Blanco near Veracruz in January 1909, and it forms a key part of what Jeffrey Bortz calls the "revolution within the revolution."[56] As these quotes show, this conflict was one of the signal events that historians point to when suggesting the inevitability of the Mexican Revolution, and also show the ways in which such events emerge out of the resistance to unjust forms of labor. As John Mason Hart writes in *Revolutionary Mexico: The Coming and Process of the Mexican Revolution*, "the Río Blanco affair began as a lockout; it turned into a workers' rebellion."[57] After the workers had lost the struggle, a contingent of them attempted to return to the job, and they appealed to the mill's company store to advance them food until their next pay came. They were refused, and as tensions rose the manager of the company store shot two workers. In response, a group of workers led by Margarita Martínez burned the company store to the ground. Fighting erupted between the workers and the federal army, and as revolutionary ferment spread through the area, workers continued to burn company stores and destroy the goods on sale.[58]

Traven tweaks key elements of the Río Blanco story—his characters are lumber workers in a *montería*, not textile workers—but he adopts others quite directly: the characters have memories of previous textile strikes,[59] and the confrontation comes to a climax at a company store when the employer, Don Félix, fires his revolver into a crowd of workers,[60] which prompts the workers to burn the store to the ground.[61] In the history, fighting erupted between the workers and the army, and by the end of the conflict, as Hart writes, "the army killed almost two hundred workers, and the number of wounded defies estimate. Four hundred workers were taken prisoner. Armed workers killed approximately twenty-five soldiers in just over twenty-four hours of fighting. They wounded between thirty and forty soldiers."[62] Traven's narrator writes that after the strike ended, the officers of the regular army refused to suppress "the now humbled and conquered men and women workers, [but] what the army officers had refused to do the *Rurales* carried out with such brutality."[63]

What makes the event reverberate so deeply, in Traven's novels as well as in Mexican labor and revolutionary history, is that the repression came after the struggle had already been defeated—it was retribution for insubordination, not an attempt to end a conflict—and that the repression afterward was indiscriminate. "Workers and non-workers, women, children, old people, the sick," Traven writes, "no distinction was made between them. And that happened, not during a strike, but days, often weeks, after the strike had ended, when the workers had returned to the factories and the whole district was entirely quiet."[64]

The stories of the conflict and subsequent fighting spread quickly—as well as into Traven's novel—and they fomented both worker revolt and revolutionary ideas. This violence is ominous, looming throughout the novels. The narrator writes that anyone "who had other ideas concerning human rights was whipped or otherwise tortured until he changed his opinion, or was, with the blessing of the Church, shot if he spread such ideas."[65] Such violence is not only shown in whispers of past events. The Mahogany Novels are filled with vivid scenes of torture, such as the hanging of *montería* workers. The workers are not hanged by their necks, but rather by their limbs, and sometimes by their ears and noses. Kenneth Payne, one of the few scholars who has written on Traven's fiction, comments on this moment. In his essay *"The Rebellion of the Hanged*: B. Traven's Anti-Fascist Novel of the Mexican Revolution,"* Payne writes that the "worker found 'guilty' of not reaching his quota [of four tons of mahogany per day] is taken out into the forest at night and hung from a tree by his four limbs.[. . .] [T]he victim's nostrils and ears are smeared with fat in order to attract insects—a refinement introduced to ensure that an uncooperative victim will cooperate fully in his own punishment on future occasions.[66] This torture is designed to coerce the workers into submission, but it is also designed in such a way that it would not do them permanent damage. "These hangings were all the more terrifying and destructive of any resistance," Traven's narrator writes, "because they were not deadly.[. . .] A dead man would not have brought them any money."[67] Any challenge to the authority of the *montería* owners or managers is met with a torturous response, and the point of hanging is to cultivate a high degree of submissive behavior in the workers. This domination is very effective, but even this method of coercion, extreme though it may be, has its limitations.

Santiago, one of the *montería* workers, says that "human beings can become like oxen or donkeys and remain impassive when they're beaten or goaded, but only if they've succeeded in suppressing all their natural instinct to rebel."[68] This "natural instinct to rebel" is not suppressed completely. When these workers begin to cooperate, they find that, as Santiago says in *The*

Rebellion of the Hanged, "[t]he day will come when we too will be hanging and unhanging. And when we approach them it will be not to accept blows, but to give them."[69] When hanged and smeared with fat, the workers fight against the insects. When the workers become rebels, they will learn from their example.

⑥   ⑥   ⑥

Therefore the early Mahogany Novels illustrate a dystopian society, where resistance is present but easily beaten because it is not organized collectively. Traven's narrator writes that, in the early novels, "whatever the men undertook or thought of undertaking was done individually, everyone for himself and everyone in his own personal way.[. . .] There was no link of comradeship or any inclination for mutual assistance."[70] As is painfully shown in several examples, as with single ants against a lion, individual resistance is weak when compared to the power and resources of the *montería* owners or the dictator. These "link[s] of comradeship" and "inclination[s] for mutual aid" are learned slowly, but when these lessons are finally learned, the rebels discover that they possess a remarkable degree of power and a particular kind of intelligence.

The authority figures laugh at the idea that they should take these tiny ants seriously; they believe that this swarm is chaotic and weak.[71] Lieutenant Bailleres, a spy for the federal army, says, "[H]ow [Juan Mendez] can be their general, I can't understand.[. . .] No one respects him. They all address him as an equal. Eats like the rest of the gang with his fingers. Sleeps on a mat like the other swine. We can finish off that collection of animals in three hours."[72] One can understand Bailleres's confidence—as noted above, the Mahogany Novels are haunted with stories about how the federal army and the *rurales* repress strikes and mutinies, doling out severe retribution for even small acts of resistance against the authorities. One can also understand why Martín Trinidad uses the metaphor of many ants against a lion, however, especially because Bailleres's confidence eventually seems more like hubris: the atrophied intelligence and rigidity of the federal army ultimately leads to its defeat.

Richard Mezo writes that in the world of the novels, "[w]e see only a land of human misery, a land of corruption, injustice, murder, and slavery. [. . .] Encouraging foreign 'development' (read 'exploitation') in any country, regardless of the boon it may at first seem, has always resulted in chaos, misery, and human tragedy."[73] What Traven communicates, Mezo notes, is that such human tragedy cannot be perpetuated indefinitely. "When these problems become intolerable," he writes, "a government will be forced to notice them, because reform, rebellion, or revolution will inevitably follow. In *Government*, we see such a process and a foreshadowing of the Mexican Revolution."[74] It takes systematic and sustained violence for constituted powers to preserve their hegemony. The ideological structures present in Traven's novels have great force and can be sufficient to control many people for extended periods of time, but, as the novels show, they are not sustainable without accompanying demonstrations of force and violence.

Indeed, Traven shows, to a considerable degree, the logic the dictatorship uses, but also that at a certain point, that logic becomes intolerable to those who suffer under it. By doing so, Traven provides material to understand that logic and therefore to begin to imagine a substantive alternative to it. What is at stake here is what I call the Riot Act situation and Derrida calls "the revolutionary situation": a scenario where a constituted power is overthrown in favor of a new ruling power. What we will see in the Mahogany Novels is not what Walter Benjamin calls "pure violence": a coup that could end a cycle of violence. Instead, what the novels show is that constituent powers can, and sometimes do, transform into new constituted powers. The new power rules, it sets laws, and it decides on matters of life and death, because it can do so. What was strongest in a given situation may not be the strongest for long. As Payne writes, "Traven's novel[s] spoke loudest as a statement of revolutionary inevitability, albeit grounded in the actualities of Latin-American history. In the words of the character Martín Trinidad, the novel[s] demonstrate that 'the Dictatorship and tyranny are neither invulnerable nor invincible.'"[75] The braid of ruling power is quite strong, but it can be cut or unraveled if faced with the right conditions and a counterbalancing force. How this braid is cut is the story of Traven's swarm; what happens after that braid is cut is a problem to which I return in this chapter's conclusion.

⑥　⑥　⑥

The rebels eventually cooperate in an effective group, but it is difficult to convey how slowly these cooperative links of mutual aid are built—it takes nearly eight hundred pages to move from isolated, comparatively limited resistance to effective collective action. With such space, however, Traven can show how the links of mutual aid are built through slow trial and error. One of the earliest moments where group cooperation begins to emerge is in *March to the Montería*, the third novel in the series. At this point, an overseer, Don Anselmo, is driving a "large group" of Indians to the *montería* known as La Harmonia—"harmony."[76] Don Anselmo's mind begins to wander when some in the group begin to shout at him. At this point he realizes that he is outnumbered. Anselmo is "a good enough marksman to shoot six of them, but the twenty left alive would not give him time to recharge his gun."[77] If these workers were to cooperate, their combined force could overpower him. At this stage in the group's evolution, however, these rebels in waiting are more like individual ants who decide to take on the lion. Two of the group attack him. Sensing that this attack is imminent, Don Anselmo reaches for his gun; as he does, one of the workers "hit him a blow with the sharp edge of his machete straight across the face. Then another Indian came from behind and struck Don Anselmo a terrific blow on the right shoulder. The blow had been aimed at the head. If it had landed true that would have been the end of the fight."[78] This last machete blow did not hit its expected target, however, and Don Anselmo is able to fight off his two attackers.

Once the rest of the "large group" sees that Don Anselmo has survived, they sit idly by. It is a painful learning experience. Traven writes, "Unable to keep the final end in view, all those who had not actively participated in the fight simply sat where they had been sitting before the struggle started. [. . .] If one of them had had the sense to yell: 'Now, come on, let's finish him,' that would have signaled the end. But nobody did anything."[79] Such effort has to be learned, often in the face of violence designed precisely to keep these workers isolated from one another. This episode is the beginning of the characters' growing awareness. Once the group reaches the *montería*, the story of the fight spreads quickly. "In the *montería* [Don Anselmo] was asked how he had gotten his wounds. He said that one of the men had hit him with a machete and then ran away. He did not go into details. In due time, however, the circumstances of the case became known, because some of the men told them to fellow workers at the *montería*."[80] The story continued to circulate, playing a formative role in the group's evolving method of cooperation.[81]

Don Anselmo knows that the workers make up a superior force, and they know it too. This moment is not quite an epiphany for them, because the awareness of their power evolves slowly over the course of the novels, rather than in a single moment of illumination. This is a tipping point in the narrative, however. By the end of the next novel, *Trozas*, the fourth in the series, the workers' cooperation becomes more practiced; in the fifth and sixth novels, *Rebellion of the Hanged* and *General from the Jungle*, the rebels' cooperation is quite polished. As their collective power builds, the rebels "would destroy every form of authority they met."[82] They burn debt records and destroy anything they believe contributes to their domination.

The first time the rebels are characterized as a swarm is also the first time they fight their domination in a way that shows successful cooperation. From this moment in the novels, the characteristics of their cooperation and of their particular intelligence come into view. When the overseer nicknamed El Gusano—the worm—threatens to rape Modesta, Celso's companion, Celso spontaneously attacks El Gusano. At first, it looks as if Gusano might escape. As opposed to the earlier attack on Don Anselmo, however, the rebels realize that the "comedy has lasted long enough,"[83] and they join Celso to kill Gusano. For a moment the rebels seem like a stereotypical mob—crazy with the blood of Gusano, they immediately, magnetically start off to find the other overseers on the *finca*. Celso, however, interjects:

> "Hey!" Celso shouted. "Come on, everybody. We have to think. We must make plans.[. . .] First we're going to think what we must do and how to do it. If we rush in crazily it won't cost us anything to take over the office. But then? You know very well that there are overseers in every corner of the jungle and that the other men don't yet know anything about our plans. The overseers can all get together and finish us off easily.[. . .] Let's stay here and talk it over. If we make useful decisions now, we won't have to regret them later."[84]

The rebels "sat in a circle" to discuss their plans, which include methods of stealing arms and ammunition, the degree of "pity," if any to have toward the overseers, and, importantly, the ideas that motivate the rebellion.[85] The rebels discuss the meaning of "Land and Liberty," the phrase that communicates their vision, at some length in this moment. "We must raise all the men suffering in the camps," Martín Trinidad says. "The peons must be free—all of them, absolutely all.[. . .] All of them must have their patches of land that they can cultivate in peace, and the harvests must be for them only and for nobody else. That is land and liberty!"[86] Trinidad's insistence that "absolutely all" of the workers must be free is an echo of the universal emancipation of the Haitian Revolution, and like that earlier effort, the ideas stated here as "land and liberty" were born in the resistance to labor exploitation.

On this point, Brian Gollnick, in one of the few recent pieces of scholarship on the Mahogany Novels, writes that "Traven's rebels undergo no growth in their consciousness anterior to the decision to take up arms against their oppressors. According to this logic, peasant rebellion can only be a direct unnecessary consequence of physical privation and misery."[87] It would have been useful for Traven to expand upon the ideologies that motivate the rebels' vision, but nevertheless, this categorical description of the rebels' consciousness overstates the case. The moment referenced here, with its emphasis on a discussion of tactics, illustrates how this group of rebels begins to move beyond individual impulse, to think and act together—they grow and adapt, adjusting their tactics to their situation. They are a diverse group, which allows them to see many perspectives on the problems they face as they discuss and debate together, a method that provides them with a mechanism for aggregating those ideas and perspectives. As Celso's insistence on debate shows, if an idea is quickly proposed and followed without such a conversation, the results could be disastrous. This is the advantage of a thousand heads.

Yet Traven's narrator does state that the rebels' "idea of the rebellion [is] limited to the simple thoughts: 'Down with the dictatorship!' 'Down with tyrants and oppressors!'"[88] While several characters are shown to have considerable individual intelligence—the rebels named General, Martín Trinidad, and Celso—the ideas about "*¡Tierra y Libertad!*" facilitate the rebels' cooperation. The rebels insist that they "have no chiefs or officers"; while this claim is more complicated than the rebels insist, the slogan functions in a way that gives the group coherence.[89] As in the other rebellions we have seen, it is reasonable to assume that each participant had different, sometimes contrasting interpretations of these ideas, but flexible, adaptable ideas provide an intellectual scaffolding upon which to build something much larger. If the ideas were rigid, they would bind the rebels' actions rather than offering the parameters that facilitate their cooperation.

So it is significant that the first mention of the swarm in the novels comes at this moment. After some additional preparation, the rebels begin their attack on one of the large debt-slavery plantations. When they arrive at the main house, its overseer, Don Severo, realizing that something grave is about to happen, "[sticks] out his chest, and trie[s] to look as though he believe[s] in his own authority."[90] When the rebels laugh in response, Don Severo shouts, "But, men, what is it you want?" The rebels shout in return that they "want to go back to our people. We don't want to work now! We want our freedom! We're going to set free all the men on the *fincas* and in the lumber camps! Land and Liberty!"[91] As Don Severo falls, he is sure that he had fired seven times at the rebels, "because the chamber of his pistol was empty when the men burst into the office. They swarmed in a mass from the open space and the slope. Not one of those who had arms fired a shot. They attacked the foremen with sticks and rocks."[92] This type of collective action is not homogeneity, but cooperative diversity. The group's members contribute according to their skills and abilities—some contribute to debate more than others, some fight in particular ways—but it is clear that the rebels begin to fight effectively because they now do so collectively. Traven's coupling of swarm imagery and the rebels' first successful collective act of resistance is more than just a coincidence—it is, rather, indicative of a change in how the rebels relate to one another. They are no longer single ants fighting against lions, but now a swarm. As such, they coordinate their activities, confer together, and act in cohesive ways—all without the authorities that formerly directed them.

From this point on, there is no way to contain the rebels. On their march, "they would destroy every form of authority they met. They would kill all the *finqueros*, bosses, aristocrats, and white men and would enlist all the peons and workers being held as slaves."[93] More formal aspects of organization begin to emerge, such as a council of war, which deliberates and decides the direction of the rebellion.[94] Were Traven to have written a less complicated story, the Mahogany Novels might have ended here in celebration, but at the moment when their organization emerges, so does the ambivalence of their actions: "nobody seemed to ask himself what would happen once everything had been destroyed. Even Martín Trinidad had only a vague picture of what might happen later."[95] Although the rebels "argued animatedly" about the tasks that were ahead of them, they also began to devalue the characteristics that made them successful, especially the need for discussion and debate. They mock the "windbags of revolution," who "talk and talk."[96] One of the complicated aspects to analyze about Traven's novels is the relation between the violence the rebels use, even if it is justified, and the forms of hierarchy they hope to abolish. This swarm is an army, not a debating society, but compared to the federal army, a hierarchical organization that has very little value for debate or discussion, the swarm seems like it takes with it a mobile commons, and at moments of relative calm, the rebels discuss and debate—albeit in limited ways, the narrator always points out—their strategy, tactics, and especially their set of seditious ideas, "¡*Tierra y Libertad!*"

Nevertheless, the latter Mahogany Novels illustrate how "a thousand heads and two thousand vigorous arms make up a superior force."[97] Building to a crescendo, the rebels "swarm out fanlike over the terrain."[98] When confronted, "the well-drilled, smartly riding *Rurales* [believe] that nothing could bring order out of this panic-stricken mob," and they are partly right.[99] The *rurales* can no longer bring "order" to these rebels, but they are no mob. They are a swarm, and this misunderstanding is costly. This assumption of disorder, of irrationality, this assumption that any effective organization would need to be "led by knowledgeable officers" proves fatal.[100] When the first real battle is over, literal ants pick up where the rebels end: moments after the rebels successfully end their fight, "the mangled remains of the *Rurales* were already swarming thickly with red ants."[101]

Although the swarm's "two thousand vigorous arms make up a superior force," what do the novels suggest about the swarm's "thousand heads"?[102] The answer, in part, is in how Traven's narrator contrasts the intelligence of the rebel group and the intelligence of the federal army. If strength counts toward determining the intelligence of the swarm, the swarm itself clearly possesses some intelligence. Strength is not evidence of higher-level intelligence, however, so there must be other characteristics of the swarm that make it intelligent.

The rebel army has several characteristics in common with the federal army, not the least of which is that it too has a general. But the rebels express their power in different ways, perhaps seen most clearly in how they discuss and debate. Although Traven's narrator argues that independent thought takes time to develop,[103] at several moments we see the rebels engaged in discussion, debating tactics and strategy, but also discussing their views on the revolution's goals. The narrator frequently points out how the rebels "had never been allowed freedom of expression; every possibility of communication and discussion had been denied them."[104] This is clearly a lament, but it is also meant as a wedge to distinguish the type of intelligence in the rebel swarm from the type of intelligence in the federal army. Traven's narrator suggests that this activity is not just liberatory, but also what unleashes the group's intelligence and aggregates that intelligence in ways that make the group itself smart.

Just as there is strength in numbers, the same idea might hold for intelligence: multiple brains are better than a single brain, just as "two thousand vigorous arms" make up a superior force. But this idea also leads to a dead end—in the federal army, too, there are multiple brains. The difference is in how intelligence is aggregated in different groups. In more hierarchical organizations, where decision-making power resides at the top, the judgment of a relatively few experts almost always has opportunities for expression, and the lower that one goes, those opportunities become more seldom. This is a generalization, of course, but it is a generalization supported by ample evidence in the Mahogany Novels. That evidence suggests that the Federal General's unwillingness to incorporate his soldiers' ideas causes his defeat.

Whereas the Rebel General is portrayed as contemplative and empathetic,[105] the Federal General consistently refuses to admit that the rebels pose a military threat. In "an example of the atrophied powers of thought of all those who occupy a public office or a position of responsibility under a dictatorship,"[106] the Federal General is approached by one of his sergeants, who, after first asking permission to speak, offers the most tepid of comments: "I think, sir, that there's something not quite right in this whole affair, if I may put it like that, sir."[107] With a "paternal smile still on his fat, rosy lips," the General "said indulgently and patronizingly, 'Sergeant Morones, your question and your observation do you credit. They show that you are an excellent soldier, able to think for yourself and weigh unusual occurrences."[108] The General dismisses the Sergeant, however, by saying that the rebels "are yellow cowards, and they all behave just as one would expect of such riffraff."[109] The Sergeant is unsatisfied by the General's response, but

> as a dutiful and experienced soldier who, moreover, knew that his promotion to officer depended on always conceding one's superiors to be in the right, always being tactful toward higher-ups, and not concerning oneself with matters not expressly entrusted to one, he carefully avoided even mentioning any doubts that still lingered in his mind after his commanding officer had expounded his opinion.[110]

Hubris, sycophancy, and submission to authority make a deadly combination for the federal army. Traven's narrator writes, "Muddled thinking becomes a virtue under a dictatorship, but in a democracy it is simply regarded as laziness."[111] Traven's narrator suggests that the weaknesses of hierarchical organizations are that they stifle free thinking and that they cannot aggregate the collective intelligence of their members. The federal army has no debate, and therefore no mechanism to raise and examine diverse perspectives. Its strength is in the experience and expertise of a few people, which is not insignificant, but which will often come up short in comparison to groups that can aggregate many different ideas effectively.

If the weakness of "the windbags of revolution" is the weariness of participants and the need to make decisions quickly when the stakes are as high as they are in the Mahogany Novels, then the weakness of the reliance on command and obedience, to the exclusion of any debate and discussion, is that relevant ideas will be missed, and this will sharply curtail the range of possibilities that a group will consider. There are situations where decisions need to be made quickly, and no debate is possible. But when debate is possible, a swarmlike intelligence has the potential to outperform considerably a more centralized form of intelligence. These are the consequences that the Federal General ignores when he silences his Sergeant. The narrator shows that individual actors inside the swarm are smart—the Rebel General, for example, "had been, without knowing it himself, born with the gifts and talents of a great general"[112]—but the decentralized nature of the group's power and intelligence makes the group smarter than the sum of its individual members.

The Problems of Solipaz

At the end of the novels, after a tremendous volume of materials showing the relations between the domination of constituted power and the resistance to it, Traven leaves readers with difficult problems. In the final scenes, the rebels discover that the dictatorship was already overthrown before they began to fight. The complex nature of constituted power, the fact that it has many interacting parts, comes here to mean that those powers are not overthrown with the ouster of one dictator, as important as that one part of the machine may be. In this case, old hierarchies have already been dismantled, or at least temporarily destabilized, but a new hierarchy is ascendant. In the closing scene of *The General from the Jungle*, the last novel in the series, the rebels enter the town of Solipaz—sun and peace. They have defeated the federal army, and Traven's narrator leaves little doubt that the rebels are justified in their attempts to dismantle the structures of empire that dominate them, but the situation grows murky when the rebels find out that the goal they sought all along, once achieved, has not produced the effects they had wished to produce.

The situation proves even more difficult when one sees that Traven had sown the seeds of this problem throughout the last novel. Earlier, in addition to their wavering commitments to discussion and debate, the rebels also begin to display characteristics that resemble the structures of domination that they had sought to dismantle. The rebels are committed to the idea of an egalitarian society, one in which "land and liberty" are the goals, and where all are equal. In early interactions between the rebels and the others they meet, the rebels quickly correct any deference to their authority. The Rebel General consistently voices his devotion to the egalitarian ideals of the revolution: "I'm not your chief!" General says to a group of workers. "I'm your friend and comrade. We are all comrades. There are no more bosses, no patrons, no major-domos, no *capataces*."[113] The situation is more difficult, however, than General wishes it to be. Besides the fact that the rebel army has several hierarchical features—a fact that undercuts General's claim of an abolition of hierarchy—there is also the uncomfortable fact that "whoever came riding on such fine horses, and had revolvers and rifles, and fought with *Rurales* must be a new master, probably a crueler, more relentless and unjust master than the former one."[114] This new set of relationships, Traven states, was replicated throughout the country. The workers were not liberated by the revolution. "They remained slaves, with the single difference that their masters had changed."[115]

What began, therefore, as a justified attempt to abolish a particular constituted power becomes a new and different constituted power. As was noted above, for Carl Schmitt, after constituting itself, constituent power does not evaporate, but rather, the newly constituted representatives become the "bearer[s] of *pouvoir constituant*" through the process of representation.[116] Schmitt gives no indication that the collapsing together of constituent power and constituted power through the process of consensual representation is problematic theoretically, but he does spend considerable time—indeed, the bulk of *Dictatorship*—outlining the problems inherent in situations where the "bearers" of constituent power, or, more accurately, their agents—police, usually—meet the *demos* and confront them with force. Once in place, the newly constituted power retains perhaps the ideologies, shapes, or tenors of that constituent power, but it has a new role to play—to maintain itself, rather than to overthrow another power. The distinction in these roles is not trivial.

Traven's narrator seeks to put this situation in perspective by arguing that the rebels' "acts could not be taken as proofs of cruelty, because their adversaries and oppressors were a hundred times more savage and cruel than they when safeguarding their interests."[117] This is undoubtedly true, but neither is it satisfactory. The Mahogany Novels show the rebels challenging a hierarchy they find unjust, but while they seek to dismantle a particular constituted power, they do not ultimately dismantle constituted power as such.

CHAPTER FIVE

Repression and Cooperation
in Marie Vieux Chauvet's *Love*

By the end of the US military occupation of Haiti, which lasted from 1915 to 1934, Haiti's institutions of representative government lay in tatters. National independence, fought for by Toussaint and Dessalines, and secured by 2,000 leaders, had evolved into a series of civil wars, coups d'etat, and neocolonial aggression that had put these institutions in a state of perpetual instability. Marie Vieux Chauvet's novella *Love* is set in the aftermath of the occupation and is a picture of authoritarian force consolidating itself as a constituted power. It is also a text that shows the relations between the modes of power in both spectacular and subtle ways.

Love is the first of a trilogy of novellas that also includes *Anger* and *Madness*; they are set directly after the US occupation, but they are also an unmistakable indictment of François Duvalier's regime, under which Chauvet lived. The novellas were immediately banned, and Chauvet left Haiti soon after they were published, to avoid Duvalier's retaliation.[1] As Elizabeth Walcott-Hackshaw notes, *Love, Anger, Madness* is "unquestionably revolutionary and courageous in its use of a first-person narrative that dared to say what others stifled."[2] Chauvet notes both the instability before the US occupation and also how the US Marines attacked the Palais National,[3] an event that was precipitated by the US Marines removing $500,000 worth of gold from the Banque Nationale d'Haiti (the equivalent of $11 million today), and taking it to New York, an act that Laurent Dubois writes "can only be described as an international armed robbery."[4] The novella is therefore an opportunity to see, in many of its bloody details, the lingering repercussions of a national occupation by a hostile force and, in the wake of that occupation, the way a particular authoritarian regime constitutes and sustains itself. Walcott-Hackshaw writes,

> What the Duvalier regime created and promoted in its culture of terror was
> an arbitrariness that prevented any social group from feeling that it would be
> excluded. Therefore, organized resistance by groups or individuals was effectively
> undermined.[. . .] Chauvet describes the process of distancing and isolation, the
> aim of which is to avoid contamination.[5]

A reader sees the difficulties the regime presents to any form of collective action, through juridical means, like outlawing sedition and using quarantine for a punishment, and extrajuridical means, like cultivating isolation and a nearly omnipresent sense of fear—although the line between those two means is hardly clear. The only effective check on systematized injustice is what is on display in Traven's Mahogany Novels: people building networks of mutual aid smart and strong enough to destabilize such a regime. But the regime in *Love* knows this fact, and therefore the logic that guides its action is dedicated to severing or disrupting those networks.

These dynamics are viewed through the journal writings of Claire Clamont, the main character and narrator. Claire is the oldest daughter in the family, is unmarried, and has a skin color that is darker than the rest of her family's, a characteristic that marks her as somewhat separate from others in her society's racial and economic aristocracy.[6] It is difficult, though not impossible, to see Claire in a heroic mold, although this is a complicated assessment, as we will see. For much of the novel, Claire sequesters herself in her bedroom and in fantasy—she dreams, and practices at, killing her sister so that she could begin an affair with her brother-in-law, Jean Luze.[7] These fantasies are coping mechanisms, not positive, certainly, but they are helpful to her. Along these lines Claire writes that "freedom is an inmost power,"[8] which is a tragic retrenchment of the concept, but nevertheless one onto which she can hold—external freedom in the world in which she lives has been restricted so severely that she defines it in inward ways, rather than forgoing it altogether.

In *Love*, two facts, though at odds with each other, are still true: first, as Claire writes, "[m]isery, social injustice, all the injustices in the world, and they are countless, will disappear only with the human species. One remedies hundreds of miseries only to discover millions of others[. . .] To defend himself, man refines the meanness of his heart."[9] Claire calls the hope for a world without injustice a "lost cause,"[10] and she may be right—what she observes around her is almost ever-present brutality, including random murders and extreme sexual violence against women. As Colin Dayan writes in a recent issue of *Yale French Studies*, Chauvet "sets out to test the limits of decency, common sense, and even good writing."[11] But the second fact is that

Chauvet's work insists that even in the midst of this misery and injustice, a person's power, the willingness to rebel, the urge not to be complicit in one's own domination, is never completely extinguished. Yet in the face of such thoroughgoing violence, the wish to rebel seems alive only in the faintest of flickering light: what Claire suggests about the "meanness of heart" is a coping strategy to reduce one's own pain and to turn away from the pain others suffer. As she writes, "[s]elfishness becomes our way of life. We wallow in cowardice and resignation."[12] There are limits, Chauvet seems to suggest, to how much pain and coercion a person can take before she or he submits to a torturer who possesses a greater degree of physical force. In other words, repression produces resistance, but that resistance may not always have an opportunity or sufficient power to mount an effective challenge: Claire writes, "It's just that our weapons are not comparable."[13] Injustice in *Love* is ascendant, and the most common path to self-preservation is through isolation, even if it means ignoring someone else's suffering.

Warren Montag writes that "absolute power, then, is nothing more than a juridical fiction, based on the separation of the sovereign's rights from his power. And sovereigns tend to ignore the fiction for the fact: few fail to recognize the irreducible limits of their power and the inescapable fragility of sovereignty itself."[14] *Love* puts this idea to a severe test. When one considers the thoroughgoing brutality of the constituted powers in the novella, it can be difficult to think that the comment is correct, but it is. We might look from a different perspective. Chauvet's *Love* shows a situation where a constituted power has expressed its authority to an extremely substantial degree. But, as Carl Schmitt does, it is important to look at what may be exceptions to usual ways of operating, to look at the most extreme cases–even though doing so may be difficult–because in these moments, the dynamics of power can be clarified.[15] In *Love*, direct democracy and constituted power show themselves quite clearly, both in spectacular clashes and in quieter moments.

The cunning, merciless genius of *Love* is to show a regime that knows that collective resistance is the only effective way to challenge systematized injustice—the characters in *Love* are two or three generations removed from the Haitian Revolution, and none have forgotten its lessons, although they interpret those lessons quite differently. The current regime knows the moves that destabilize a constituted power, and it has put techniques into practice that break the bonds of cooperation wherever possible. Therefore, the issue is not so simple as choosing, or not choosing, to cooperate. The regime uses fear and violence to impede the cooperation direct democracy requires.

In her essay "Madness and the *Mulâtre-Aristocrate*: Haiti, Decolonization, and Women in Marie Chauvet's *Amour*," Hellen Lee-Keller traces a line of scholars, including Frantz Fanon, Elizabeth Walcott-Hackshaw, and Martin Munro, who have investigated the ways authoritarian regimes cultivate isolation and alienation in order to divide people from one another and from their sense of themselves as human beings, both of which aid the regime in ruling.[16] In this chapter I invert that idea in order to build upon it. Gilles Deleuze uses the terms *active* and *reactive* to describe forces that, respectively, affirm and negate; *active* and *reactive* are not value judgments, but rather are terms that describe the effects of power.[17] In this terminology, Lee-Keller and the scholars she mentions show how such regimes produce things that are reactive—isolation and alienation. I will add to this by arguing that the regime also represses things that are active, namely, the cooperation and mutual aid that could multiply the characters' power into direct democracy. But even though repression is throughout the text, it has limits, and the resistance that it ultimately cannot squash shows important aspects of the relation between the two modes of power.

For the characters in *Love* who resist the regime, how to build cooperative links of mutual aid is among the most pressing problems they face. As she listens to the screams coming from the nearby prison, screams that she cannot entirely drown out by playing music on her record player, Claire writes that a "kind of mysterious tremor stirs the town like the hushed sound of a wing slowly gliding over our heads. This shudder that courses through me cannot be merely personal, I know this now. Like me, all of them must be secretly working to free themselves from the constricting fear. I am not alone."[18] This is an important recognition, but recognizing it and being able to act upon that recognition are two different things. There are particular effects to the violence in *Love*; while it takes many forms, and it is motivated by revenge, gender domination, and racial and class hatred, one of its most salient characteristics is that it is designed to weaken the networks of mutual aid. Claire is not alone, but networks of mutual aid are material things, and when the links of those networks are suppressed, a person can feel very much alone. In that way, *Love* is bitter proof of Spinoza's idea from the *Political Treatise*: "Individuals alone do not possess sufficient power to preserve themselves and thus of necessity unite with others to survive."[19] Spinoza here is speaking about community in the abstract, but for the world in which Claire lives, that survival is an immediately pressing concern.

Most other chapters in this book show spectacles, eruptions of the power I call direct democracy. Those are valuable examples because in that spectacle, such power looms large and, in cases like the 2,000 leaders in the Haitian

Revolution, it shows its potential. But while remarkable, most are affirmations of Derrida's comment in "Force of Law" that such spectacles are most often bloody affairs, made inevitable by accumulated injustices. Like the rocks in Lucy Parsons's metaphor, they must be removed before a person can travel down a road. The power of ability, what I call direct democracy when multiplied by cooperation, is certainly blocked by accumulated injustices in Chauvet's *Love*; it is perhaps blocked by a more vicious expression of constituted power than any other example here. There is, at the end of the novella, a representation of the Riot Act situation, and it is one in which a group of people overcome a constituted power by force, in this case the police, and then proceed to the prison to free all who are held there. The novella's main character, Claire, plays a key role in this *coup de force*, as we will see. Quite understandably, this spectacular scene has attracted much of the scholarly attention given to the novella. But in *Love*, there are quieter moments that express the power of cooperative ability in different, but no less insightful, ways. These moments are easy to miss, but they illustrate Claire's power—even as events and "thoughts [are] swarming within the hellish complexity of the soul"—perhaps in a better way than any of the other examples.[20]

In this chapter, I present two readings of *Love*—first, a fuller examination, and second, a shorter reprise—looking at the novella's content from different perspectives. As I will show, for the characters in *Love*, especially its narrator, Claire, mounting an effective resistance is not a simple matter of choosing, or not choosing, to cooperate: the violence that they face is specifically designed to check that cooperation, to repress the networks of mutual aid. The novella includes spectacles that catch a reader's eye, and also quieter elements that are no less important. Both the spectacle and the subtle illustrate the relations between the two modes of power in the novella, and I consider each in turn.

First Reading of *Love*: The Spectacle

The characters in *Love* feel the regime's presence in both public and private, and at no moment are its effects very far from their daily experiences. This state of affairs leads Claire to ask an honest, important question about "what could have brought us to hang our heads and resign ourselves."[21] Not all the characters in *Love* hang their heads in resignation, but almost all of them feel the impulse to do so. This impulse is widespread and therefore is a signal that its cause is systemic, that there is a dynamic at work that elicits this result. Yet it would be a mistake to suggest that the community Chauvet describes had much unity before the rise of the regime. Claire writes that around 1900, when she was born, "[t]hree groups emerged, isolated from each other like enemies: the 'aristocrats' to whom I belonged, the petty bourgeois, and the common people."[22] The legacy of slavery, with its racial, class, and gender hierarchies, had already fractured the community, but Chauvet's novellas show this uneasy arrangement in rapid collapse. Old hierarchies are everywhere unstable, and new ones are asserting themselves in ways that seem ubiquitous.

Two characters in *Love* represent the structures of constituted power: Calédu, the local commandant of the police, who is the regime's representative in the town where Claire's family lives, and M. Long, the American corporate executive whose export business keeps commodities like fish, coffee, and wood flowing from Haiti to the United States.[23] Calédu and M. Long are individual characters, but they are also synecdoches for larger forces, present but not always visible in the novella. Two people alone could not wield the level of oppression that they inflict: thus, Calédu is a stand-in for both a militarized police force and a reminder of the Tonton Macoute, Haiti's dictatorship-era paramilitary. M. Long, the American capitalist, is a stand-in for the resource extraction of neocolonialism, for the foreign expropriation of Haitian coffee, timber, and labor. By the time a reader meets Chauvet's characters, Calédu and M. Long have been exercising their power for a decade.[24] Claire notes that Calédu "wields the right of life and death over us, and he abuses it."[25] M. Long, Claire writes, "has cleverly found shelter under the wings of the authorities in order to better suck our blood."[26] Claire sees lessons for her current situation in her national history and wonders what will happen when the natural resources that M. Long exploits run out: "Avalanches of soil slid down the mountains and piled around their feet," she writes. "Coffee is nothing but a memory for all of us. Timber export has replaced that business. When the wood is gone, he will go after something else. The slave trade, perhaps."[27] This neocolonialism does not have the same characteristics that French colonialism did, but their dynamics are similar enough to make Claire see the parallel.[28] That Calédu and M. Long work together so closely is a sign that once again, constituted powers are complex—they are a braid made stronger by being woven together.

Calédu and M. Long rule by using a violence that is vicious enough to freeze people in their tracks and to turn away from basic impulses like caring for others who need help. Chauvet illustrates this in an insightful scene early in the book, during a church procession. As the procession makes its way past Calédu and M. Long, a person Claire calls "Jacques the madman" comes running up to Calédu, screaming, calling Calédu "a devil" and "Satan," yelling that "the gates of hell" have been opened on the community.[29] Calédu grabs Jacques by the collar and slaps him; when he cannot make Jacques stop screaming, "Calédu pulls his revolver from his belt and shoots the lunatic point-blank. Jacques falls to his knees without a protest."[30] The children in the procession cry, but the adults are still: the only movement is the nuns clutching their rosaries. After a moment, Dr. Audier, one of Claire's family friends, takes a step toward Jacques, but "a bullet whistling near his feet nails him to the ground, terrified."[31] Claire writes, "[W]e remain frozen in place."[32] The priest humbly begs Calédu to leave. When he does, it "was the signal for a mad dash. The trembling nuns gathered their students. Men, women and children rushed home."[33] The scene illustrates the relations of power—when Calédu wants to overpower another, such as Jacques, he can. He can also project his power over others to bend them to his will. Violence, and the threat of further violence, freezes people in this scene. The nuns do not step between Calédu and their students; parents do not dare gesture that they would protect their children. Social and familial bonds come up short in a test of strength against Calédu's gun and his capacity to use violence. Although they outnumber him, the characters here do not act collectively, because they have learned through hard experience that to act against Calédu is to invite reprisals. They unfreeze only after he leaves.

To show this scene is not to fault the nuns and the parents—it is to show that the effects of Calédu's violence have penetrated the whole community's minds so thoroughly that they are afraid even to act to protect the people they care about deeply. This characterization is consistent throughout much of the novella, and it is a reminder to think of people both as they are and as they could be, which is both mired in violence and also capable of living lives that more fully express their potential.[34] Chauvet's characters are multilayered and often contradictory; none are simply heroic or simply flawed, but are rather caught in situations where intense violence complicates those relations and influences their actions.

This multilayered relation of characters' power is perhaps most clearly on display in Claire's family and its history. Her father had owned a substantial coffee plantation on Lion Mountain, and after he died, it fell to Claire to manage, a task for which her father did not adequately prepare her. When she suspected that the workers on the plantation were withholding payments due to her family, her frustrations devolved into fury. Claire arranged to sell the coffee at a cut rate, leaving no wages for her workers, an act that led to increased hostility between Claire and those workers. But while the fiercest the workers' retaliation got was to shake their fists at Claire's house,[35] Claire responded to the exchange with disproportionate anger. She writes that her "father's farmers paid with their lives for my brilliant idea [to cut the rate], because about twenty planters armed with machetes descended on our land and slaughtered them."[36] The people who committed the murders were found and jailed, but Claire writes, "No one dared openly attack me, the daughter of a great despotic and merciless landowner, but I was responsible for everything and everyone knew it."[37] Years later, during the present events of the story, Calédu taunts Claire with the history of her act: "'I have heard, Miss Clamont,' he whispered wickedly, 'that in the old days a bloody incident took place up there on your land, on Lion Mountain. So it seems you and I both have killing on our conscience. Mine doesn't bother me much. Does yours?'"[38] The way Calédu taunts Claire leads her, rather hypocritically, to lament the lack of national unity in the face of M. Long's neocolonial exploitation: "Are we losing our pride and our solidarity to such an extent that we betray one another out of fear?" she asks. "Don't they realize that they are giving our enemies ammunition against us?"[39] It is rather shocking that Claire could cite the memory of her actions as the fault for a lack of solidarity, rather than the act itself, but in this ambiguous moment, Claire shows that she is mired in the violence of her past, violence that she caused, but also that she sees solidarity and collective resistance as the key tools to use to combat the domination she now faces. Claire has killing on her conscience, but she also promises to act, according to her abilities and opportunities, to secure some measure of justice in her community.

Similar comments could be made about Jean Luze, Claire's brother-in-law. Jean Luze is the object of Claire's somewhat secret affection, and he is also French, and a veteran of the First World War; he also knows the history of the French Revolution well and sees parallels between it and his current situation.[40] His most admirable characteristic is his attitude: his eyes are oriented in the direction of rebelling against Calédu. Yet he works for M. Long's export business and therefore hopes to fray one of the threads in the braid of constituted power while lashing another of its threads ever tighter. In conversation with Dr. Audier after the scene in which Calédu kills Jacques, Jean Luze says,

> "You have to protest, respond to this with a demonstration, face the danger together. They would never destroy an entire town. These murders, these tortures, are meant to terrorize you. But let one person here lead an uprising and the other side will tremble . . ."
>
> "You don't understand anything," Dr. Audier said laconically, softly resting his trembling hand on Jean Luze's arm.[41]

Although Claire calls him, correctly, an "idealist," Jean Luze is not just a dewy-eyed dreamer.[42] His head has been filled with too many stories about heroic leaders and unimportant followers, and they have led him to the incorrect conclusion that such a movement could topple the regime. He is, however, correct to suggest that the best strategy is collective resistance. In *Love*, it is as useless to look to leaders for salvation as it is to appeal to the regime for some kind of leniency.[43] What he also misses is that the context from which he draws his experience—French resistance to German aggression—is dissimilar to the context to which he would apply the lessons of his experience. As Dr. Audier implies, the violence the characters in *Love* face is designed to inhibit the cooperation Jean Luze advocates. These characters are in horrifically violent circumstances: for his part, Jean Luze never comes to see the contradiction in hating Calédu yet working for M. Long. Claire has to unlearn the isolation that has enveloped her, and may, in fact, never be successful in doing so, regardless of the type of person the novella hints she could become. Yet to the degree that she is able, Claire sees, as the novella progresses, that isolation, both for herself and for others, is a more difficult matter.

In addition to Claire and Jean Luze, several other characters demonstrate that they know that some form of solidarity is the only effective counter to this domination. The workers who shout to the crowds to "stick together" as Calédu beats them for going on strike against M. Long see the idea especially clearly.[44] Claire makes several notes about the idea in her journal, one of which quotes a worker shouting to a crowd: "We should have created a coalition and refused all offers," but, Claire then writes, "black hill folk never stick together."[45] As in the moment when Calédu taunts her for murdering her workers, Claire's racial and class privilege come to the surface here, leading her to think that the situation for "black hill folk" is just a matter of choosing to cooperate, and to insinuate that they rarely make the right decision. However, the "black hill folk" know what to do, as we will see below; it is Claire and Jean Luze—who have been, in comparison, comfortable in their privilege—who have a difficult time seeing the ways that collective resistance is repressed by violence.

⑥　⑥　⑥

In particular, though the line between them is not quite clear, there are juridical and extrajuridical tools that the regime uses to repress mutual aid. Of the juridical tools, the use of quarantine as a punishment and laws against sedition and subversive activities are the most prominent. The regime defines sedition or "subversive activities" simply as any speech or act it does not like; as I will show, it uses charges of sedition to isolate people and also as a thin veneer to cover any abuses it wants to perpetrate, including its sexual violence against women. The crimes and the punishment go together in the logic of the regime: sedition is the contaminant, and quarantine is the cure. Quarantine is a literal way to isolate people from one another, and Claire mentions how the state used this method to remove two characters, Tonton Mathurin and Agnès Grandupré, from the community altogether.[46] Agnès Grandupré, Claire writes, for example, "grew up under quarantine. She was erased from our lives, and I sometimes forgot she even existed."[47] Similarly, to be charged with sedition is to be an open suspect of the regime, to be a person with whom others dare not associate unless they also want to be considered suspect. This too, fits the logic of the regime: laws against sedition are among its most flexible tools, and also are tools that strike at one of the necessary aspects of collective resistance. The two uses of sedition are, first, to limit the circulation, to the degree that it is able, of any criticism of the regime, and second, as a blanket law to justify any method of repression that it sees fit to use, at any time.

For example, sedition is the pretense that Calédu uses to commit what is perhaps the most brutal act in a novella that is full of brutal acts. Dora Soubiran is Claire's childhood friend and neighbor, whom Claire describes as "a completely harmless zealot."[48] Perhaps Chauvet intends Dora to be a rather unsympathetic character: her religiosity is manifested in a pious disdain for others. Even though Claire, like Dora, is a member of the aristocracy, Claire's fullest description of her friend and neighbor seems to begrudge the fact that Dora's family is clearly more accomplished than Claire's is, and she holds Dora in some level of contempt for the ways that Dora keeps those privileges in the forefront of the minds of the people around her.[49] Like Claire, Calédu also openly begrudges Dora's privilege, only to a greater degree than Claire does.

Perhaps because of her piety or because she thought that her old privileges would protect her, one day Dora follows Calédu down the street, saying the rosary and, as Claire writes, "looking down her nose" at Calédu.[50] Using a sedition charge as a pretext, he arrests her; over the course of the next two days, Calédu and four other unnamed men take turns raping her.[51] Chauvet represents the rape somewhat obliquely, but it is nevertheless unmistakable: after those two days, Dora was "haggard and unrecognizable, followed by the taunts of the beggars roaring with laughter to see her walk with open legs like a cripple."[52] This is not, as Jean Luze might suggest, "well-behaved fatalism,"[53] but rather an act of the power to overpower another. It is a particularly vicious form of bodily violence, and acting alone, there is little that Dora, Claire, Jean Luze, or any other could do to stop it, even if they were to choose to intervene, which is questionable. In the aftermath, Dora's pain is an open secret: she "hobbles along with legs spread apart like a maimed animal."[54] Dora may be unsympathetic to the other characters, but she has been tortured, then released so that all can see the effects of that torture; she would benefit immensely from even a small act of caring. Fear represses mutual aid, however, and that is one of the points of the rape: while it is inflected with gender, class and race hatred—as he rapes her, Calédu shouts, "Snobs, you bunch of snobs, mulatto snobs, I'll make cripples of you all, you snobs"[55]—it is also an act designed to discipline everyone around Dora as well. Calédu sends out an unmistakable signal that to care for Dora after he rapes her is to risk his retaliation, and the other characters do not miss this message.

After Calédu releases Dora, Claire's sister warns her against visiting Dora; at first, Claire follows her advice. "We hear her sob at night," Claire writes in her journal. "No one dares rescue her. She's a suspect. One of those who has been marked by Calédu, a man chosen expressly by the police to tame this little town famous for its arrogance and prejudices."[56] Chauvet implies that Dr. Audier treats Dora's wounds, but she immediately follows that implication with a declarative statement that the doctor will not do more: he "is brave enough for looking after a victim, Dr. Audier must tell himself. The reign of terror has broken his spirit. The politician, the great champion of freedom and the rights of man that he was when my father was alive, is dead in him."[57] The greater dilemma in the Clamont household after the rape is how to deal with Calédu, specifically, whether to invite him to a party. Claire's sister Félicia suggests inviting him to the party because she is "prudent" and because she blames the rape on its victim, stating that Dora "has always been heedless"; her sister Annette suggests that Calédu is "not a bad guy," but just following his orders.[58] These reactions are testimony to how thoroughly Calédu and the regime have overpowered the other characters—he has reached into their home, their thoughts, their strategies for survival. They are nearly agreed that their survival depends on placating Calédu rather than resisting him.

So unlike the earlier scene where the nuns and parents rush to protect their children after Calédu's threat has passed, few characters rush to Dora's aid—as Claire writes, no one else wants to be suspected of sedition and to suffer a similarly horrific punishment. The reverberations in the community show that it has a profound effect—the social capital that Dora previously possessed as a mixed-race upper-class woman no longer protects her, and this realization sends shock waves through Claire's social circle. Mme. Camuse, after delivering a second-hand description of the way Calédu raped Dora, says, "I'm seventy-five years old. I have seen revolutionaries walk into this town, bandits;[59] I've witnessed bloody battles, lived through civil war, but never, you hear me, never have I felt as evil and foul a curse hovering over this town as I feel it today . . ."[60] It is understandable, of course, that seeing Dora so wounded would make Claire, in her words, refine the meanness of her heart and dwell on the possibility that the privileges that she shares with Dora will also no longer protect her from Calédu.[61] "I don't like these lingering looks Calédu keeps giving me each time I run into him in the street," Claire writes. "No matter how much contempt I muster, I'm not able to maintain the aristocratic composure that had kept the necessary distance between us and had forced him to lower his eyes in shame."[62] Claire's old privileges no longer work to keep down those she thinks are lower than her in the social hierarchy, and while hierarchy based on the privileges of class and color is unjust, so is the new hierarchy of race, gender, and force, and it rightly makes Claire fearful.

Furthermore, Calédu rapes Dora as part of a program to maintain and project the regime's power; it is not a whim or the act of a single despotic official. It is, rather, one important element of a larger system of domination. As Lee-Keller suggests, the political strife in *Love* is part of "the continual and unfinished process of decolonization," and therefore the violence in the novella, especially the sexual violence against women, "cannot be understood as a political anomaly, but as the logical consequences of colonialism."[63] Furthermore, Lee-Keller writes that the "explicit, violent actions are not limited to black male characters, but Chauvet includes scenes in which other various male characters inflict violence on women in order to illustrate that patriarchal violence is not limited to a few aberrant men. Rather, masculinity is demonstrated—across national, racial, and cultural lines—through violence."[64]

Patriarchal violence is systemic, not anomalous. For all of these reasons, the suggestions that Claire's sisters make to isolate themselves from Dora out of self-interest and self-preservation are understandable, but under different circumstances, they may not have blocked Claire or the other characters from acting immediately upon some level of sympathy for Dora. This is because, as I have argued, the violence in *Love* is designed to hamper the links of mutual aid in the community. Claire knows that if she were to display a private act of sympathy—to say nothing of a public act of solidarity—she would risk retaliation if Calédu were to learn about it. The violence that Calédu inflicts on Dora comes with a warning to everyone in the community that Dora is to be left to suffer alone, and to violate that warning is to invite similar violence. It is remarkable, then, that Claire will disregard that warning, as we will see.

⑥　⑥　⑥

At the end of the novella, Claire stabs and kills Calédu on her veranda. Many of the scholars whom Lee-Keller cites in "Madness and the *Mulâtre-Aristocrate*" have focused on this act as the example of Claire's bravery and the novella's poetic justice. This focus is consistent with the framework that this scholarship uses, namely, an examination of how the regime produces things that are reactive—isolation and alienation—and this work shows how the scenes leading to the stabbing are multilayered, to say the least. In this chapter's next section, I will suggest a different reading of these events, one that highlights other aspects of the story, but this is meant to complement, not undermine, the work that has focused on Claire's acts at the novella's end.

To a significant degree, Claire prefers the isolation of her bedroom, where she writes in her journal and where her imagination can run in many directions. In her fantasies Claire pictures her brother-in-law Jean Luze as her lover, and by the latter parts of the novella, Claire steps to the edge of delusion and makes plans to kill her sister Félicia so that Jean Luze would be released from their marriage and, ostensibly, be free to begin a relationship with Claire. These are fantasies, but they border on becoming real: Jean Luze has given her a "paper dagger"—which J. Michael Dash suggests is a "double-edged letter opener, a wickedly ironic weapon for effecting political transformation."[65] Claire practices, and perhaps tests herself, by referring to it simply as a dagger, and by using it to kill the neighbor's cat.[66]

At some point afterward, Claire is once again in her bedroom, with the dagger, now vacillating between killing her sister and committing suicide. She is unaware that a crowd has formed, and that it intends to avenge itself on Calédu and M. Long. Before she can decide what to do with her dagger, she hears the crowd in the street outside her house. The "black hill folk" that Claire suggests never stick together have in fact stuck together, and as a crowd, together with Jean Luze, they attack Calédu and M. Long. "The street is lit by the peasants' torches," Claire writes. "They are hollering, 'Down with Mister Long,' and walking toward the American. He immediately aims a submachine gun: twenty fall."[67] Claire writes that Calédu then

> is afraid, alone in the dark, hounded by the beggars he himself armed. He is moving backward toward my house. Does he realize that? Behind the blinds of the living room, I watch and wait for him. I take my dagger from my blouse and open the door partway. He is on my veranda. I see him hesitate and turn his head in every direction. He is within reach. With extraordinary strength, I plunge the dagger into his back once, twice, three times. The blood spurts.[. . .] No one has seen me, except perhaps Dora Soubiran, whose house is so close to mine."[68]

Claire's act is justified, considering all the pain that Calédu has caused. It is extrajudicial, of course, but that has no bearing on whether her acts are just—it would be difficult to imagine Claire securing much justice from the regime in *Love*. The stabbing is also quite clearly an example of the power to overpower another. It is spectacular, delivered in a flash of action in the novella's final pages, so the scene clearly deserves the amount of scholarly attention that it has received. While there is debate about how to read Claire's act, much of this scholarship focuses on its collective nature.[69] As Valerie Kaussen writes, "once Claire can voice and accept the validity of her own (often negative) desires, she is able to recognize the links between her own demands and those of others, and act in solidarity, in coalition, with other groups and individuals who likewise pursue their freedom."[70] This is undoubtedly correct—Claire's act is made possible because she makes it in tandem with others: the crowd has pursued Calédu to the point where they have put him into a place where Claire can kill him. Claire has the fortitude to kill Calédu when she is presented with the opportunity, and that is to her credit; she secures this measure of justice in the way she is able and when she sees a practical opportunity. But at minimum, the way Claire kills Calédu is ambiguous, a fact that is seen in the substantial scholarly debate about the act. It is not premeditated or planned; Claire has not chosen to be part of the crowd that confronts Calédu and M. Long, but rather participates by happenstance. Killing Calédu takes courage and strength, but they are the courage and strength of only a moment. Claire happens to be in the right place at the right time to kill Calédu, but the place and time she is in are made right because the crowd makes them right. Once Calédu is dead, Claire writes, "Jean Luze appears with a smoking gun. I hear Joël Marti holler: 'To the prison! Free the prisoners!' A vast clamor rises in response.[. . .] From the window, I catch a glimpse of the torches wavering in the wind. The doors of the houses are open and the entire town has risen."[71] The crowd moves on, but Claire does not follow.

Claire's act to kill Calédu, done in tandem with the crowd's attempt on M. Long's life, then freeing the prisoners, is remarkable. It is a reaction to Calédu's domination, and it is well deserved. It is an act to end the production of isolation and alienation. A reader could speculate that for some period of time, the community can rest without Calédu, and his prisoners will live without their shackles. As Melissa Sande suggests, "Claire's final action is then hopeful in that Chauvet is suggesting a break from prescribed roles for Haitian women in the future. [. . . This] ending unites the masses, bringing them out of hiding in their homes and back into the streets of their town, where they can now usurp the power from the hands of a violent dictator."[72] This is a hopeful, plausible conclusion to draw from the end of *Love*. The novella is historical fiction, however; while it is strongly implied that the crowd of workers kills M. Long—that is the crowd's announced intent—a reader does not see his end. The last moment a reader sees M. Long is when he kills twenty people in the crowd. It is plausible, then, to imagine him to be killed by the crowd or to be hiding until quieter times. Yet even if the crowd avenges itself on M. Long, such an act would not bring the neocolonial exploitation that he represents to an end. Furthermore, it is as possible to suggest that Calédu will be replaced, that the regime will reassert itself, perhaps in ways that will be worse than under Calédu. Perhaps Claire, or the crowd of workers, would kill Calédu's replacement, too, and perhaps Claire's kindness to Dora will not be reciprocated, but these are speculations for which there is no evidence in *Love*: the novella ends after Claire stabs Calédu. Yet, at least for a moment, the town can rest: much of the repression that drives the forces of isolation and alienation has been checked. This is quite considerable, and it is another reason, as mentioned in previous chapters, to distinguish between direct democracy and constituent power: this group of people does not constitute its power in new law or a new regime, but it does nevertheless express its power, its ability to act and to multiply that power collectively. This power is strong enough to surmount the fear Calédu has cultivated so widely in the community and to survive the literal and symbolic force of M. Long's submachine gun and the neocolonialism it represents.

Second Reading of *Love*: The Collective Power to Care

In Calédu's murder and the march to the prison, the novella's end plays out the Riot Act situation: constituted power tries to preserve itself against a crowd and finds its power insufficient to prevail. Here is where the novella ends, but given that it links to *Anger* and *Madness*, the two novellas that follow *Love*, it is strongly implied that these acts do not alter the constituted power under which the characters live. The celebration in the street and the act freeing the prisoners are notable and important, and they are a *coup de force*, but not a coup d'etat.

Put a bit differently, the end of *Love* leaves the representative of constituted power dead, but constituted power itself only damaged. No other evidence in the novella will suggest any other outcome—to do so would have to ignore that *Love* is linked to *Anger* and *Madness*, stories that plunge their characters even further into violence, as well as the recognition that the three novellas are works of historical fiction and therefore must hew, to some degree, to the fact that dictatorships not unlike those in *Love, Anger, Madness* governed Haiti well beyond the historical moment in which the novellas are set. But as I show in this section, not only does Claire resist Calédu by overpowering him, she also does so in a way that takes more courage and strength than the stabbing does: her act of caring for Dora. I wish not to overstate the situation—material force needs to be overthrown with material force, to paraphrase Marx; again, at the end of the novella, we see a *coup de force* that goes some distance to reducing the degree to which Claire, Dora, and their peers are debased.[73] But Claire's act of solidarity with Dora also deserves attention, and although it is different, it deserves to be seen as having an equal if not greater importance than the stabbing. To show why requires a reading of *Love* from a second perspective, a reprise of material that, for being subtle, may have otherwise been missed.

In the *Ethics*, Spinoza defines friendship as a state of mutual freedom.[74] This is perhaps a bit too strong to describe Claire and Dora's relationship—it would be difficult to describe the world in which they live as permitting any satisfying degree of freedom, and if one uses the term *friend* as a layperson's term, not in the technical sense that Spinoza uses it, it would also be difficult to say that Claire and Dora show a friendship that is very deep. Additionally, as noted above, Spinoza writes that if two people "come together and join forces, they have more power over Nature, and consequently more right, than either one alone; and the greater the number who form a union in this way, the more right they will together possess."[75] Nevertheless, in the technical sense of these terms, Claire and Dora present a striking example of collective power and of friendship. They increase their power together—the power to survive, of course, but more importantly, the power to openly, premeditatedly, defy the constituted powers in their community.

As mentioned above, Calédu rapes Dora not only to punish her, but as a warning to everyone else as well. Dora's supposed crime is sedition—a meaningless word in this context, unless that word is so broadly defined as to include everything that the regime does not like. Anyone, at any time, could be accused of sedition, and that mere accusation could lead immediately to punishment at Calédu's discretion. It is remarkable, then, that Claire builds slowly toward disregarding this warning, and when she finally does, she breaks it fearlessly and repeatedly. "I saw Dora Soubiran fall," Claire writes.

> She was walking with legs spread apart, a basket on her arm; she stumbled on a stone and fell. I ran down the stairs. I gave her my hand in the middle of the street and walked her home. Calédu happened to go by just then. He stopped. I did not look at him. Eyes glinted behind closed blinds.[. . .] "Watch out for the commandant," she whispered suddenly, "watch out for him." "I will come back every day," I repeated firmly. The whispers from behind the blinds followed me home.[76]

What could the eyes and whispers from behind the blinds mean? Shock, probably, at the fact that Claire is willing to dare Calédu's anger. Perhaps those eyes and whispers are signs of hope that such an open act of disobedience could lead to destabilizing Calédu's power over the community; they could equally be cursing Claire out of fear that her disobedience will lead to more violence. But regardless of what those eyes and whispers convey, they are the manifestation of the fact that Claire has broken Calédu's rules and has actively chosen care for another person over self-preservation. After this first spontaneous meeting, Claire does visit Dora regularly, even though Claire's sister Félicia frowns on it.[77] Claire visits Dora in private and public,[78] in direct disobedience of Calédu's threats.

In this comparatively small but incredibly meaningful set of acts, Claire chooses community over isolation. Andrew Asibong writes that "Claire may be deeply disturbed (and disturbing) in many ways, but the steadily emerging psychic strength by which her narrative is characterized lies in her capacity for learning, experimentation and, crucially, empathetic, survivable relationality."[79] In these small but meaningful acts, Claire takes an active, affirmative step to build a community by establishing one link in a larger network of mutual aid. Again, neither this nor any other act in the novella topples the regime—to suggest so would be to overstate the case significantly. It would be more precise to say that in this moment, a reader can see the resistance to the isolated and fearful society that Calédu enforces, and also an act that, if multiplied out many more times, looks like a network of mutual aid, a group of people cooperating for a common purpose, much like the 2,000, Nat Turner and his peers, and Traven's swarm of rebels. Certainly those groups show a scale far larger than any similar group in *Love*—with the exception of the assembled crowd at the end of the novella—but Claire's act of caring for Dora is a hand extended in solidarity, a building block for a larger structure.

If the production of reactive effects—isolation and alienation—is the framework with which one views the novella, clearly Claire's act to kill Calédu is the key moment. However, if one looks from the equal and opposite angle, to see the active thing that the regime suppresses, the key moment is not the murder, justified though it is, but rather a set of moments, distributed throughout the novella, in which Claire cares for Dora, in direct rebellion against Calédu's threats, his laws against sedition, and his violence. The ways that Claire cares for Dora are subtler, far less spectacular, but they are, in Deleuze's terms, active: her acts help to build affirmative bonds of mutual aid. As opposed to the spontaneous opportunity to kill Calédu that Claire receives from the crowd, Claire cares for Dora in a planned, considered manner. Visiting Dora, in public and private, repeatedly, after she has been raped, when all know that Dora has been accused of sedition and therefore that to associate with her is to make one also suspect in the eyes of the regime, is a premeditated, sustained act of courage. It is also a connection built between two people who suffer horribly.

The stabbing is unpremeditated, it is spontaneous—this is not to devalue it, but rather to say that it is categorically distinct from Claire's premeditated, open defiance of Calédu in a subtle series of repeated acts of kindness. Her hand extended in solidarity is not a flourish or the act of someone heroic or idealized beyond being human, but the act of a human being recognizing the price she might pay at the hands of powerful people who want to see her stay isolated, to keep her fearful. No one will mistake Claire for a great hero, certainly not the families and friends of the workers she arranged to have murdered on her father's coffee plantation. The legacy of slavery in Haiti has left too strong an imprint on Claire to allow her to be treated with anything approaching uncritical veneration. But even withstanding the violence in which she is mired, a violence to which she has contributed and perhaps would continue to contribute if she felt her privilege threatened, she has the capacity to act kindly to a friend even when that act expressly defies an authority that could punish her severely for that act. This is not nothing: as she writes, "[m]any a spine has been bent by all this scraping."[80] People far stronger than Claire often genuflect with little hesitation to people who are far weaker than Calédu.

Claire's offer of mutual aid is not just about character and acting ethically—it is difficult to see her as much of a moral example. Networks of mutual aid are material things—the connections between people allow for sharing ideas and resources, and for many other purposes. By choosing to help Dora rather than to keep her isolated, Claire may have saved Dora's life. In writing that misery and injustice will always exist, Claire is half right. Her acts prove the other half of this idea: injustice will produce resistance. This does not mean that resistance will be successful—in *Love*, it is nearly everywhere checked, disrupted. When Claire writes, "Freedom is an inmost power,"[81] she may be trying to persuade herself of something that she knows is not actually true. The freedom she writes about is repressed by particular forms of systemic violence, a violence that is meant to repress the networks of mutual aid that are the only real hope of securing that freedom. Claire keeps that hope alive in the pages of her diary, which is an inmost power, but one cannot simply think that one is free—there are material barriers to freedom, and they pen Claire in her room. These comforting stories about freedom are useful, but freedom is an external thing, in this case one with hard limits enforced by Calédu. In showing a seditious act of caring for Dora, Claire builds back, even if in a small way, a link in a network of mutual aid that, if it could overcome the regime's violence to suppress it, could be built into a larger community.

EPILOGUE

Since C. L. R. James made the call for further research on the Haitian Revolution's 2,000 leaders in his "Lectures on *The Black Jacobins*," a number of scholars have written about the event from a variety of archival and theoretical perspectives and have, therefore, done much to advance our understanding of the Haitian Revolution's many complexities. These scholars often mention the 2,000 leaders prominently; this book has built from their work by analyzing the example of the 2,000 and the implications of their example at length, especially as James represented them in *The Black Jacobins*, and also by following their trajectory through other similar movements. As I hope to have shown, the other examples here deepen and extend the logic of collective action that the 2,000 displayed.

The purpose of this book has been to show a literary history of the concept I call direct democracy and to analyze that concept in a comparative light. By direct democracy, I do not mean what is usually meant—the term usually describes the government of ancient Athens or the forms of organization often found in maroon colonies, worker cooperatives, or the like.[1] This study might be analogous in some ways, but it has sought to put conversations about direct democracy on a different trajectory. In the etymology of democracy, there is governing, rule, and authority, but there is also power. I have no wish to return to some ancient past, but rather to broaden the ideas about what democracy could be, and in the process, to widen the literary archive to include a set of texts that is still too frequently ignored in conversations about democracy, labor, and slavery.

In my interpretation, direct democracy is the power of ability when multiplied by cooperation; in certain situations, that cooperative power shows emergent properties. It is analogous to, but distinct from, what Schmitt and others call constituent power, Agamben calls destituent power, and Rancière calls politics. To paraphrase Aristotle, Spinoza, and Marx, even though abilities atrophy or increase with neglect or practice, such capacities are a part of the human experience—the builder does not lose her ability when she is not building; the player does not lose his ability when he is not playing. People increase their power to act when they cooperate, and under certain conditions a group's power can come to be greater than the sum of its parts—these are the characteristics of the power I call direct democracy.

That has been my first claim—that direct democracy can be understood as a complex and collective type of power; its best example, though not its only example, is the Haitian Revolution's 2,000 leaders. My second claim has been that a range of writers have recognized this power, and when they represented it in their texts, they used the swarm metaphor to describe it. The uses of the swarm metaphor have always been contested—like other animal metaphors, it has been used to dehumanize what it describes, but it has also been used to describe collective intelligence and cooperative communities. From the German *Schwärmerei*, it has meant enthusiasm or zealotry; a type of irrational fervor. As an insult, used by thinkers like Carl Schmitt and Thomas Carlyle, *Schwärmerei* stands opposed to the constituted powers they believe are right and just; therefore, any challenge to them seemed irrational and unjust. In their use, *Schwärmerei* is a term wielded in order to protect the privilege of the enfranchised against the disenfranchised. But the insult proves the point just as well as other, more positive uses of the swarm metaphor by writers like James and B. Traven. The power the metaphor is meant to convey is palpable to all these writers, present in such a way that it must be recognized. Whether to contribute to its repression or its flourishing, the use of a swarm metaphor is like a signpost pointing to the presence of the power I call direct democracy.

The literary history of direct democracy in my project is about cooperation in response to exploitation, about the vital need to theorize the meanings and expressions of power, a term that in English may seem singular, but which is actually multiple. What I have called the two modes of power—that is, the power inherent in human capacity and the power of human relations, the power to act and the power to overpower—names a distinction that may otherwise be missed. Consider, for example, a famous phrase from *The Black Jacobins*. James writes that for "two centuries the higher civilization had shown [the insurgents] that power was used for wreaking your will on those whom you controlled. Now that they held power they did as they had been taught.[. . .] The cruelties of property and privilege are always more ferocious than the revenges of poverty and oppression. For the one aims at perpetuating resented injustice, the other is merely a momentary passion soon appeased."[2] James means to make a distinction here, to show that the two types of power—the power to overpower another indefinitely and the power to act to end that exploitation—are not precisely the same. Nor are they, however, completely different: the roles of domination and submission have been reversed, and from that perspective only, the revenges of poverty and oppression may look quite similar to the cruelties of property and privilege. But even with that similarity, the importance of making the distinction, the importance of recognizing that power has two modes, is clear in this example. For two centuries, colonizers had stolen millions of people and had generated tremendous amounts of wealth from that theft of lives and labor. It was a system that these colonizers had hoped would continue in perpetuity. James writes that colonizers dream dreams of an eternity of exploitation,[3] but the revenges of poverty and oppression have different ends in mind. After eleven years of struggle, the Haitian Revolution stopped this theft, not globally, certainly—as a system, the slave trade continued to thrive for decades after Haitian independence—but between 1697 and the end of the revolution, approximately 774,000 people disembarked at Saint Domingue in bondage; once the revolution was complete, this trafficking was stopped completely.[4] The Haitian Revolution includes many of the same ambiguities that accompany similar events, but these facts are considerable and deserve the attention that they have recently received. In the story of the Haitian Revolution, we can see the beams that built the house of colonialism and slavery, as well as the axe that could dismantle it.

While the 2,000 leaders in the Haitian Revolution are perhaps the best example of the power I call direct democracy, they are not the only ones to show its logic of collective action. It is the logic that Carl Schmitt needed to theorize, but also to minimize, in order to build a theory of sovereignty. It is in the labor unions that Thomas Carlyle wished would be repressed, and in Lucy Parsons's agitation as part of the movement for the eight-hour workday. It is in Nat Turner and his peers' efforts to free themselves, and in the ways that B. Traven's rebels and Marie Vieux Chauvet's characters hope for and work for, in ways that are spectacular and subtle, a world that is substantially different from, and better than, the worlds they inhabit. These characters do not appeal to a higher power to change their world for them, but rather act directly, in concert with others, to make the world a bit less miserable and a bit more free.

These struggles were rooted in the fact that enslaved people, women, and workers were part of a *demos*, the same as any other people, and as such, they could express their abilities in the degrees and in the ways that their situations made possible. The questions of democracy's *demos* are no less complicated than the questions of its *kratos*, and include far more nuances than I have been able to treat here: there are many more aspects of the conversation that need further attention. The various examples here show that constituted powers retain their hegemony through a variety of means, not merely through brute repression. The literature on this point includes prominent voices, but more is necessary to show specifically how direct democratic power has been repressed.[5] Looking from another perspective, there has been rekindled interest in Spinoza and the Radical Enlightenment in recent years, a trend I hope to see continue.[6] Spinoza's ethics is an ethics of power, not a devotion to any particular cultural norm; it is complicated territory, and while it has been valuable here, additional work that focuses at length on the problems of Spinoza's ethics and its relation to direct democracy as I have described it would be a useful compliment to this project. All human beings are capable of both kindness and cruelty, and it is always valuable to study which institutions, structures, and communities facilitate which of these outcomes. One current coming from Spinoza's *Theological-Political Treatise*, for example, the idea that the range of freedom built upon human capacity is larger than the range of freedom built upon the power to overpower another, or at least that the realm of freedom that does not necessitate overpowering another is actually much larger than is commonly thought, would be particularly useful to put to an extended test. Whether this second understanding of freedom is even worthy of the name is also open to question: privilege may feel like freedom, but it is ultimately vacant.

In the introduction to this book, I noted that the interpretation of democracy as a type of power and the interpretation of democracy as a form of government are like two different but parallel paths. The question remains about how the power I call direct democracy could function, flourish, or be diminished in a state that also calls itself democratic. The modes of power are situated in communities, and in places and institutions that can either hamper or facilitate those powers. In the *Political Treatise*, work left unfinished when he died, Spinoza began to theorize what he called absolute democracy, by which he meant a form of democracy that was not based on an alienation of peoples' power through representation.[7] What that community may look like in practical terms is a difficult problem to think through, but that difficulty means that the task is all the more important. One of the tasks of literary analysis is to sketch the problems and possibilities of such issues; communities, however, are made by the people who live in them.

But in that work of community building, there is much to be learned from literary history, the work of analyzing and imagining worlds that are a bit less miserable and a bit more free. This project has been rooted in the long nineteenth century, and among the ideas it hopes to convey is that the writers and movement activists of our generation are not the first to be profoundly dissatisfied by inequalities of race, gender, and class, injustices that may seem to bind people impossibly tightly. In these pages, I have referred to constituted powers as braids woven of many different threads. Braids make individual threads stronger, but they also show that these threads are not homogenous, and they can, under certain circumstances, fray and unravel. The parts that make them up can contradict one another, be in tension with one another, be made up of strands with differing strengths and weaknesses. They are not always as tightly bound as they seem to be.

Each generation has its own specific situation, yet in the work of making a better world, each generation looks back to the ones before it to gather ideas and tools in order to remake them for its own purposes, and each generation also makes initial use of new ideas and tools. The long nineteenth century was a particularly creative period, filled with the resistance to exploitation that led to innovations in the ways we understand democracy. The power I call direct democracy circulated in networks, through the Americas, the Atlantic world, and beyond. The literary history of the long nineteenth century, with its ties to the radical aspects of the Enlightenment, the resistance to slavery, and the direct action of people struggling against hierarchical domination reveals considerable insight and provides the opportunities to ask many new questions about the literary representations of political movements, about the potential and limits of those movements, and about the intersection of direct democracy and the various forms of democratic organization. To assemble the relevant parts of this history, my sources for thinking about direct democratic power have come from the transnational currents of the slave trade, the inevitable resistance that the slave trade provoked, and the ideas that emerged as a part of that resistance, from sources that go beyond a Western-centric framework and also beyond the thinking of writers who would reduce the contradictions and failures of the Enlightenment to caricature, instead of picking up its radical legacy and remaking it.[8]

In this literary history, there are ideas that made real contributions to bettering the human condition (such as universal emancipation from the Haitian Revolution or the reduction of the working day from twelve hours or more to eight), and they were produced collectively by the very people who needed them most. Direct democracy and its related concepts—power and creativity, domination and disenfranchisement, among others—are the ideas we can see in this history. The response to domination need not be different types of domination—it can also be cooperative resistance.

The movements of our historical moment, acting in cooperative networks and including diverse arrays of people committed to universally inclusive ideas of liberty, community, and justice, have inherited the legacies of the movements analyzed in this book, both the failures and the successes. To hope that the movements of both eras, and the power and ideas that motivate them, propose models for experimentation that are substantive alternatives to the injustices and inequalities of the world in which we live is to justify further efforts to research them.

NOTES

Prologue

1. Statistics in this paragraph are taken from David Eltis and David Richardson, *Atlas of the Atlantic Slave Trade* (New Haven: Yale University Press, 2010).

2. C. L. R. James, *The Black Jacobins: Toussaint L'Ouverture and the San Domingo Revolution* (New York: Vintage, 1989) 46. James uses the Spanish name for the colony, San Domingo.

3. Laurent Dubois, *Avengers of the New World: The Story of the Haitian Revolution* (Cambridge: Belknap Press, 2004) 152–54, 166–68.

4. Philip Kaisary, *The Haitian Revolution in the Literary Imagination* (Charlottesville: University of Virginia Press, 2014).

5. Sibylle Fischer, *Modernity Disavowed: Haiti and the Cultures of Slavery in the Age of Revolution* (Durham: Duke University Press, 2004) 9.

6. Nick Nesbitt, *Universal Emancipation: The Haitian Revolution and the Radical Enlightenment* (Charlottesville: University of Virginia Press, 2008) 1.

7. Dubois, *Avengers*, 277–78; James, *Black Jacobins*, 291, 334.

8. Carolyn E. Fick, *The Making of Haiti: The Saint Domingue Revolution from Below* (Knoxville: University of Tennessee Press, 2004) 216.

9. James, *Black Jacobins*, 341.

10. Ibid., 346.

11. Ibid., 346–47.

12. Laurent Dubois, *A Colony of Citizens: Revolution and Slave Emancipation in the French Caribbean, 1787–1804* (Chapel Hill: University of North Carolina Press, 2004) 369, 402.

13. Ibid., 403.

14. Dubois, *Avengers*, 280–81.

15. Fick, *Making of Haiti*, 52.

16. James, *Black Jacobins*, 346.

17. Ibid., 127. See also 109, 117, 314, 324.

18. C. L. R. James, "Lectures on *The Black Jacobins*," *Small Axe* 8 (September 2000): 108.

Introduction

1. "David Cameron Criticized Over Migrant 'Swarm' Language." BBC News, 30 July 2015 <www.bbc.com/news/uk-politics-33716501>.

2. Peter Linebaugh and Marcus Rediker, *The Many-Headed Hydra: Sailors, Slaves, Commoners and the Hidden History of the Revolutionary Atlantic* (Boston: Beacon, 2000) 39, 62, 68, 69, 102.

3. Michel Foucault, *Discipline and Punish: The Birth of the Prison* (New York: Vintage, 1995) 200.

4. Edward Said, *Orientalism* (New York: Vintage, 1979) 93.

5. John Plotz, *The Crowd: British Literature and Public Politics* (Berkeley: University of California Press) 15.

6. Roger Scruton, *Spinoza: A Very Short Introduction* (Oxford: Oxford University Press, 2002) 81.

7. From the Greek δημοκρατία.

8. Giorgio Agamben, *Homo Sacer: Sovereign Power and Bare Life* (Stanford: Stanford University Press, 1998) 176. Agamben here is writing of a history with ample examples of excluding people from the body politic. As Carl Schmitt notes in his critique of Hobbes, Locke, and Rousseau, when most writers "talk about the people, whose rights they defend against the prince, it is beyond question that they do not mean either the *plebs* or the *incondite et confusa turba* [the confused and disordered crowd], but only the people who are represented by the organization of the estates" (19). Hobbes, for example, calls the included a *persona*, who, Schmitt writes, is always strictly distinguished from the "shapeless multitude," the "*multitudo dissoluta*" (23). The necessary response, given with irrefutable logic, comes from Frederick Douglass, in his speech "The Meaning of July 4th for the Negro": "The Southern statute books are covered with enactments forbidding, under severe fines and penalties, the teaching of the slave to read or to write. When you can point to any such laws in reference to the beasts of the field, then I may consent to argue the manhood of the slave. When the dogs in your streets, when the fowls of the air, when the cattle on your hills, when the fish of the sea, and the reptiles that crawl, shall be unable to distinguish the slave from a brute, then will I argue with you that the slave is a man!"

9. Thinking about democracy as a form of government as well as a type of power can shed light on many questions. For example, the distinction could build from a conversation with Jeremy Popkin, David Geggus, and others that Sibylle Fischer describes in her essay "History and Catastrophe." The conversation asked why the Haitian Revolution should be considered democratic, especially after seeing its authoritarian legacy in the twentieth century. She writes that the Haitian Revolution "has come to constitute the ground on which questions are raised about the emancipatory nature of those Western revolutions that took place in the name of liberty but had little to say about racial slavery, with some scholars now declaring the Haitian Revolution the most universalist, radical, and democratic revolution of the eighteenth and nineteenth centuries." David Geggus asked why should "an antislavery revolution be included under the heading of democratic revolutions when the resulting state was notoriously militaristic and autocratic?" If governance is the only framework within which we can have conversations about democracy, then the Haitian Revolution certainly seems not to be very democratic. Seen as an expression of a people's power, on the other hand, the Haitian Revolution is profoundly democratic. Sibylle Fischer, "History and Catastrophe," 164–65, emphasis in original.

10. Ursula K. Le Guin, *The Tombs of Atuan* (New York: Saga, 2012) 217, italics in original.

11. See Gilles Deleuze, *Spinoza: Practical Philosophy* (San Francisco: City Lights, 1988), in particular the discussion here of Spinoza's use of the terms *potestas, potentia, aptus, conatus, affectus,* and *affectio,* all terms relevant to this discussion (99).

12. Melanie Mitchell, *Complexity: A Guided Tour* (Oxford: Oxford University Press, 2011) 4.

13. Linebaugh and Rediker, *Many-Headed Hydra,* 26–28.

14. Deleuze, *Spinoza,* 104.

15. *Ibid.,* 125.

16. In a similar vein, about the concept of cooperation, which will be one of this study's main concepts, see David Harvey's comment: "Marx casts neither corporation nor division of labor in an inherently negative light. He views them as potentially creative, beneficial and gratifying for the laborer. Cooperation and well organized divisions of labor are wonderful human possibilities that add to our collective powers. Socialism and communism would presumably have great need of them. What Marx will seek to show is how these positive potentialities are seized on by capital to its own particular advantage and thereby turned into something negative for the laborer." David Harvey, *A Companion to Marx's Capital* (London: Verso, 2010) 172, xxx.

17. Agamben, *Homo Sacer,* 45.

18. See Warren Montag's reading of Spinoza's *Ethics,* prop. 50, on this point: "Power, especially physical power, can never be alienated as if it were property, or surrendered as if it were a possession of a subject." Warren Montag, *Bodies, Masses, Power: Spinoza and His Contemporaries* (London: Verso, 1999) 70.

19. James, *Black Jacobins,* x, 25, 91.

20. Linebaugh and Rediker, *Many-Headed Hydra,* 14.

21. Frédéric Lordon, *Willing Slaves of Capital: Spinoza and Marx on Desire* (London: Verso, 2014) x.

22. Brian Massumi, "Translator's Preface," Gilles Deleuze and Félix Guattari, *A Thousand Plateaus: Capitalism and Schizophrenia* (Minneapolis: University of Minnesota Press, 1987) xvii.

23. Karl Marx, *Capital: A Critical Analysis of Capitalist Production,* trans. Samuel Moore and Edward Aveling (New York: International, 1967) 171.

24. Walter Benjamin, "A Critique of Violence," *Reflections: Essays, Aphorisms, Autobiographical Writings* (New York: Schocken, 1986) 277–300.

25. Carl Schmitt, *Dictatorship: From the Beginning of the Modern Concept of Sovereignty to the Proletarian Class Struggle* (Cambridge: Polity, 2014) 119, 123.

26. Benjamin considers the problem only in relation to violence—he does not consider whether analogous forms of power could be seen apart from violent manifestations.

27. Michael Hardt, "Foreword: Three Keys to Understanding Constituent Power," Antonio Negri, *Insurgencies: Constituent Power and the Modern State* (Minneapolis: University of Minnesota Press, 2009) viii–xii.

28. Priscilla Wald, *Constituting Americans: Cultural Anxiety and Narrative Form* (Durham: Duke University Press, 1995).

29. Ibid., vii–viii. See also Hardt's discussion of these terms in the "Translator's Foreword" to *The Savage Anomaly: The Power of Spinoza's Metaphysics and Politics* (Minneapolis: University of Minnesota Press), 1999, xi–xvi.

30. Giorgio Agamben, "What Is Destituent Power?" *Environment and Planning D: Society and Space*, 32.1 (February 2014): 65–74. Agamben writes: "If the fundamental ontological question today is not work but inoperativity, and if this inoperativity can, however, be deployed only through a work, then the corresponding political concept can no longer be that of 'constituent power' [*potere constituente*], but something that could be called 'destituent power' [*potenza destituente*]. And if revolutions and insurrections correspond to constituent power, that is, a violence that establishes and constitutes the new law, in order to think a destituent power we have to imagine completely other strategies, whose definition is the task of the coming politics. A power that was only just overthrown by violence will rise again in another form, in the incessant, inevitable dialectic between constituent power and constituted power, violence which makes the law and violence that preserves it" (70, translations in original).

31. Jacques Rancière, *Dissensus: On Politics and Aesthetics* (London: Continuum, 2011) 53. There is a certain elegance and applicability to the vocabulary Rancière uses, especially the terms "politics," or dissensus, on one hand, and "police," or the distribution of the sensible, on the other, which are analogous to constituent power and constituted power. In NWA's song "Fuck the Police," we find the lyrics: "Ice Cube will swarm / over any motherfucker in a blue uniform." This is interesting, and not only because Ice Cube and Rancière share the same term as their object of critique. (Even though the meanings of the terms differ—to Rancière, the police to whom Ice Cube refers are merely the *basse police*, or the low police. The *basse police* for Rancière are just one tool available to the more comprehensive police order, the distribution of the sensible). The pairing is also interesting because even Ice Cube's singular voice, as the speaker of the lyric, presents as multiple, as complex: he sings of himself in the third person, making himself double, at least, and therefore consistent with the collective nature of the swarm metaphor. For more on this point, see Eugene Wofford, "Who the Fuck Is Jacques Rancière?" 28 March 2013 <www.critical-theory.com/who-the-fuck-is-jacques -ranciere/?> 24 January 2016.

32. Jacques Derrida, "Force of Law: The 'Mystical Foundations of Authority,'" *Acts of Religion* (London: Routledge, 2001) 228–98.

33. William Lloyd Garrison, cited in George Fitzhugh, *Cannibals All! Or, Slaves without Masters* (Richmond: A. Morris, 1857), 309 <docsouth.unc.edu/southlit/fitzhughcan/fitzcan .html>.

34. William Lloyd Garrison, "No Union with Slaveholders," *Liberator* 7 July 1854, 106. The relevant text of the article is: "Mr. Garrison said he should now proceed to perform an action which would be the testimony of his own soul to all present, of the estimation in which he held the pro-slavery laws and deeds of the nation. Producing a copy of the *Fugitive Slave Law*, he set fire to it, and it burnt to ashes.[. . .] Then holding up the U.S. Constitution, he branded it as the source and parent of all the other atrocities—'a covenant with death, and an agreement with hell,'—and consumed it to ashes on the spot, exclaiming, 'So perish all compromises with tyranny!'"

35. Derrida, "Force of Law," 268–69. Derrida writes, quoting from Benjamin: "What the state fears, the state being law in its greatest force, is not so much crime or robbery, even on [a] grand scale . . . The state is afraid of *founding* violence—that is, violence able to justify, to

legitimate (*begründen*), or transform the relations of law (*Rechtsverhältnisse*) and so to present itself as having the right to law.[. . .] The general strike thus provides a valuable guiding thread, since it exercises the conceded right to contest the order of existing law and to create a revolutionary situation in which the task will be to found new law, if not always[. . .] a new state." See also Georges Sorel, *Reflections on Violence* (Mineola: Dover, 2004).

36. Nick Nesbitt, ed., *Toussaint Louverture: The Haitian Revolution* (London: Verso, 2008) 59.

37. Schmitt, *Dictatorship*, 156.

38. Nesbitt, *Caribbean Critique*, 35.

39. Ibid., 176–77. See also 114, 123, 124, 139, 174.

40. The relationship between constituent power and constituted power has many facets, only some of which will be mentioned here. To follow other threads in the conversation, see Agamben's *State of Exception* on the debates between Benjamin and Schmitt, including both an "exoteric" and an "esoteric" dossier—texts in which the others refer to one another directly and indirectly (52–64).

41. Ibid., 88.

42. Ibid., 126.

43. Ibid., 37. Schmitt traces the idea's history thoroughly. Writing of Durandus's *Speculum iuris*, published circa 1272, he notes the argument that a legate "had a mission he had to fulfill, and if he was prevented from fulfilling it he was entitled to punish all those who hindered him or did not obey him, since his *potestas* would of course be '*delusoria*' ['imaginary'] if he did not have *coercitio* [the right to impose it by coercion]."

44. Ibid., xxvi. In their introduction, Hoelzl and Ward provide the clearest statement of Schmitt's view of the difference between dictatorship and totalitarianism: "When does this dictatorial intervention turn into totalitarianism? Answer: whenever the dissolution of the separation of legislative, judicial and executive powers leads to their being taken by a single agent and the duration of a clearly defined period of dictatorship becomes unlimited. The Appendix [to this edition, which consists of Schmitt's extended critique of the relevant law, Article 48 of the Weimar Constitution] warns about this possibility by insisting that to postpone formulating a law for the implementation of the state of emergency (Article 48, 2.5) opens the space for it" (xxvi).

45. Ibid., 175–76.

46. Ibid., 177.

47. Ibid., 123.

48. Agamben writes in *State of Exception*, "Jurists and political philosophers have generally directed their attention chiefly to the theory of sovereignty contained in the book from 1922 [*Political Theology*], without realizing that this theory acquires its sense solely on the basis of the theory of the state of exception already elaborated in *Dictatorship*" (35).

49. Schmitt, *Dictatorship*, xliii. Schmitt writes that the goal of *Dictatorship* is to "give a theoretical account of the transition from the older 'dictatorship of reformations' to the 'dictatorship of revolutions,' on the basis of the *pouvoir constituant* of the people.[. . .] As a consequence of the constituted, and not the constitutive, nature of the people's power, he remains a direct commissar of the people—a dictator who also dictates to his superior,

without ceasing to legitimize himself through that superior" (xliv). Furthermore, the "content of the legislator's action is right [*Recht*], but devoid of legal power: it is powerless right. Dictatorship is omnipotence without law [*Gesetz*]: it is lawless power.[. . .] The legislator is nothing but right that is not yet constituted; the dictator is nothing but constituted power. When a relationship emerges that makes it possible to give the legislator the power of a dictator, to create a dictatorial legislator and a constitutional dictator, then the commissary dictatorship has become a sovereign dictatorship. This relationship will come about through an idea that is, in its substance, a consequence of Rousseau's *Contrat social*, although he does not name as a separate power: *le pouvoir constituant* [the constituting power]" (110–11).

50. In this respect, the relation between constituent power and constituted power is not unlike the relation that Marx showed between labor and capital in his famous vampire metaphor: capital is dead labor, that, vampire-like, only lives by sucking living labor, and lives the more, the more labor it sucks. One might paraphrase Schmitt to say that as the "bearer" of constituent power, constituted power lives on in a similar relationship. See Montag, *Bodies, Masses, Power*, 92–95.

51. Agamben, *Homo Sacer*, 41–42.

52. Schmitt, *Dictatorship*, 13, 203.

53. Three moments in Schmitt's *Dictatorship* help to clarify his use of the terms. First, he writes that *pouvoir constituant* can be associated with an existing constitution, and is foundational to it and subsumed by it, but it cannot be negated by a constitution—this power exists even when paper constitutions are overthrown (119). In his discussion of the state of exception, Schmitt writes that the state of exception "is above the ordinary constituted forces [*Gewalten*]—it, the constituting force [*Gewalt*] that contains in itself the power [*Macht*]—and it operates in most cases like the omnipotence of the *pouvoir constutitant* in the modern state" (13). On the relations between these powers, Schmitt writes that "all constituted powers are opposed to a constituent power, which lays down the foundations of the constitution. This constituent power is in principle unlimited and can do everything, because it is not subject to the constitution: it provides the foundation for the constitution itself" (121).

54. Agamben, *State of Exception*, 4–5, 11.

55. Lucy Parsons, *Freedom, Equality, and Solidarity: Writings and Speeches, 1878–1937* (Chicago: Charles H. Kerr, 2004) 113.

56. See, for example, Marina Sitrin, *Horizontalism: Voices of Popular Power in Argentina* (Oakland: AK Press, 2006), an oral history of the efforts by workers to "recuperate" factories that were previously shuttered by their former owners, and John Curl, *For All the People: Uncovering the Hidden History of Cooperation, Cooperative Movements, and Communalism in America*, which includes a very useful bibliographic essay about cooperative histories, worker cooperatives, farmer cooperatives, and consumer cooperatives (469–82). Importantly, see W. E. B. Du Bois, *Economic Co-operation among Negro Americans*, and Jessica Gordon Nembhard, *Collective Courage: A History of African American Cooperative Economic Thought and Practice*. Some of the most important ideas to study are detailed in David Montgomery's scholarship, especially *Worker Control in America*. On maroon colonies, see Alvin O. Thompson, *Flight to Freedom: African Runaways and Maroons in the Americas*. See

also Immanuel Ness and Dario Azzellini, *Ours to Master and to Own: Workers' Control from the Commune to the Present*; Richard Wolff, *Democracy at Work: A Cure for Capitalism*; Gar Alperovitz, *America beyond Capitalism*.

57. Agamben, *Homo Sacer*, 11, 178.

58. Spinoza writes that if two people "come together and join forces, they have more power over Nature, and consequently more right, than either one alone; and the greater the number who form a union in this way, the more right they will together possess." Baruch Spinoza, *Political Treatise, Spinoza: Complete Works*, ed. Michael L. Morgan (Indianapolis: Hackett, 2002) 686.

59. In *Capital*, Marx writes, "When numerous labourers work together side by side, whether in one and the same process, or in different but connected processes, they are said to co-operate, or to work in co-operation. Just as the offensive power of a squadron of cavalry, or the defensive power of a regiment of infantry is essentially different from the sum of the offensive or defensive powers of the individual cavalry or infantry soldiers taken separately, so the sum total of the mechanical forces exerted by isolated workmen differs from the social force that is developed, when many hands take part simultaneously in one and the same undivided operation, such as raising a heavy weight, turning a winch, or removing an obstacle. In such cases the effect of the combined labour could either not be produced at all by isolated individual labour, or it could only be produced by a great expenditure of time, or on a very dwarfed scale. Not only have we here an increase in the productive power of the individual, by means of co-operation, but the creation of a new power, namely, the collective power of masses. Apart from the new power that arises from the fusion of many forces into one single force, mere social contact begets in most industries an emulation and a stimulation of the animal spirits that heighten the efficiency of each individual workman. Hence it is that a dozen persons working together will, in their collective working-day of 144 hours, produce far more than twelve isolated men each working 12 hours, or than one man who works twelve days in succession. The reason of this is that man is, if not as Aristotle contends, a political, at all events a social animal" (*Capital*, ch. XIII). What Marx notices here is what contemporary writers call complexity, in the technical sense of that term, not as a synonym for difficulty, but rather as a synonym for multiplicity, and how a multiplicity can, under certain circumstances, become more than the sum of its parts. Marx calls this a new power, the collective power of masses; whether it is a "single force," as he suggests, I do not think is correct. It is a coherent phenomenon, yes, but it is produced only precisely because it is the combination of many interacting people. Take away those interactions, and one takes away the power. Therefore, I would not call it singular but, rather, complex.

60. Arthur Herzog, *The Swarm* (New York: Author's Choice Press, 1974); Hilda M. Ransome, *The Sacred Bee in Ancient Times and Folklore* (Mineola: Dover, 2004).

61. "Look to the ant, thou sluggard; / Consider her ways, and be wise: / Which, having no chief, overseer, or ruler, / Provides her meat in the summer, / And gathers her food in the harvest" (Proverbs 6:6, KJV).

62. James Surowiecki, *The Wisdom of Crowds: Why the Many Are Smarter than the Few and How Collective Wisdom Shapes Businesses, Economies, Societies, and Nations* (New York: Anchor, 2005), and Peter Miller, *The Smart Swarm: How to Work Efficiently, Communicate*

Effectively, and Make Better Decisions Using the Secrets of Flocks, Schools, and Colonies (New York: Avery, 2011).

63. David Harvey writes that "the 'despotism' of labor control depends on some mix of coercion and persuasion as well as upon the successful organization of a hierarchical structure of authority in labor relations. Plainly, any breakdown in this control presages a crisis, and Marx emphasizes the implicit power of workers to disrupt, sabotage, slow down or simply to cease altogether the production of value upon which the capitalist necessarily relies" (*Companion to Marx's* Capital, 326).

64. Frederick Douglass, *Autobiographies* (New York: Library of America, 1994) 390.

65. Aristotle, *A History of Animals*, D'Arcy Wentworth Thompson, trans. <classics.mit .edu/Aristotle/history_anim.html>.

66. Jan Swammerdam, *The Book of Nature; or the History of Insects* (London: C. G. Seyggert, 1758) 159. Swammerdam was one of the early researchers to use the new microscope technology in scientifically rigorous ways, and therefore he was able to make the discovery about the queen's role in reproduction. Swammerdam writes, "I proposed in my book on insects published in the year 1669, at some other time to read expressly on the structure of insects, and in that work to give the particular history of bees; saying, by way of anticipation, that the king, as commonly called, was a female, the drone a male, and that the common Bees belonged to neither sex" (159).

67. Charles Butler, *The Feminine Monarchie, or The Historie of Bees* (Oxford: Joseph Barnes, 1609); Joseph Warder, *The True Amazons: Or, the Monarchy of Bees* (London: John Pemberton, 1713).

68. Warder, *True Amazons*, iii. In addition to the examples listed, there are practically innumerable references to bees and ants and their swarms in literary history. The following provides a sampling. In Aesop's fable "The Ant and the Grasshopper," ants are shown to be industrious and forward thinking—they stockpile food for the winter and distribute resources equitably, as opposed to the grasshopper, who thinks only of leisure. On the other hand, ants in a swarm are often represented as particularly dangerous. Achilles' soldiers were called myrmidons; myrmeciinae is a subfamily of red ant. From the ancient texts to the present, authors have used the metaphor to convey a range of cultural and political ideas. Aesop's ants are industrious and forward looking. Achilles' myrmidons, who come from ants, as described in Ovid's *Metamorphoses*, are loyal but are also unthinking and vicious followers. Mark Twain writes in *What Is Man?* that "[a]s a thinker and planner the ant is the equal of any savage race of men; as a self-educated specialist in several arts she is the superior of any savage race of men; and in one or two high mental qualities she is above the reach of any man, savage or civilized" (106–7). Mark M. Moffett's book *Adventures among Ants: A Global Safari with a Cast of Trillions*, includes fascinating close-up photos of various ants as individuals and as colonies. Moffett tells the story of having no point of reference to begin his photographic work, so he approached the ants with the material he had on hand: the fashion magazines in the grocery store checkout aisle.

69. John Burroughs, "The Pastoral Bees," *Birds and Bees, Sharp Eyes, and Other Papers*, 25 January 2016 <www.gutenberg.org/files/3163/3163-h/3163-h.htm>.

70. See Brian Massumi, *What Animals Teach Us about Politics* (Durham: Duke University Press, 2014), for a recent and nuanced theoretical discussion of this problem.

71. My primary concern is with the swarm as metaphor, but I also wish to point out that the dynamics of actual swarms are fertile grounds for political thinkers who see in those dynamics an alternative to the hierarchy found in so much human organization. On that point, see Manuel DeLanda's work, especially *A New Philosophy of Society: Assemblage Theory and Social Complexity.* Humans cannot take moral or philosophical guidance from bees and ants, but contemporary work on swarm dynamics has led to remarkable insights. Swarms have no leader; cooperation, not command, is what allows them to perform difficult tasks; the aggregation of all their decisions makes the group more than just the sum of its parts. That swarms organize themselves without a leader is, of course, due to centuries of evolutionary adaptation. It is now, however, an accepted fact among those who study bees that their swarms have no leader. Thomas Seeley writes in *Honeybee Democracy*, "There is one common misunderstanding about the inner operations of a honeybee colony that I must dispel at the outset, namely that a colony is governed by a benevolent dictator, Her Majesty the Queen. The belief that a colony's coherence derives from an omniscient queen (or king) telling the workers what to do is centuries old, tracing back to Aristotle and persisting until modern times. But it is false.[. . .] The work of a hive is instead governed collectively by the workers themselves, each one an alert individual making tours of inspection looking for things to do and acting on her own to serve the community (5–6). In particular, see chapter 10 of *Honeybee Democracy*, "Swarm Smarts," in which Seeley discusses how the lessons he derives from the bees' collective decision making could be applied in other contexts, including in town meetings and academic department meetings.

72. Previously, we have only had hunches to explain the cooperative dynamics of swarms and other nonhierarchical assemblages. In the *Metaphysics*, for example, Aristotle notes situations where "the totality is not, as it were, a mere heap, but the whole is something besides the parts" (Book H 1045a 8–10). Why, Aristotle might ask, or under what conditions, do groups become more than a sum of their parts? What separates the often-elegant collective dynamics of such groups—perhaps the most remarkable example is the murmuration of starlings—from the hostile or inefficient group? The answers to these questions are still up for debate, but what was for Aristotle a curious observation has become an interdisciplinary field of research on what are called complex systems. As I noted above, in the technical sense of the term, *complexity* is not a synonym for *difficulty*, but for *multiplicity*, and the patterns and ideas that emerge from that multiplicity. In language that echoes Aristotle's, M. E. J. Newman writes that "most researchers in the field would probably agree that [complex systems are] composed of many interacting parts, such that the collective behavior of those parts together is more than the sum of their individual behaviors. The collective behaviors are sometimes also called "emergent" behaviors, and a complex system can thus be said to be a system of interacting parts that displays emergent behavior" (par. 2).

73. See also Negri's play *Swarm: Didactics of the Militant,* in *Trilogy of Resistance* (Minneapolis: University of Minnesota Press, 2011).

74. Michael Hardt and Antonio Negri, *Multitude: War and Democracy in the Age of Empire* (New York: Penguin, 2005) 92.

75. Frantz Fanon, *The Wretched of the Earth* (New York: Grove, 2005) 42–43.

76. Michael Lundblad, *The Birth of a Jungle: Animality in Progressive-Era U.S. Literature and Culture* (Oxford: Oxford University Press, 2013). Lundblad writes that the "history of animality, from my perspective, can be focused productively on its cultural significance in relation to human oppression, violence, and exploitation. But it needs to pay attention to various ways of thinking about 'real' animals as well, including the ways that various kinds of animals have been treated historically by various human groups.[. . .] Most people would presumably object to constructing or treating various human groups as 'animals,' but we also need to pay critical attention to problematic histories of animalizing *animals*, in which they are seen as driven essentially, if not exclusively, by instincts for violence and heterosexuality" (11).

77. Ibid., 11. *Swarm* is the language I track throughout this book, but the terms for other assemblages are interesting: flocks of starlings, crowds of people, an army of toads, a murder of crows, a parliament of owls. See Deleuze and Guattari's comments about swarms and packs of wolves in *A Thousand Plateaus*, especially the chapter "1914: One or Several Wolves?" For Nietzsche, herds were the collectivities of reactive forces (Deleuze, *Nietzsche and Philosophy* [New York: Columbia University Press, 2006] 138).

78. Karl Marx, "Marx to Ruge," *Deutsch-Französische Jahrbücher*, emphasis in original. On Napoleon at the Berezina, see Tolstoy's *War and Peace* (1189–1190, 1222), as well as Rancière's comments about Tolstoy in "On the Battlefield," *The Politics of Literature* 72–79. In his invasion of Russia, ca. 1812, eight years after his loss in the Haitian Revolution, Napoleon was retreating from Moscow and had an army of approximately 28,000 soldiers, down from 50,000 before crossing the Berezina River, and down from 422,000 at the start of his Russian invasion. Nearly 400,000 French lost their lives in this campaign, to say nothing of the Russians and others, and here Napoleon can only mock those to whom he gives orders. The situation is breathtaking in its audacity and in its flippant attitude toward human life. This is perhaps why it attracted attention from Tolstoy, Marx, and Rancière.

79. David F. Ericson, *The Debate Over Slavery: Antislavery and Proslavery Liberalism in Antebellum America* (New York: NYU Press, 2000) 110–11.

80. Fitzhugh, *Cannibals All!*, 188.

81. Ibid., 102–3. For more information on Fitzhugh's views, see Ericson, who writes that Fitzhugh "defends [slavery] as part of a broader family of protective institutions" and also as an institution "specially fitted for the members of an allegedly inferior race" (107, 108).

82. Fitzhugh, *Cannibals All!*, 293.

83. Alberto Toscano, *Fanaticism: On the Uses of an Idea* (London: Verso, 2010) xiv–xv; Friedrich Engels, *The Peasant War in Germany* (New York: International, 2000).

84. Andrew Poe, "The Sources and Limits of Political Enthusiasm," PhD diss., University of California, San Diego, University of California E-Scholarship, 2010, Web, 19 January 2016.

85. Poe, "Sources and Limits," xv.

86. Karl Marx, *The Marx/Engels Reader*, 2nd ed. Ed. Robert C. Tucker (New York: W.W. Norton, 1978) 475.

87. Montag, *Bodies, Masses, Power*, 53–54.

88. Nesbitt, *Caribbean Critique*, 38.

89. Schmitt, *Dictatorship*, 114.

90. Hoelzl and Ward, "Translators' Introduction," xiii.

91. Schmitt, *Dictatorship*, 7.

92. Michael Foucault, *Fearless Speech* (Los Angeles: Semiotext(e), 2001), 78–79.

93. Schmitt, *Dictatorship*, 7, 91, 235. See especially p. 235, note 18 of Hoelzl and Ward's translation of *Dictatorship*, where Schmitt traces the idea "reason dictates" through works by St. Thomas, Hugo Grotius, Hobbes, Locke, Kant, Montesquieu, Rousseau, and others.

94. For a contemporary thought on the matter, see Michael Gould-Wartofsky, "When Rioting Is Rational." Gould-Wartofsky writes that "the 'riot effect' narrative contains a fatal flaw betrayed in the terminology itself: it rests on the assumption that 'riots' are essentially random occurrences. For those who blame black America for black poverty, riots are distinguished not by their contingency or their spontaneity or their political cast, but by their irrationality. On this misreading of history, civil resistance has nothing to do with the underlying conditions that make it rational to rebel, or with the relations of power that make other avenues of action unavailable to the urban poor."

95. Le Bon, *Crowd*, 119. For more on these ideas, see part I of Laclau's book *The Populist Persuasion*, especially chapter 2, "Le Bon: Suggestion and Distorted Representations."

96. Plotz, *Crowd*, 5.

97. Ibid., 5.

98. If one does want a refutation of the claims made by Le Bon, one of the best that exists is in Bill Buford's book on football supporters, *Among the Thugs*. Buford undermines the pseudopsychology of crowds in a swift and insightful paragraph: "The crowd does not tell us its histories; it is the observers of the crowd, listening to each other as much as to the shouting outside their windows: Edmund Burke, removed in London, weighing the gravity of a revolution that he sees only through other people's eyes; Hippolyte Taine, preparing lectures in Oxford, where he reads in the English papers of the violence of the Commune and fears for his family and his property in Paris; Gustave Le Bon, the 'father of crowd theory,' eleventh-hour sociologist, effortless plagiarist, lifting passages from Scipio Sighele, Gabriel Tarde, and (inevitably) Hippolyte Taine (it is possible that the only crowd seen by the father of crowd theory was in Paris on a shopping day); Freud, two years after the great crowd massacres of the Great War, the streets outside his window already alive with the sounds of restless nationalism and anti-Semitism, advancing his own theories about the crowd and its leaders, based (inevitably) on the work of the 'justly famous' Le Bon" (184).

99. Le Bon, *Crowd*, x.

100. Linebaugh and Rediker, *The Many-Headed Hydra*, 330.

101. Nesbitt, *Universal Emancipation*, 37.

102. Cedric Robinson, *Black Marxism: The Making of the Black Radical Tradition* (Chapel Hill: University of North Carolina Press, 2000) xxxii.

Chapter One

1. Dubois, *Avengers*, 255.

2. See Fick, *Making of Haiti*, 210, for a fuller discussion of the French strategy.

3. James, *Black Jacobins*, 273.

4. See, for example, *The Battle of Algiers*, a thorough examination of a similar strategy, prosecuted by French colonial forces in Algeria. *The Battle of Algiers*, dir. Gillo Pontecorvo (Criterion, 2013).

5. James, *Black Jacobins*, 346.

6. Ibid., 353, 456.

7. Nesbitt, *Caribbean Critique*, 30.

8. Fick, *Making of Haiti*, 1.

9. Ibid., 215.

10. To answer how the revolution expanded without its leaders is beyond the scope of this chapter. However, research exists on the scalability of networked, decentralized forms of organization, and it could be the starting point for this work. See, for example, Manuel DeLanda's *A New Philosophy of Society: Assemblage Theory and Social Complexity*, in which he applies the Deleuzian notion of assemblages to groups and communities of ever-larger scales. DeLanda writes that the "bulk of this book will be spent giving concrete examples of how we can bridge the level of individual persons and that of the largest social entities (such as territorial states) through an embedding of assemblages in a succession of micro-and macro-scales" (17). Such an approach seems likely to explain the logic of how networked groups can change scale, often quite rapidly.

11. Robinson, *Black Marxism*, xxx.

12. Fick, *Making of Haiti*, 117.

13. James, "Lectures on *The Black Jacobins*," 108.

14. Ibid., 99–100.

15. Paul B. Miller, *Elusive Origins: The Enlightenment in the Modern Caribbean Historical Imagination* (Charlottesville: University of Virginia Press, 2010), 69. In addition to the scholarship cited in this chapter, see also Robin Blackburn, "*The Black Jacobins* and New World Slavery" and Kara M. Rabbitt, "C. L. R. James's Figuring of Toussaint-Louverture: *The Black Jacobins* and the Literary Hero," both in Selwyn R. Cudjoe and William E. Cain, eds., *C. L. R. James: His Intellectual Legacies*.

16. Christian Høgsbjerg, ed., C. L. R. James, *Toussaint Louverture: The Story of the Only Successful Slave Revolt in History* (Durham: Duke University Press, 2012), 127.

17. James, *Black Jacobins*, 338.

18. James, "Lectures," 106.

19. Ibid., 108.

20. David Scott, *Conscripts of Modernity: The Tragedy of Colonial Enlightenment* (Durham: Duke University Press, 2004) 10.

21. Ibid., 4, 104.

22. Ibid., 56.

23. Ibid., 209.

24. Ibid., 57.

25. Ibid., x.

26. Scott, *Conscripts*, 103–5.

27. Fick, *Making of Haiti*, v.

28. Dubois, *Avengers*, 287.

29. Susan Buck-Morss, *Hegel, Haiti, and Universal History* (Pittsburgh: University of Pittsburgh Press, 2009) 38, 105.

30. Nesbitt, *Universal Emancipation*, 205–6.

31. Fick, *Making of Haiti*, 216.

32. Ibid., 226.

33. Miller, *Elusive Origins*, 61.

34. James, "Lectures," 99–100.

35. James, *Black Jacobins*, x.

36. Ibid., 243.

37. Miller, *Elusive Origins*, 69–70.

38. Aristotle, *Metaphysics*, Book H 1045a 8–10.

39. The belief that people necessarily become homogenized in groups might be countered by Spinoza's comments in the *Ethics*, IV, Prop. 37, here paraphrased by Balibar: "Men who are guided by reason (and insofar as they are so guided) seek what is useful to them. What is most useful to any man is other men, whose strength, when combined with his own, will provide him with greater security, prosperity, and knowledge. The desire for self-preservation therefore rationally implies, for each man, that he should desire what is good for others and want to form a stable association with them.[. . .] To desire the good of others as a function of my own good (and thus to anticipate my own good through the good of others), so as to be able to use others and to be used by them, is therefore in no way to desire that those others should be like me, should act like me and adopt my opinions. On the contrary, it is to desire that they should be different, develop their own powers and know what is of use to them more and more adequately. In other words, the City that is rationally conceived and constructed through the daily activity of its members is indeed a collective individuality, bound together by the affects of friendship, morality, and religion, but it is not founded on uniformity. Thus it is itself the means by which each man can affirm and strengthen his own individuality" (110).

40. Successful narratives with multiple variables are rare, but extant. For example, in his essay "C. L. R. James: The Myth of Western Civilization," Robert A. Hill considers *The Black Jacobins* with Tolstoy's *War and Peace*, which is an insightful comparison. If there is a book that can be put in the same conversations as *The Black Jacobins* in its representation of complexity, it is Tolstoy's epic, which, in describing the "hydra of revolution" (6) and making frequent references to swarms, is insistent that it is "simple-minded certitude" that leads to a historiography of heroes (668). Tolstoy details at length that the better representation of events happens "by some complex interplay of desires, motivation, and machinations on the part of the[. . .] contenders, who had no idea of how things would turn out" (758).

41. On this point, see two insightful sources. First, Jane Jacobs's application of complexity theory to the problems of urban planning, *The Death and Life of Great American Cities*,

especially her conclusion, "The Kind of Problem a City Is." Second, see Mitchell, who writes, "Reductionism has been the dominant approach to science since the 1600s. René Descartes, one of reductionism's earliest proponents, described his own scientific method thus: 'to divide all the difficulties under examination into as many parts as possible, and as many as were required to solve them in the best way' and 'to conduct my thoughts in a given order, beginning with the *simplest* and most easily understood objects, and gradually ascending, as it were step by step, to the knowledge of the most *complex.*'[. . .] [T]wentieth-century science," Mitchell writes, "was[. . .] marked by the demise of the reductionist dream. In spite of its great successes explaining the very large and very small, fundamental physics, and more generally, scientific reductionism, have been notably mute in explaining the complex phenomena closest to our human-scale concerns" (ix–x, emphasis in original).

42. See Bruno Latour's Actor Network Theory, especially as it is rendered in *Reassembling the Social.*

43. Montag, Warren. *Bodies, Masses, Power*, 68–69. For more information, see all of Montag's third chapter, "The Body of the Multitude."

44. Miller, *Elusive Origins*, 184.

45. James, *Black Jacobins*, 292.

46. Aristotle, *Politics*, 1263 b 35.

47. Frank Rosengarten, *Urbane Revolutionary: C. L. R. James and the Struggle for a New Society* (Jackson: University Press of Mississippi, 2012) 158.

48. James, *Black Jacobins*, 116–17.

49. Robinson, *Black Marxism*, xxx.

50. James, *Black Jacobins*, 273. On the history of the term "motley crew," and its relevance here, see Linebaugh and Rediker, 27–28.

51. James, *Black Jacobins*, 108.

52. Ibid., 324.

53. Dubois, *Avengers*, 287.

54. James, *Black Jacobins*, 127.

55. Ibid., 127.

56. The fifth time James uses the swarm metaphor in *The Black Jacobins*, he does so to describe the Russian, Austrian, and German allies marching against Bonaparte in 1814: "Twelve years later Napoleon, in the greatest campaign of all his campaigns, the campaign of 1814, would attempt [a maneuver identical to Toussaint's march to the north] in face of the allies swarming on Paris" (314).

57. I paraphrase here from Marcus Rediker, *Villains of All Nations: Atlantic Piracy in the Golden Age*. Rediker writes, "[c]ontemporaries who claimed that pirates had 'no regular command among them' mistook a different social order—differing from the ordering of merchant, naval and privateering vessels—for disorder" (61).

58. James, *Black Jacobins*, x.

59. Ibid., 361.

60. Ibid., 325.

61. Ibid., 370.

62. Ibid., 339.

63. Robinson, *Black Marxism*, 314–15.

64. Ibid., 315.

65. Rosengarten, *Urbane Revolutionary*, 55.

66. Anna Grimshaw, "Introduction: C. L. R. James: A Revolutionary Vision for the Twentieth Century," in *The C. L. R. James Reader* (Oxford: Blackwell, 1992) 12. Kara M. Rabbit, "C. L. R. James's Figuring of Toussaint-Louverture: *The Black Jacobins* and the Literary Hero," *C. L. R. James: His Intellectual Legacies*, ed. Selwyn R. Cudjoe and William E. Cain (Amherst: University of Massachusetts Press, 1995) 127.

67. Rosengarten, *Urbane Revolutionary*, 36.

68. Ibid., 36.

69. Ibid., 41.

70. See Grace Lee Boggs, *Living for Change: An Autobiography* (Minneapolis: University of Minnesota Press, 1998), and James Boggs, *The American Revolution: Pages from Negro Worker's Notebook* (New York: Monthly Review Press, 1963).

71. In addition to the texts discussed, see Christian Høgsbjerg, "'A Thorn in the Side of Great Britain': C. L. R. James and the Caribbean Labour Rebellions of the 1930s," *Small Axe* 15 (2): 24–42.

72. C. L. R. James, "Every Cook Can Govern" in *A New Notion: Two Works by C. L. R. James*, ed. Noel Ignatiev (Oakland: PM Press, 2010). It is apparent that one of James's main concerns is the slide of representative democracy into a modern form of bureaucratic totalitarianism. His concerns are merited, but in that conversation, one might also see Agamben's comments in *Homo Sacer* of the "inner solidarity" between representative democracy and totalitarianism (10). Agamben writes with caution not to miss the "enormous differences that characterize their history and their rivalry," but also to show their pairing as an "idea alone will make it possible to clear the way for the new politics, which remains largely to be invented" (11).

73. James, "Every Cook," 141–42.

74. Ibid., 148.

75. James, "Lectures," 106.

76. Nesbitt, *Universal Emancipation*, 26.

77. James, *Black Jacobins*, 361.

78. Ibid., 250.

79. See, for example, Jean Casimir's concept of the "counter-plantation" in *La Cultura oprimida* and Mats Lundahl's study of "minifundia" in *Peasants and Poverty: A Study of Haiti*.

Chapter Two

1. Garraway, Doris L., ed. *Tree of Liberty: Cultural Legacies of the Haitian Revolution in the Atlantic World* (Charlottesville: University of Virginia Press, 2008), 5–8.

2. Fischer, *Modernity Disavowed*, 11.

3. Ibid., 22.

4. Du Bois, *Black Reconstruction in America*, 57, 64.

5. Marx, *Civil War in France*, 74.

6. Fischer, *Modernity Disavowed*, 16–17; Vivian Gornick, *The Solitude of Self: Thinking about Elizabeth Cady Stanton* (New York: Farrar, Straus, and Giroux, 2006), 23–28.

7. James, *Black Jacobins*, 81.

8. Rancière, *Disagreement*, 10.

9. James Anthony Froude, *Thomas Carlyle: A History of His Life in London, 1834–1881*, vol. II (New York: Charles Scribner's Sons, 1898) 598.

10. Montag, *Bodies, Masses, Power*, 93, citing Spinoza, *Political Treatise* ch. 7, para. 27.

11. Thomas Carlyle, "Shooting Niagara: And After?" (London: Chapman and Hall, 1868) 4, 52.

12. Robert Leigh Davis, "Democratic Vistas," *A Companion to Walt Whitman*, ed. Donald Kummings (New York: Blackwell, 2006) 541.

13. Carlyle, "Shooting Niagara," 9.

14. Ibid., 49.

15. Roberto Mangabeira Unger and Cornel West, *The Future of American Progressivism: An Initiative for Political and Economic Reform* (Boston: Beacon, 1998) 11.

16. Walt Whitman, *Prose Works* (New York: NYU Press, 1964) 2:382–83; *Prose Works* 2:755; hereafter, *PW*.

17. Whitman, *PW*, 2:757.

18. Whitman, *PW*, 2:389.

19. Ed Folsom, ed., *Democratic Vistas: The Original Edition in Facsimile* (Iowa City: University of Iowa Press, 2010) xv.

20. Kenneth M. Price, "'Be radical—be radical—be not too damned radical!': The Origins and Resonance of Whitman's Signature Expression," *Walt Whitman Quarterly Review* 22 (Fall 2004/Spring 2005): 126–29.

21. Carlyle, "Shooting Niagara," 35–36, 40.

22. Parsons, *Freedom, Equality, Solidarity*, 83.

23. Ibid., 31.

24. Ashbaugh, *Lucy Parsons*, 8.

25. Ibid., 226.

26. Thomas F. Haddox, "Whitman's End of History: 'As I Sat Alone by Blue Ontario's Shore,' Democratic Vistas, and the Postbellum Politics of Nostalgia," *Walt Whitman Quarterly Review* 22.1 (2004): 11.

27. Carlyle, "Shooting Niagara," 9.

28. Ibid., 49.

29. Ibid., 19, 35–36.

30. Ibid., 35, 6.

31. Froude, *Thomas Carlyle*, 300.

32. D. J. Trela, "Carlyle's 'Shooting Niagara': The Writing and Revising of an Article and Pamphlet," *Victorian Periodicals Review* 25.1 (Spring 1992): 30–34.

33. For an analysis of how these events shaped Carlyle's and Whitman's thinking, see Erkkila, *Whitman the Political Poet* (New York: Oxford University Press, 1989) 247. For an additional discussion of the British Reform Acts, see Evans, *Parliamentary Reform in Britain*.

34. Foucault, *Fearless Speech*, 78–79.

35. Carlyle, "Shooting Niagara," 31.

36. Ibid., 3.

37. Ibid., 1–2.

38. Ibid., 34–35.

39. Ibid., 22.

40. Plato 414b–415d; Rancière *Hatred* 34.

41. Carlyle, "Shooting Niagara," 46.

42. Catherine Hall, *Civilising Subjects: Metropole and Colony in the English Imagination 1830–1867* (Chicago: University of Chicago Press, 2002) 350.

43. Carlyle, "Shooting Niagara," 4.

44. Ibid., 4.

45. Ibid. With this idea, Carlyle prefigures the writing by Gustave Le Bon and his epigones.

46. Ibid., 8–9.

47. Betsy Erkkila reads "Shooting Niagara" as "Carlyle's call for an authoritarian state" (254) in a vein that is not unlike Karl Popper's critique of Plato in *The Open Society and Its Enemies*. In short, what Popper had to deduce from Plato's trajectory of ideas, Carlyle makes plain.

48. George Orwell, *A Kind of Compulsion* (London: Secker and Warburg, 2000) 196.

49. Carlyle, "Shooting Niagara," 19.

50. Carlyle writes, "With factions, suspicions, want of bread and sugar, it is verily what they call *déchiré*, torn asunder this poor country: France and all that is French. For, over seas too come bad news. In black Saint-Domingo, before that variegated Glitter in the Champs-Élysées was lit for an Accepted Constitution, there had risen, and was burning contemporary with it, quite another variegated Glitter and nocturnal Fulgor, had we known it: of molasses and ardent-spirits; of sugar-boileries, plantations, furniture, cattle and men: skyhigh; the Plain of Cap Français one huge whirl of smoke and flame! (Book II, 2.5.IV).

51. Sarah Winter, "On the Morant Bay Rebellion in Jamaica and the Governor Eyre-George William Gordon Controversy, 1865–70." *BRANCH: Britain, Representation, and Nineteenth-Century History* <branchcollective.org>, 4.

52. For a fuller treatment of these events and their many implications, see Hall, *Civilizing Subjects*, as well as Edward Said's review of that book, "Always on Top," and the dialogue between Hall, Madhavi Kale, Patrick E. Bryan, Rhonda Cobham, and Faith Smith in *Small Axe* 7.2 (September 2003). See also Kostal, *A Jurisprudence of Power*; Heuman, *"The Killing Time": The Morant Bay Rebellion in Jamaica*; and Underhill, *The Tragedy of Morant Bay*.

53. Heuman, *Killing Time*, 98.

54. Winter, "On the Morant Bay Rebellion," par. 1.

55. Heuman, *Killing Time*, 98.

56. Carlyle, "Shooting Niagara," 13.

57. Kostal, *Jurisprudence*, 187.

58. Froude, *Thomas Carlyle*, 601.

59. Carlyle, "Shooting Niagara," 18–19.

60. Ibid., 19.

61. Douglas Lorimer, *Colour, Class, and the Victorians* (Leicester: Leicester University Press, 1978) 195.

62. Whitman, *PW* 2:393.

63. Folsom, *Democratic Vistas*, xxiii–xxix.

64. See Betsy Erkkila, "'To Paris with my Love': Whitman among the French Revisited." Whitman added the passage about the Commune, only to remove it from future versions. Part of the passage reads: "only deep, vast, emotional, real affinity of America is with the cause of Popular Government [in Europe]—and especially in France" (*PW* 2: 757).

65. Whitman, *PW* 2:755.

66. Ibid., 391.

67. Ibid., 363.

68. Ibid., 365.

69. Ibid., 753.

70. Whitman, *Journalism*, 89.

71. Whitman, *PW* 1:254.

72. Erkkila, *Whitman the Political Poet*, 247. For details on the debate between Carlyle and Whitman, in addition to the texts considered in this chapter, see Paine, "The Literary Relations of Whitman and Carlyle with Especial Reference to Their Contrasting Views on Democracy"; Brooks, "What Whitman Knew"; Weisbuch, *Atlantic Double-Cross*; Grier, "Walt Whitman, the Galaxy, and *Democratic Vistas*"; and Scholnick, "'Culture' or Democracy: Whitman, Eugene Benson, and *The* Galaxy."

73. Whitman, *PW* 2:375–76.

74. Ibid., 422.

75. Ibid., 379.

76. Carlyle, "Shooting Niagara," 22.

77. Whitman, *PW* 2:363; *PW* 2:379.

78. Ibid., 396.

79. Ibid., 362.

80. For a discussion of the problem, its historical roots, and contemporary implications, see the interesting proposal by Paul Lucardie in "Let the Dice Decide! A Qualified Argument for Sortitionist Democracy," *Problems of Democracy: Language and Speaking*. Ed. Mary-Ann Crumplin (Oxford: Inter-Disciplinary Press, 2011) 103–19.

81. See Hardt, "Jefferson and Democracy," and Betsy Erkkila's and Barry Shank's responses to Hardt.

82. Stephen John Mack, *The Pragmatic Whitman: Reimagining American Democracy* (Iowa City: University of Iowa Press, 2002) 137.

83. Whitman, *PW* 2:389, 401.

84. Folsom, 113–14.

85. Whitman, *PW* 2:400–2.

86. As did the more radical writers of his time, and after. Michel Fabre points out that Emma Goldman and Eugene Debs, for example, admired *Democratic Vistas* and *Leaves of Grass* and, to varying degrees, appropriated Whitman's ideas for their projects.

87. See Luke Mancuso, *The Strange Sad War Revolving: Walt Whitman, Reconstruction, and the Emergence of Black Citizenship, 1865–1876* (Columbia: Camden House, 1997), especially chapter 2, "'Reconstruction is Still in Abeyance': Walt Whitman's *Democratic Vistas* and the Federalizing of National Identity."

88. Whitman, *PW* 2:396; *PW* 2:382; *PW* 2:753.

89. Du Bois, *Black Reconstruction*, 6, 13.

90. Ed Folsom, ed. *Democratic Vistas*, 46. See also Ed Folsom, "Lucifer and Ethiopia: Whitman, Race, and Poetics before the Civil War and After," *A Historical Guide to Walt Whitman*, ed. David S. Reynolds. (New York: Oxford University Press, 2000) 45–95. As Mischa Honeck writes in *We Are the Revolutionists*, it is important to remember a distinction between abolition and antislavery in nineteenth-century thought: white abolitionists of the era often opposed slavery as an institution but nevertheless could not bring themselves to believe in racial equality (10).

91. Whitman, *PW* 2:754.

92. Ibid., 2:754.

93. Ibid., 2:375; *PW* 2:363.

94. Ibid., 2:383.

95. I paraphrase here from Staughton Lynd, *The Intellectual Origins of American Radicalism* (Cambridge: Cambridge University Press, 2009) 160.

96. Whitman, *PW* 2:389.

97. Ibid., 2:389–90.

98. Ibid., 2:390

99. Ibid.

100. Ibid., 2:410.

101. Parsons, *Freedom, Equality, and Solidarity*, 27.

102. Ibid., 113.

103. Perhaps the best examination of the ideologies of the activists with which Parsons was affiliated in Chicago is found in chapter 8 of James Green's book *Death in the Haymarket*. In short, activists in Chicago in the era made a diverse immigrant mix, and the Chicago idea wove together various radical threads, most notably anarchism and Marxism.

104. Parsons, *Freedom, Equality, and Solidarity*, 55.

105. When Parsons uses the phrase "political methods," she means electoral politics.

106. Parsons, *Freedom, Equality, and Solidarity*, 115, emphasis in original.

107. Ibid., 32, 33.

108. Gale Ahrens, "Introduction" to *Lucy Parsons: Freedom, Equality, and Solidarity, Writings and Speeches, 1878–1937* (Chicago: Charles H. Kerr, 2004) 3. Biographical information in the following paragraphs is culled from that text; from Ashbaugh, *Lucy Parsons: An American Revolutionary* (Chicago: Charles H. Kerr, 1976); and from McKean, "A Fury for Justice: Lucy Parsons and the Revolutionary Anarchist Movement in Chicago."

109. Carolyn Ashbaugh, *Lucy Parsons: An American Revolutionary* (Chicago: Haymarket Books, 2012) 66. This disavowal perhaps led to Parsons's rather simplistic understanding of race and gender relations as subsidiary to economic relations. Robin D. G. Kelley points out

that Parsons basically took the Old Left line, which held that racism and sexism were features of capitalism: "kill the latter and the former would wither away" (41).

110. The International Working People's Association is distinct from, but grew from the demise of, the Marx's International Working Men's Association, also called the First International. The IWPA is perhaps best known for its "Pittsburgh Proclamation," a document that helped Lucy Parsons to frame her ideology considerably.

111. Kelley, *Freedom Dreams*, 42. There is some disagreement among Parsons's biographers about whether she was a lifelong anarchist or whether she joined the Communist Party late in life (Ahrens, *Lucy Parsons*, 3). Both seem possible based on the available evidence. At different times, she called herself a socialist and an anarchist, and from 1891, she was the editor and publisher of the newspaper *Anarchist-Communist Monthly* (Ashbaugh, *Lucy Parsons*, 183). She insisted on taking a political view that was not doctrinaire, and she had a consistent affinity with the poor and oppressed. It follows, then, that she could find solidarity with the groups that shared those interests when, over the course of her lifetime, different groups with ideologies that spoke to her principles came to prominence.

112. See, for example, the recent book by Timothy Messer-Kruse, *The Haymarket Conspiracy: Transatlantic Anarchist Networks*, which notes Lucy only once in the text without a simultaneous mention of Albert, and after doing so, adds an endnote to state that Lucy published Albert's biography (Urbana: University of Illinois Press, 2012) 183, 227.

113. For more information, see Nancy Bentley, "Looking at State Violence: Lucy Parsons, José Marti, and Haymarket," *The Oxford Handbook of 19th Century American Literature*, ed. Russ Castronovo (Oxford: Oxford University Press, 2012).

114. Ahrens, *Freedom, Equality, and Solidarity*, 6, emphasis in original.

115. Ibid., 114.

116. Mel Dubofsky, *We Shall Be All: A History of the Industrial Workers of the World* (Chicago: Quadrangle Books, 1969) 47.

117. Ashbaugh, *Lucy Parsons*, 226.

118. Parsons, *Freedom, Equality, and Solidarity*, 55.

119. Ashbaugh, *Lucy Parsons*, 35.

120. Lynd, *Intellectual Origins*, 35; Schmitt, *Dictatorship*, 124.

121. Lynd, *Intellectual Origins*, 35.

122. Parsons, *Freedom, Equality, and Solidarity*, 131. Parsons's theoretical views on the reduction of the workday drew from Marx, whose comments on the topic display the idea of cross-pollinated struggles against chattel and wage slavery. He writes, "In the United States of America, any sort of independent labor movement was paralyzed so long as slavery disfigured a part of the republic. Labor with a white skin cannot emancipate itself where labor with a black skin is branded. But out of the death of slavery a new vigorous life sprang. The first fruit of the Civil War was an agitation for the 8-hour day—a movement which ran with express speed from the Atlantic to the Pacific, from New England to California" (301).

123. The Illinois legislature passed a law mandating the eight-hour workday, which took effect on 1 May 1867, and the United States Congress passed a similar law for mechanics and laborers employed by the federal government on 25 June 1868. Businesses in Chicago ignored the former law, and Ulysses S. Grant's cabinet secretaries issued orders that negated

the federal law. In short, laws could not make the eight-hour workday a material reality when employers could ignore it with impunity. It took coordinated and continuous strikes to make the eight-hour workday a material reality. See Green, *Death in the Haymarket,* chapter 2, "A Paradise for Workers and Speculators."

124. Parsons, *Freedom, Equality, and Solidarity,* 158.

125. Ibid., 29.

Chapter Three

1. Sally E. Hadden, *Slave Patrols: Law and Violence in Virginia and the Carolinas* (Cambridge: Harvard University Press, 2001) 148–49.

2. Scot French, *The Rebellious Slave: Nat Turner In American Memory* (New York: Houghton Mifflin, 2003) 44–45.

3. John B. Duff and Peter M. Mitchell, *The Nat Turner Rebellion: The Historical Event and the Modern Controversy* (New York: Harper and Row, 1971) 32.

4. Thomas R. Gray was not Turner's lawyer; the court appointed William C. Parker as Turner's counsel. See David F. Allmendinger, *Nat Turner and the Rising in Southampton County* (Baltimore: Johns Hopkins University Press, 2014) 6.

5. Thomas R. Gray, *The Confessions of Nat Turner* in Herbert Aptheker, *Nat Turner's Slave Rebellion* (Mineola: Dover, 2006) 4–5.

6. Ibid., 21.

7. Ibid., 7.

8. Allmendinger, *Nat Turner,* 257.

9. Gray, *Confessions,* 3, 1.

10. Ibid., 147.

11. Allmendinger, *Nat Turner,* 8.

12. Gray, *Confessions,* 130.

13. Robin Blackburn, *The Overthrow of Colonial Slavery: 1776–1848* (London: Verso, 2011) 3.

14. Allmendinger, *Nat Turner,* 7, 245–53.

15. Ibid., 225.

16. Gray, *Confessions,* 152, 138.

17. Aptheker, *Nat Turner's Slave Rebellion,* 49.

18. Plotz, *Crowd,* 172.

19. See Du Bois, *John Brown,* 46–47; Malcolm X, *Autobiography of Malcolm X,* 79; Baker, *Nat Turner,* 6; Shakur, *Assata: An Autobiography,* (Chicago: Lawrence Hill, 2001) 175. In Martin Duberman's historical novel *Haymarket,* Lucy Parsons argues several times that Turner led a successful revolt (118, 185).

20. Shakur, *Assata,* 175–76.

21. Aptheker, *Nat Turner's Slave Rebellion,* 7–16.

22. In Southampton County in 1810, there were 5,982 whites, 1,109 free blacks, and 6,406 slaves. In 1830, one year before the rebellion, there were 6,573 whites (growth rate of 7.2%), 1,745 free blacks (growth rate of 33.6%), and 7,756 slaves (growth rate of 13.4%). In 1830

there were 293 residents in and around Jerusalem, the city closest to where the rebellion took place; of these, there were 103 whites, eight free blacks, and 182 slaves (Aptheker, *Nat Turner's Slave Rebellion*, 15; Allmendinger, *Nat Turner*, 159).

23. Robinson, *Black Marxism*, xxii.

24. Aptheker, *Nat Turner's Slave Rebellion*, 34.

25. Allmendinger, *Nat Turner*, 93.

26. Gray, *Confessions*, 142.

27. Aptheker, *Nat Turner's Slave Rebellion*, 7.

28. Douglass R. Egerton, "Nat Turner in a Hemispheric Context," *Nat Turner: A Slave Rebellion in History and Memory*, ed. Kenneth S. Greenberg (Oxford: Oxford University Press, 2003) 144.

29. Gray, *Confessions*, 13.

30. Ibid., 14.

31. Henry Irving Tragle, *The Southampton Slave Revolt of 1831: A Compilation of Source Material* (Amherst: University of Massachusetts Press, 1971) xvii.

32. Mary Kemp Davis, "'What Happened in This Place?': In Search of the Female Slave in the Nat Turner Slave Insurrection," *Nat Turner: A Slave Rebellion in History and Memory*, ed. Kenneth S. Greenberg (Oxford: Oxford University Press, 2003) 176.

33. Daniel S. Fabricant, "Thomas R. Gray and William Styron: Finally, a Critical Look at the 1831 Confessions of Nat Turner," *American Journal of Legal History* 37.3 (July 1993): 332, 333.

34. Ibid., 343, 349.

35. Allmendinger, *Nat Turner*, 191.

36. Ibid., 96–101.

37. French, *Rebellious Slave*, 2.

38. Ibid., 37–38.

39. Ibid., 4.

40. Allmendinger, *Nat Turner*, 239.

41. Ibid., 144.

42. Ibid., 102–4.

43. Ibid., 100–101.

44. Ibid., 102.

45. Ibid., 104, 117.

46. Gray, *Confessions*, 132.

47. Ibid., 138.

48. Allmendinger, *Nat Turner*, 14, 20, 74, 78–83.

49. Ibid., 74.

50. Gray, *Confessions*, 149.

51. Thomas Wentworth Higginson, "Nat Turner's Insurrection," *The Nat Turner Rebellion: The Historical Event and the Modern Controversy*, ed. John B. Duff and Peter B. Mitchell (New York: Harper and Row, 1971) 61.

52. Almendinger, *Nat Turner*, 199–207. See also Alfred L. Brophy, "The Nat Turner Trials," *North Carolina Law Review* 91 (June 2013): 1831–1836.

53. Almendinger, *Nat Turner*, 209.

54. Tragle, *Southampton Slave Revolt*, 17.

55. Edward E. Baptist, *The Half Has Never Been Told: Slavery and the Making of American Capitalism* (New York: Basic Books, 2014) 208.

56. Aptheker, *Nat Turner's Slave Rebellion*, 33.

57. Patrick H. Breen, "A Prophet in His Own Land: Support for Nat Turner and His Rebellion within Southampton County's Black Community," *Nat Turner: A Slave Rebellion in History and Memory*, ed. Kenneth Greenberg (Oxford: Oxford University Press, 2003) 105.

58. Gray, *Confessions*, 147.

59. Scot French, "A Conversation with Scot French," 4 December 2012 <www .houghtonmifflinbooks.com/booksellers/press_release/french/>.

60. Allmendinger, *Nat Turner*, 220.

61. Thomas C. Parramore, "Covenant in Jerusalem," Greenberg, *Nat Turner*, 75; Allmendinger, *Nat Turner*, 219.

62. Allmendinger, *Nat Turner*, 275.

63. Gray, *Confessions*, 146.

64. Ibid., 128.

65. Copyright, of course, also means that Gray could profit from Turner's story. Even in death, Turner's labors would be manipulated so that the produce of those labors would benefit the slavocracy.

66. Ibid., 129.

67. Allmendinger, *Nat Turner*, 230.

68. Gray, *Confessions*, 128–32.

69. French, *Rebellious Slave*, 4.

70. Gray, *Confessions*, 152.

71. French, *Rebellious Slave*, 4.

72. Ibid., 37.

73. Gray, *Confessions*, 3.

74. French, *Rebellious Slave*, 46.

75. Ibid., 46.

76. Gray, *Confessions*, 128, 129.

77. Raphael Dalleo writes in *Caribbean Literature and the Public Sphere: From the Plantation to the Postcolonial* that the majority of research on *The History of Mary Prince*, including an important essay by A. M. Rauwerda, has "centered on the nature of the collaborative process that produced the text" (35), which is a gentle way of expressing the fact that Prince's narrative was filtered through the "prunings" made by Susanna Strickland and Thomas Pringle, the abolitionists who published Prince's text (*History*, 3). In Prince's case—not to minimize the clumsiness and limited vision of the writers—the story was written and published by allies. This is not to say that the theoretical issues of speaking for others are less difficult than in Turner's case, only that they are different. Gray, I think that it is fair to suggest, hides malevolence behind a veil of objectivity, whereas in Prince's case, one needs to overcome the obstacles of representation that were put in place by good will.

78. Gray, *Confessions*, 133.

79. On this point, compare also the different starting points of *The Confessions* and Kyle Baker's impressive graphic novel *Nat Turner*. Baker's novel begins in Africa, with a scene of people being stolen into slavery, followed by scenes from the Middle Passage and also from Turner's childhood. Baker shows a long chain of events; Gray, by wishing to contain the narrative to the rebellion and its immediate aftermath, merely shows some of the links in that chain.

80. Allmendinger, *Nat Turner*, 101.

81. French, *Rebellious Slave*, 46.

82. Gray, *Confessions*, 130.

83. Stephen H. Browne, "'This Unparalleled and Inhuman Massacre': The Gothic, the Sacred, and the Meaning of Nat Turner," *Rhetoric and Public Affairs* 3 (2000): 314.

84. Gray, *Confessions*, 147.

85. Ibid., 147.

86. Fischer, *Modernity Disavowed*, 111.

87. Gray, *Confessions*, 147.

88. Duff and Mitchell, *Nat Turner Rebellion*, 34–35.

89. Egerton, "Nat Turner in a Hemispheric Context," 134.

90. Gray, *Confessions*, 133.

91. Ibid., 147.

92. Eugene Genovese, *Roll, Jordan, Roll: The World the Slaves Made* (New York: Vintage, 1976), 594–95.

93. Aptheker, *Nat Turner's Slave Rebellion*, 107.

94. Gray, *Confessions*, 4–5.

95. Ibid., 150.

96. Bryan Rommel-Ruiz, "Vindictive Ferocity: Virginia's Response to the Nat Turner Rebellion," *Enemies of Humanity: The Nineteenth Century War on Terrorism* (New York: Palgrave Macmillan, 2008) 69.

97. Parramore, "Covenant," 71.

98. Corey Robin, *The Reactionary Mind: Conservatism from Edmund Burke to Sarah Palin* (Oxford: Oxford University Press, 2013) 45.

99. Kenneth S. Greenberg, "Name, Face, Body" *Nat Turner: A Slave Rebellion in History and Memory*, Kenneth Greenberg (Oxford: Oxford University Press, 2003) 10.

100. Tragle, *Southampton Slave Revolt*, 21.

101. Ibid., 22.

102. Aptheker, *Nat Turner's Slave Rebellion*, 1. In the opening line of what Allmendinger calls the "memoir" section of *The Confessions*, Turner seems to dismiss the term Gray had used for the event: Turner says, "the late insurrection, as you call it" (Gray 133; Allmendinger, *Nat Turner*, 101).

103. It is a repeating pattern: when the Paris Commune erupted, its critics were certain that Karl Marx, the "Red Professor," was directing the communards' actions remotely from London. Opposite of a picture with the caption "Crowd Swarms around Toppled Vendôme Column," Donny Gluckstein writes in *The Paris Commune: A Revolution in Democracy* that "the [French] establishment had such contempt for ordinary people that it could not

conceive of revolts truly happening from below. Mass actions had to be the result of outside agitators manipulating gullible followers. So the "Red Professor," Karl Marx, was accused of orchestrating the Commune from his London office of the International Working Men's Association (later known as the First International)" (11). The same assumption about the fundamental need for leadership led Napoleon and Leclerc to pursue their strategy of decapitating the Haitian Revolution by removing its leaders, a strategy that did not break the revolution, but rather made it evolve into the 2,000 leaders. The authorities in Chicago followed a similar strategy after the Haymarket bombing: rather than pursue people who were suspected of throwing the bomb, the police rounded up the area's radical labor leaders, including Lucy Parsons's spouse, Albert, and tried them for inciting the public to violence. The police did not squelch the movement for the eight-hour workday or ever find the person who threw the bomb; their actions elevated a few people to leadership status, and then, in sentencing them to death, they created martyrs who inspired the others who ultimately won the eight-hour workday. Such examples show that it is apparent to many people how leaders and hierarchies structure both movements and the stories written about them. Leaders take up the pinnacle of a reader's attention in such stories and leave most others to be mere supporters.

Chapter Four

1. Jonah Raskin, "B. Traven's Revolution in Latin America," *B. Traven: Life and Work*, ed. Ernst Schürer and Philip Jenkins (University Park: Pennsylvania State University Press) 226.

2. B. Traven, *The General from the Jungle* (Chicago: Ivan R. Dee, 1995) 64.

3. Traven, *General*, 147.

4. Ibid., 275.

5. Judy Stone, "Conversations with B. Traven," *Ramparts* (1967): 57.

6. B. Traven, *The Rebellion of the Hanged* (Chicago: Ivan R. Dee, 1994) 231.

7. Spinoza, *Political Treatise*, ch. 2, para. 3.

8. Montag, *Bodies, Masses, Power*, 91–92.

9. Traven, *General*, 19.

10. Ibid., 7, 20.

11. Bill Weinberg, *Homage to Chiapas: The New Indigenous Struggles in Mexico* (London: Verso, 2000).

12. Karl Guthke, *B. Traven: The Life behind the Legends* (Brooklyn: Lawrence Hill, 1987) 25, 202–4.

13. Ibid., 41.

14. Ibid., xii.

15. Ibid., 23.

16. Ibid., 221–22.

17. Ibid., 224.

18. Ibid., 279.

19. Ibid., 23–24.

20. Ibid., 249.

21. Ibid., 209.

22. Jud Newborn and Annette Dumbach, *Sophie Scholl and the White Rose* (London: Oneworld, 2007) 58.

23. Ibid., 300.

24. Ibid., 301.

25. B. Traven, *The Treasure of the Sierra Madre* (New York: Farrar, Straus, and Giroux, 2010).

26. Guthke, *B. Traven*, 3.

27. Ibid., 211–12.

28. Richard E. Mezo, *A Study of B. Traven's Fiction: The Journey to Solipaz* (San Francisco: Mellen Research University Press, 1993) xiv.

29. Brian Gollnick, *Reinventing the Lacandón: Subaltern Representations in the Rain Forest of Chiapas* (Tucson: University of Arizona Press, 2008) 96.

30. As they did for Traven, the ambivalences of the end of the Mexican Revolution present problems and inspirations for many other writers. See, for example, Adolfo Gilly's history of the Mexican Revolution, *La revolucíon interrumpida*—the "interrupted revolution." For fictional explorations of this ambivalence, see, for example, Mariano Azuela's novel *The Underdogs*, Martin Luis Guzmán's *The Eagle and the Serpent*, and Carlos Fuentes's *The Death of Artemio Cruz*.

31. Mezo, *Study*, 136.

32. B. Traven, *The Carreta* (Chicago: Ivan R. Dee, 1994) 150; B. Traven, *General*, 142; B. Traven, *Government* (Chicago: Ivan R. Dee, 1993) 126–27.

33. Traven, *Government*, 71.

34. Ibid., 71.

35. Ibid., 12.

36. B. Traven, *March to the Montería* (Chicago: Ivan R. Dee, 1994) 159.

37. Ibid., 160–61.

38. As their name implies, the "*científicos*" brought their special talents and expertise to the "science" of government in Porfirio Díaz's dictatorship. As Frank McLynn writes in *Villa and Zapata: A History of the Mexican Revolution*, "[d]uring the *Porfiriato*, Díaz's most influential advisers were the so-called *científicos* or Mexican positivists, who believed in capitalism, industrialism, and modern technology; they despised Mexico's colonial past and Indian heritage. Most of the Mexican elite—politicians, bankers, editors, businessmen, generals—subscribed to *científico* ideals" (10).

39. Traven, *Government*, 228–29.

40. Ibid., 128.

41. Ibid., 133.

42. Traven, *Rebellion*, 200.

43. Traven, *Government*, 27.

44. Traven, *General*, 210.

45. Traven, *Rebellion*, 213.

46. Traven, *General*, 47. The characters that eventually form the swarm are variously referred to as peasants, peons, workers, proletarians, agriculturists, and other names over

the course of the novels. Most come from the various indigenous communities—Tzotzil, Tseltal, Bachajontec, Huasteca, and Chol are ones Traven mentions specifically—in Chiapas and neighboring states. For the sake of consistency, I use the word "worker" to describe these characters previous to the emergence of the swarm and "rebels" to describe them afterwards.

47. B. Traven, *Trozas* (Chicago: Ivan R. Dee, 1994) 37.

48. Traven, *General*, 107.

49. Ibid., 208.

50. Traven, *Government*, 26–29.

51. Ibid., 126–27.

52. Traven, *March to the Montería*, 198.

53. Traven, *Trozas*, 165.

54. Traven, *General*, 5. The *rurales* in the Mahogany Novels are represented as terror personified. Historians have taken a more nuanced view, however. The *rurales* were brutal in their repression of strikes and mutinies, but they were also highly symbolic with their new weapons and sharp uniforms. They were also frequently less than an efficient fighting force—Frank McLynn calls the *rurales* "corrupt and incompetent," and as such, they "were a fitting symbol of a lazy, corrupt and unpopular regime" (22, 23).

55. Traven, *Rebellion*, 195.

56. Jeffrey Bortz, *Revolution Within the Revolution: Cotton Textile Workers and the Mexican Labor Regime, 1910-1923* (Stanford: Stanford University Press, 2008), 2.

57. John Mason Hart, *Revolutionary Mexico: the Coming and Process of the Mexican Revolution* (Berkley: University of California Press, 1997), 71.

58. Bortz 88. See also Gilly 52; Hart 69–72; McLynn 19–20; Turner 167–75.

59. Traven, *Rebellion* 195; Traven, *General* 5.

60. Traven, *Rebellion* 181.

61. Ibid., 205.

62. Hart, *Revolutionary Mexico*, 71.

63. Traven, *General*, 5.

64. Ibid., 5–6.

65. Traven, *March to the Montería*, 159.

66. Kenneth Payne, "*The Rebellion of the Hanged*: B. Traven's Anti-Fascist Novel of the Mexican Revolution," *International Fiction Review* 18.2 (1991): 101.

67. Traven, *March to the Montería*, 72–73.

68. Traven, *Rebellion*, 64–65.

69. Ibid., 72.

70. Traven, *March to the Montería*, 109, 111.

71. Traven, *General*, 217.

72. Ibid., 182–83.

73. Mezo, *Study*, 130.

74. Ibid., 130.

75. Payne, "Anti-Fascist Novel," 106.

76. Traven, *Trozas*, 87.

77. Traven, *March to the Montería*, 123–24.

78. Ibid., 128.

79. Ibid., 129–30.

80. Ibid., 142.

81. The story of this fight spreads through the montería in much the same way it spread into Traven's fiction. As Heidi Zogbaum points out, this episode is taken almost verbatim from Chiapas folklore (125–26).

82. Traven, Rebellion, 199.

83. Ibid., 166.

84. Ibid., 164, 165–66.

85. Ibid., 164.

86. Ibid., 165.

87. Gollnick, Reinventing the Lacandón, 111.

88. Traven, General, 67.

89. Traven, Rebellion, 171. The rebels in the Mahogany Novels, like Emiliano Zapata and many of the Mexican revolutionaries, adopt the phrase "¡Tierra y Libertad!" as coined by Ricardo Flores Magón, a radical journalist and activist for the Mexican Liberal Party. For more information, see the collections of Flores Magón's writings, especially Dreams of Freedom: A Ricardo Flores Magón Reader and Land and Liberty: Anarchist Influences in the Mexican Revolution. For a scholarly study of Flores Magón's influence on the Mexican Revolution and his subsequent persecution, see Colin M. MacLachlan, Anarchism and the Mexican Revolution: The Political Trials of Ricardo Flores Magón in the United States.

90. Traven, Rebellion, 178.

91. Ibid., 179.

92. Ibid., 180.

93. Ibid., 199.

94. Ibid., 198–99.

95. Ibid., 199.

96. Ibid., 239, 238.

97. Ibid., 231.

98. Traven, General, 44.

99. Ibid., 46.

100. Ibid., 47.

101. Ibid., 54.

102. Traven, *Rebellion*, 231.

103. Traven, *General*, 19.

104. Traven, *Rebellion*, 200.

105. Traven, *General*, 42.

106. Ibid., 208.

107. Ibid., 207.

108. Ibid., 207–8.

109. Ibid., 208.

110. Ibid., 209.

111. Ibid., 214.

112. Ibid., 85.

113. Ibid., 69.

114. Ibid., 60.

115. Ibid., 61.

116. Schmitt, *Dictatorship*, 174.

117. Traven, *Rebellion*, 200–201.

Chapter Five

1. Hellen Lee-Keller, "Madness and the Mulâtre-Aristocrate: Haiti, Decolonization, and Women in Marie Chauvet's *Amour*," *Callaloo* 32.4 (2009): 1293.

2. Elizabeth Walcott-Hackshaw, "My Love Is like a Rose: Terror, *Territoire*, and the Poetics of Marie Chauvet," *Small Axe* 18 (September 2005): 41.

3. Marie Vieux Chauvet, *Love, Anger, Madness: A Haitian Triptych* (New York: Modern Library, 2010) 100, 108.

4. Laurent Dubois, *Haiti: The Aftershocks of History* (New York: Metropolitan, 2012) 204.

5. Walcott-Hackshaw, "My Love," 43.

6. Chauvet, *Love*, 4.

7. Ibid., 151, 153.

8. Ibid., 69.

9. Ibid., 8.

10. Ibid.

11. Colin Dayan, "The Gods in the Trunk, or Writing in a Belittered World," *Yale French Studies*, issue *Revisiting Marie Vieux Chauvet: Paradoxes of the Postcolonial Feminine* 128 (2015): 93.

12. Chauvet, *Love*, 45.

13. Ibid., 154.

14. Montag, *Bodies, Masses, Power*, 92.

15. Schmitt, *Political Theology*, 15.

16. Lee-Keller, "Madness and the *Mulâtre-Aristocrate*," 1293–94; 1296.

17. Gilles Deleuze, *Nietzsche and Philosophy*, 52.

18. Chauvet, *Love*, 20, 148.

19. Spinoza, *Political Treatise*, ch. 2, para. 3.

20. Chauvet, *Love*, 69.

21. Ibid., 44.

22. Ibid., 4.

23. Ibid., 8, 9. As Madison Smartt Bell notes in a review of *Love, Anger, Madness*, Calédu's name "recalls the French colonist Caradeux, renowned for his imaginative cruelty to his slaves." "Calédu" is also Kreyòl for "one who beats hard" (Lee-Keller 1310, quoting Dayan and Larrier).

24. Chauvet, *Love*, 8, 5.

25. Ibid., 8

26. Ibid., 18.

27. Ibid., 129.

28. As Lee-Keller argues, "[w]hile the plantation system as such no longer existed in Chauvet's day, hunger, unemployment, and poverty still did, and the novel explicitly describes this" (1308).

29. Chauvet, *Love*, 40–41.

30. Ibid., 41.

31. Ibid.

32. Ibid.

33. Ibid., 41–42.

34. Nesbitt, *Universal Emancipation*, 26.

35. Chauvet, *Love*, 112.

36. Ibid., 112.

37. Ibid., 113.

38. Ibid., 49.

39. Ibid., 50.

40. Ibid., 43.

41. Ibid., 42.

42. Ibid., 126.

43. The second novella in Chauvet's trilogy, *Anger*, in which a father prostitutes his daughter Rose to the regime in order to save his family's property, shows both the danger and the futility of appealing to the regime for leniency. As Joan Dayan writes, "[a]ll that ultimately remains of Rose is a heap of dead flesh that testifies to the efficacy of state tyranny" (121).

44. Chauvet, *Love*, 73, 127.

45. Ibid., 46.

46. Ibid., 89, 107.

47. Ibid., 107.

48. Ibid., 14.

49. Ibid.

50. Ibid.

51. Ibid.

52. Ibid.

53. Ibid., 55.

54. Ibid., 17.

55. Ibid., 136.

56. Ibid., 14.

57. Ibid., 17.

58. Ibid., 15.

59. See Dubois, *Haiti*: "bandit" is the word that the American occupation forces dictated that their people use to describe the Caco rebels (232). Using the word "bandits" in the past tense, as if the bandits that Mme. Camuse references have come and gone, is an indication that Chauvet levels a critique at the Duvalier dictatorship.

60. Chauvet, *Love*, 32.

61. Ibid., 8.

62. Ibid., 142.

63. Lee-Keller, "Madness and the *Mulâtre-Aristocrate*," 1297.

64. Ibid., 1302.

65. Chauvet, *Love*, 46; J. Michael Dash, *The Other America: Caribbean Literature in a New World Context* (Charlottesville: University of Virginia Press, 1998) 111.

66. Chauvet, *Love*, 152.

67. Ibid., 155.

68. Ibid.

69. See Martin Munro, who writes that the "Haitian antihero also has an important anti-ideological function, for he transforms an individual decline into a collective deliverance" (36). See also Dash, *The Other America*, who reads Claire's act as ambiguous (111). Chauvet implies that the "black hill folk" have overcome a great, perhaps even greater, amount of violence in order to "stick together" at the end of the novella. On this specific point it would be interesting to imagine what information an omniscient narrator could provide about the inner workings of the Clamont household and its circle of acquaintances and also the dynamics of the groups of people who eventually come to form the crowd on the street at the end of the novella.

70. Valerie Kaussen, "Irrational Revolutions: Colonial Intersubjectivity and Dialectics in Marie Chauvet's *Amour*," *Tree of Liberty: Cultural Legacies of the Haitian Revolution in the Atlantic World*, ed. Doris L. Garraway (Charlottesville: University of Virginia Press, 2008) 140.

71. Chauvet, *Love*, 156.

72. Melissa Sande, "Cultural Memory for the Political Present: Examining Marie Chauvet's *Love* in the Aftermath of Haiti's Earthquake," *Otherness: Essays and Studies* 2.1 (August 2011).

73. In a famous passage from the "Contribution to the Critique of Hegel's *Philosophy of Right*," Marx writes that "the arm of criticism cannot replace the criticism of arms. Material force can only be overthrown by material force. [The aim of certain kinds of criticism] ends, therefore, with the categorical imperative to overthrow all those conditions in which man is an abased, enslaved, abandoned, contemptible being" (60).

74. Spinoza, *Ethics*, IV P70–73.

75. Spinoza, *Political Treatise*, 686.

76. Chauvet, *Love*, 135–36.

77. Ibid., 143.

78. Ibid.

79. Andrew Asibong, "Three Is the Loneliest Number: Marie Vieux Chauvet, Marie NDiaye, and the Traumatized Triptych." *Yale French Studies. Revisiting Marie Vieux Chauvet: Paradoxes of the Postcolonial Feminine* 128 (2015): 157.

80. Chauvet, *Love*, 9.

81. Ibid., 69.

Epilogue

1. There are a number of communities and movements putting these ideas and political forms into practice in our era; they have received some scholarly attention and deserve to receive a great deal more. See, for example, two prominent examples among many: the widespread movement in Argentina to build *empresas recuperadas*, or "recovered enterprises," in which employees of formerly shuttered workplaces expropriate the buildings and machinery and reopen those workplaces under the democratic management of the employees, and the contemporary Zapatista movement in Chiapas, Mexico, where B. Traven's Mahogany Novels were set. On the *empresas recuperadas*, see Marina Sitrin, *Horizontalism: Voices of Popular Power in Argentina*. Sitrin writes that the term *horizontalism*, as the movement uses it, "does not imply just a flat plane for organizing or non-hierarchical relationships in which people no longer make decisions for others. It is a positive word that implies the use of direct democracy and the striving for consensus, processes in which everyone is heard and new relationships are created.[. . .] As its name suggests, *horizontalidad* implies democratic communication on a level plane and involves—or at least intentionally strives towards—non-hierarchical and anti-authoritarian creation rather than reaction (vi, 3). Valeria Wagner and Alehandro Moreira write that the Zapatistas' commitment to the "nonauthoritarian foundations of democracy" is widely influencing contemporary political struggles (190). "Whether considered as the 'model' for antiglobalization movements or as representing the transition from armed to symbolic struggle that characterizes them," Wagner and Moreira write, "the Zapatista insurgence clearly emerges as paradigmatic of the new forms of resistance, political organization, and transformation that have been called for, with growing consensus, to understand and cope with globalization" (187). From a different perspective, see also *Swarming and the Future of Conflict*, John Arquilla and David Ronfeldt's study of the Zapatista movement for the Rand Corporation, the Department of Defense's think tank. Arquilla and Ronfeldt write that "the Zapatista movement in Mexico, which fused the Zapatista National Liberation Army (EZLN) with a transnational network of sympathetic nongovernmental organizations[. . .], kept the Mexican government and army on the defensive for years by means of aggressive but peaceful information operations" (2). Also see Arquilla and Ronfeldt's other two works on related topics, *Networks and Netwars: The Future of Terror, Crime, and Militancy* and *The Zapatista Social Netwar in Mexico*.

2. James, *Black Jacobins*, 88–89.

3. Ibid., 376.

4. Eltis and Richardson, *Atlas*, 202, 248.

5. See, for example, Hadden, *Slave Patrols* and Robin, *Reactionary Mind*.

6. See, for example, Justin Rogers-Cooper, "Crowds and Spinoza's Concept of the Political," *Meditations* 25.2 (Winter 2011): 37–59, and other essays in this issue of *Meditations*, all of which focus on the relations between the work building from Spinoza and the work building from Marx.

7. Spinoza, *Political Treatise*, 754. See also Nesbitt, *Caribbean Critique*, 33, 122, and 173–74; also Montag, *Bodies, Masses, Power*, 68–69.

8. On this point, see Jonathan Israel's work, especially *Radical Enlightenment: Philosophy and the Making of Modernity, 1650–1750*, but also the other two volumes in his trilogy, *Enlightenment Contested* and *Democratic Enlightenment*.

BIBLIOGRAPHY

"An Act in Addition to the Act, Entitled 'An Act for the Punishment of Certain Crimes against the United States'" <avalon.law.yale.edu/18th_century/sedact.asp>. 4 December 2012.

Agamben, Giorgio. *Homo Sacer: Sovereign Power and Bare Life*. Stanford: Stanford University Press, 1998.

———. *State of Exception*. Chicago: University of Chicago Press, 2005.

———. "What Is Destituent Power?" *Environment and Planning D: Society and Space* 32, no. 1 (February 2014): 65–74.

Ahrens, Gale, ed. *Lucy Parsons: Freedom, Equality, Solidarity; Writings and Speeches, 1878–1937*. Chicago: Charles H. Kerr, 2004.

Asibong, Andrew. "Three Is the Loneliest Number: Marie Vieux Chauvet, Marie NDiaye, and the Traumatized Triptych." *Yale French Studies. Revisiting Marie Vieux Chauvet: Paradoxes of the Postcolonial Feminine* 128 (2015): 146–60.

Allmendinger, David F. *Nat Turner and the Rising in Southampton County*. Baltimore: Johns Hopkins University Press, 2014.

Alperovitz, Gar. *America beyond Capitalism: Reclaiming Our Wealth, Our Liberty, and Our Democracy*. Tacoma Park: Democracy Collaborative Press, 2011.

Aptheker, Herbert. *Nat Turner's Slave Rebellion, Including the 1831 "Confessions."* Mineola: Dover, 2006.

Aristotle. *The Basic Works of Aristotle*. New York: Modern Library, 2011.

———. *A History of Animals*. Trans. D'Arcy Wentworth Thompson. <classics.mit.edu/Aristotle/history_anim.html>.Arquilla, John. *Swarming and the Future of Conflict*. Santa Monica: RAND, 2000.

Arquilla, John, and David Ronfeldt. *Networks and Netwars: The Future of Terror, Crime, and Militancy*. Santa Monica: RAND, 2001.

Ashbaugh, Carolyn. *Lucy Parsons: An American Revolutionary*. Chicago: Charles H. Kerr, 1976.

Azuela, Mariano. *The Underdogs*. New York: Signet, 1962.

Baker, Kyle. *Nat Turner*. New York: Abrams, 2006.

Balibar, Etienne. *Spinoza and Politics*. London: Verso, 1998.

Baptist, Edward E. *The Half Has Never Been Told: Slavery and the Making of American Capitalism*. New York: Basic Books, 2014.

The Battle of Algiers. Dir. Gillo Pontecorvo. Criterion, 2013. DVD.

Baumann, Michael *L. B. Traven: An Introduction*. Albuquerque: University of New Mexico Press, 1976.

Bell, Madison Smartt. "Permanent Exile." Review of *Love, Anger, Madness*. *Nation*. 26 January 2010. Web. 27 February 2013.

Benjamin, Walter. "A Critique of Violence." *Reflections*: *Essays, Aphorisms, Autobiographical Writings*. New York: Schocken, 1986.

Bentley, Nancy. "Looking at State Violence: Lucy Parsons, José Marti, and Haymarket." *The Oxford Handbook of 19th Century American Literature*. Ed. Russ Castronovo. Oxford: Oxford University Press, 2012.

Blackburn, Robin. "*The Black Jacobins* and New World Slavery." *C. L. R. James: His Intellectual Legacies*. Ed. Selwyn R. Cudjoe and William E. Cain. Amherst: University of Massachusetts Press, 1995.

———. *The Overthrow of Colonial Slavery: 1776–1848*. London: Verso, 2011.

Boggs, James. *The American Revolution*: *Pages from a Negro Worker's Notebook*. New York: Monthly Review Press, 2009.

Bortz, Jeffrey. *Revolution within the Revolution*: *Cotton Textile Workers and the Mexican Labor Regime, 1910–1923*. Stanford: Stanford University Press, 2008.

Breen, Patrick H. "A Prophet in His Own Land: Support for Nat Turner and His Rebellion within Southampton County's Black Community." *Nat Turner: A Slave Rebellion in History and Memory*. Ed. Kenneth Greenberg. Oxford: Oxford University Press, 2003.

Brooks, David. "What Whitman Knew." *Atlantic Monthly* 291 (May 2003): 32–33.

Brophy, Alfred L. "The Nat Turner Trials." *North Carolina Law Review* 91 (June 2013): 1831–36.

Browne, Stephen H. "'This Unparalleled and Inhuman Massacre': The Gothic, the Sacred, and the Meaning of Nat Turner." *Rhetoric and Public Affairs* 3 (2000): 309–31.

Bryan, Patrick E. "Aiding Imperialism: White Baptists in Nineteenth-Century Jamaica." *Small Axe* 7.2 (2003): 137–49.

Buck-Morss, Susan. *Hegel, Haiti, and Universal History*. Pittsburgh: University of Pittsburgh Press, 2009.

Buckler, William E., ed. *Prose of the Victorian Period*. Boston: Houghton Mifflin, 1958.

Buhle, Paul. *C. L. R. James: The Artist as Revolutionary*. New York: Verso, 1989.

Buford, Bill. *Among the Thugs*. New York: Vintage, 1993.

Bunge, Wiep van, ed. *The Early Enlightenment in the Dutch Republic, 1650–1750*: *Selected Papers of a Conference, Held at the Herzog August Bibliothek Wolfenbüttel*. Boston: Brill, 2003.

Burroughs, John. "The Pastoral Bees." *Birds and Bees, Sharp Eyes, and Other Papers*. 25 January 2016. <www.gutenberg.org/files/3163/3163-h/3163-h.htm>.

Butler, Charles. *The Feminine Monarchie, or The Historie of Bees*. Oxford: Joseph Barnes, 1609.

Carlyle, Thomas. *The French Revolution: A History*. New York: Modern Library, 2002.

———. *On Heroes, Hero-Worship, and the Heroic in History*. Ed. Henry David Gray. New York: Longmans, Green, 1906.

———. "Shooting Niagara: And After?" London: Chapman and Hall, 1868.

Casimir, Jean. *La Cultura oprimida*. Mexico, D.F.: Editorial Nueva Imagen, 1980.

Césaire, Aimé. *Discourse on Colonialism*. New York: Monthly Review Press, 2000.

Chancey, Myriam J. A. *Framing Silence: Revolutionary Novels Written By Haitian Women*. New Brunswick: Rutgers University Press, 1997.

Chauvet, Marie Vieux. *Love, Anger, Madness: A Haitian Triptych*. New York: Modern Library, 2010.

Cobham, Rhonda. "Fishers of Men: Catherine Hall's Narrative and the Framing of History." *Small Axe* 7.2 (2003): 150–58.

Cudjoe, Selwyn R., and William E. Cain, eds. *C. L. R. James: His Intellectual Legacies*. Amherst: University of Massachusetts Press, 1995.

Curl, John. *For All the People: Uncovering the Hidden History of Cooperation, Cooperative Movements, and Communalism in America*. Oakland: PM Press, 2009.

Curran, Andrew S. *The Anatomy of Blackness: Science and Slavery in an Age of Enlightenment*. Baltimore: Johns Hopkins University Press, 2011.

Dalleo, Raphael. *Caribbean Literature and the Public Sphere*. Charlottesville: University of Virginia Press, 2011.

Dash, Michael J. *The Other America: Caribbean Literature in a New World Context*. Charlottesville: University of Virginia Press, 1998.

Davis, Mary Kemp. *Nat Turner before the Bar of Judgment: Fictional Treatments of the Southampton Slave Insurrection*. Baton Rouge: Louisiana State University Press, 1999.

———. "'What Happened in This Place?': In Search of the Female Slave in the Nat Turner Slave Insurrection." *Nat Turner: A Slave Rebellion in History and Memory*. Ed. Kenneth Greenberg. Oxford: Oxford University Press, 2003. 162–78.

Davis, Robert L., "Democratic Vistas." *A Companion to Walt Whitman*. Ed. Donald Kummings. New York: Blackwell, 2006.

Dayan, Colin. "The Gods in the Trunk, or Writing in a Belittered World." *Yale French Studies*. Issue *Revisiting Marie Vieux Chauvet: Paradoxes of the Postcolonial Feminine* 128 (2015): 92–114.

Dayan, Joan. *Haiti, History, and the Gods*. Berkeley: University of California Press, 1995.

DeLanda, Manuel. *A New Philosophy of Society: Assemblage Theory and Social Complexity*. London: Continuum, 2006.Deleuze, Gilles. *Nietzsche and Philosophy*. New York: Columbia University Press, 2006.

———. *Spinoza: Practical Philosophy*. San Francisco: City Lights, 1988.

Deleuze, Gilles, and Félix Guattari. *A Thousand Plateaus*. Minneapolis: University of Minnesota Press, 1987.

Douglass, Frederick. *Autobiographies*. New York: Library of America, 1994.

———. "The Meaning of July 4th for the Negro." *History Is a Weapon*. 24 January 2016. <www.historyisaweapon.com/defcon1/douglassjuly4.html>.

Du Bois, W. E. B. *Black Reconstruction in America, 1860–1880*. New York: Free Press, 1999.

———. *Economic Co-operation among Negro Americans*. Atlanta: Atlanta University Press, 1907.

———. *John Brown*. New York: Modern Library, 2001.

Duberman, Martin. *Haymarket: A Novel*. New York: Seven Stories Press, 2003.

Dubois, Laurent. *Avengers of the New World: The Story of the Haitian Revolution*. Cambridge: Belknap Press, 2004.

———. *Haiti: The Aftershocks of History*. New York: Metropolitan, 2012.

Duff, John B., and Peter M. Mitchell. *The Nat Turner Rebellion: The Historical Event and the Modern Controversy*. New York: Harper and Row, 1971.

Egerton, Douglass R. "Nat Turner in a Hemispheric Context." *Nat Turner: A Slave Rebellion in History and Memory*. Ed. Kenneth S. Greenberg. Oxford: Oxford University Press, 2003.

Eltis, David, and David Richardson, eds. *Atlas of the Transatlantic Slave Trade*. New Haven: Yale University Press, 2010.

Engels, Friedrich. *The Peasant War in Germany*. New York: International, 2000.

Ericson, David F. *The Debate over Slavery: Antislavery and Proslavery Liberalism in Antebellum America*. New York: NYU Press, 2000.

Erkkila, Betsy. "Radical Jefferson." *American Quarterly* 59.2 (June 2007). 277–89.

———. "'To Paris with My Love': Whitman among the French Revisited." *Revue française d'études américaines* 108 (2006): 7–22. *Whitman the Political Poet*. New York: Oxford University Press, 1989.

Evans, Eric J. *Parliamentary Reform in Britain, c. 1770–1918*. New York: Longman, 2000.

Fabre, Michel. "Walt Whitman and the Rebel Poets: A Note on Whitman's Reputation among Radical Writers during the Depression." *Walt Whitman Review* 12 (December 1966): 88–93.

Fabricant, Daniel S. "Thomas R. Gray and William Styron: Finally, a Critical Look at the 1831 *Confessions of Nat Turner*." *American Journal of Legal History* 37.3 (July 1993): 332–61.

Fanon, Frantz. *The Wretched of the Earth*. New York: Grove, 1963.

Fick, Carolyn E. *The Making of Haiti: The Saint Domingue Revolution from Below*. Knoxville: University of Tennessee Press, 2004.

Fischer, Sibylle. "History and Catastrophe." *Small Axe* 14.3 (November 2010): 163–72.

———. *Modernity Disavowed: Haiti and the Cultures of Slavery in the Age of Revolution*. Durham: Duke University Press, 2004.

Fitzhugh, George. *Cannibals All! Or, Slaves without Masters*. Richmond: A. Morris, 1857. <docsouth.unc.edu/southlit/fitzhughcan/fitzcan.html#fitz306>.

Flores Magón, Ricardo. *Dreams of Freedom: A Ricardo Flores Magón Reader*. Oakland: AK Press, 2005.

———. *Land and Liberty: Anarchist Influences in the Mexican Revolution*. Comp. David Poole. Sanday, Orkney, UK: Cienfuegos Press, 1977.

Folsom, Ed, ed. *Democratic Vistas: The Original Edition in Facsimile*. Iowa City: University of Iowa Press, 2010.

———. "Lucifer and Ethiopia: Whitman, Race, and Poetics before the Civil War and After." *A Historical Guide to Walt Whitman*. Ed. David S. Reynolds. New York: Oxford University Press, 2000.

Foner, Eric, ed. *Nat Turner*. Englewood Cliffs: Prentice-Hall, 1971.

Foucault, Michel. *Discipline and Punish: The Birth of the Prison*. New York: Vintage, 1995.

———. *Fearless Speech*. Los Angeles: Semiotext(e), 2001.

French, Scot. "A Conversation with Scot French" <www.houghtonmifflinbooks.com/book sellers/press_release/french/>. 4 December 2012.

———. *The Rebellious Slave: Nat Turner in American Memory*. New York: Houghton Mifflin, 2003.

Froude, James Anthony. *The English in the West Indies, or the Bow of Ulysses*. London: Longmans, Green, 1888.

———. *Thomas Carlyle: A History of His Life in London, 1834–1881*, vol. II. New York: Charles Scribner's Sons, 1898.

Fuentes, Carlos. *The Death of Artemio Cruz*. Trans. Alfred MacAdam. New York: Farrar, Straus, and Giroux, 1991.

Fung, Archon, and Erik O. Wright. "Thinking about Empowered Participatory Governance." *Deepening Democracy: Institutional Innovations in Empowered Participatory Governance*. London: Verso, 2003. 3–42.

Garraway, Doris L., ed. *Tree of Liberty: Cultural Legacies of the Haitian Revolution in the Atlantic World*. Charlottesville: University of Virginia Press, 2008.

Genovese, Eugene. *Roll, Jordan, Roll: The World the Slaves Made*. New York: Vintage, 1976.

Gilly, Adolfo. *The Mexican Revolution*. New York: New Press, 2005.

Gluckstein, Donny. *The Paris Commune: A Revolution in Democracy*. London: Bookmarks, 2009.

Gollnick, Brian. *Reinventing the Lacandón: Subaltern Representations in the Rain Forest of Chiapas*. Tucson: University of Arizona Press, 2008.

Gornick, Vivian. *The Solitude of Self: Thinking about Elizabeth Cady Stanton*. New York: Farrar, Straus, and Giroux, 2006.

Gray, Thomas R. *The Confessions of Nat Turner*. Baltimore: Lucas and Deaver, 1831. <digitalcommons.unl.edu/etas/15/>. 24 September 2012.

Green, James. *Death in the Haymarket: A Story of Chicago, the First Labor Movement, and the Bombing That Divided Gilded Age America*. New York: Pantheon, 2006.

Greenberg, Kenneth S. "Name, Face, Body." *Nat Turner: A Slave Rebellion in History and Memory*. Ed. Kenneth Greenberg. Oxford: Oxford University Press, 2003.

———, ed. *Nat Turner: A Slave Rebellion in History and Memory*. New York: Oxford University Press, 2003.

Grier, Edward F. "Walt Whitman, the Galaxy, and *Democratic Vistas*." *American Literature* 23 (November 1951): 332–50.

Grimshaw, Anna, ed. *The C. L. R. James Reader*. Oxford: Blackwell, 1992.

Guthke, Karl. *B. Traven: The Life behind the Legends*. Brooklyn: Lawrence Hill, 1987.

Guzmán, Martín Luís. *The Eagle and the Serpent*. New York: Knopf, 1930.

Hadden, Sally E. *Slave Patrols: Law and Violence in Virginia and the Carolinas*. Cambridge: Harvard University Press, 2001.

Haddox, Thomas F. "Whitman's End of History: 'As I Sat Alone by Blue Ontario's Shore,' *Democratic Vistas*, and the Postbellum Politics of Nostalgia." *Walt Whitman Quarterly Review* 22.1 (2004): 1–23.

"Haitian Constitution of 1801." *Toussaint L'Ouverture: The Haitian Revolution*. Ed. Nick Nesbitt. London: Verso, 2008. 45–61.

Hall, Catherine. *Civilising Subjects: Metropole and Colony in the English Imagination 1830–1867*. Chicago: University of Chicago Press, 2002.

———. "Narratives of Empire: A Reply to Critics." *Small Axe* 7.2 (2003): 168–78.

Hardt, Michael. "Jefferson and Democracy." *American Quarterly* 59.1 (2007): 41–78.

———. "Translator's Foreword." Antonio Negri, *The Savage Anomaly: The Power of Spinoza's Metaphysics and Politics*. Minneapolis: University of Minnesota Press, 2008.

Hardt, Michael, and Antonio Negri. *Declaration*. <www.scribd.com/doc/93152857/Hardt -Negri-Declaration-2012>. 4 December 2012.

———. *Multitude: War and Democracy in the Age of Empire*. New York: Penguin, 2004.

Harris, W. C., "Whitman's Leaves of Grass and the Writing of a New American Bible." *Walt Whitman Quarterly Review* 16.3–4 (1999): 172–90.

Hart, John M. *Anarchism and the Mexican Working Class, 1860–1931*. Austin: University of Texas Press, 1978.

———. *Revolutionary Mexico: The Coming and Process of the Mexican Revolution*. Berkeley: University of California Press, 1987.

Harvey, David. *A Companion to Marx's* Capital. London: Verso, 2010.

Herzog, Arthur. *The Swarm*. New York: Author's Choice Press, 1974.

Heuman, Gad. *The Killing Time: The Morant Bay Rebellion in Jamaica*. Knoxville: University of Tennessee Press, 1995.

Higginson, Thomas Wentworth. "Nat Turner's Insurrection." *The Nat Turner Rebellion: The Historical Event and the Modern Controversy*. Ed. John B. Duff and Peter B. Mitchell. New York: Harper and Row, 1971.

Hill, Robert A. "C. L. R. James: The Myth of Western Civilization." *Enterprise of the Indies*. Ed. George Lamming. Port of Spain: Trinidad and Tobago Institute of the West Indies, 1999. 255–59.

Hoelzl, Michael, and Graham Ward. "Translator's Introduction." Carl Schmitt, *Dictatorship*. Cambridge: Polity, 2014.

Høgsbjerg, Christian. "'A Thorn in the Side of Great Britain': C. L. R. James and the Caribbean Labour Rebellions of the 1930s." *Small Axe* 15.2: 24–42.

———, ed. *Toussaint Louverture: The Story of the Only Successful Slave Revolt in History, A Play in Three Acts*. Durham: Duke University Press, 2013.

Hugo, Victor. *Les Misérables*. London: Penguin, 1976.

Israel, Jonathan. *Democratic Enlightenment: Philosophy, Revolution, and Human Rights, 1750–1790*. Oxford: Oxford University Press, 2011.

———. *Enlightenment Contested: Philosophy, Modernity, and the Emancipation of Man, 1670–1752*. Oxford: Oxford University Press, 2011.

———. *Radical Enlightenment: Philosophy and the Making of Modernity, 1650–1750*. Oxford: Oxford University Press, 2002.

———. *A Revolution of the Mind: Radical Enlightenment and the Intellectual Origins of Modern Democracy*. Princeton: Princeton University Press, 2010.

Jacobs, Harriet. *Incidents in the Life of a Slave Girl*. 14 July 2013. <www.gutenberg.org/cache/ epub/11030/pg11030.html>.

Jacobs, Jane. *The Death and Life of Great American Cities*. New York: Vintage, 1992.

James, C. L. R. *American Civilization*. Cambridge: Blackwell, 1993.

———. *The Black Jacobins: Toussaint L'Ouverture and the San Domingo Revolution*. New York: Vintage, 1989.

———. "Every Cook Can Govern." *A New Notion: Two Works by C. L. R. James*. Ed. Noel Ignatiev. Oakland: PM Press, 2010.

———. "Lectures on *The Black Jacobins*." *Small Axe* 8 (September 2000): 65–112.

———. *Mariners, Renegades, and Castaways: The Story of Herman Melville and the World We Live In*. Dartmouth: University Press of New England, 2001.

———. "Every Cook Can Govern: A Study of Democracy in Ancient Greece and Its Meaning for Today." In *A New Notion: Two Works by C. L. R. James*. Oakland: PM Press, 2010.

James, C. L. R., Grace C. Lee, and Cornelius Castoriadis. *Facing Reality: The New Society, Where to Look for It, and How to Bring It Closer*. Chicago: Charles H. Kerr, 2006.

Kaisary, Philip. *The Haitian Revolution in the Literary Imagination*. Charlottesville: University of Virginia Press, 2014.

Kale, Madhavi. "Subject to Question: Empire and Catherine Hall's *Civilizing Subjects*." *Small Axe* 7.2 (2003): 127–36.

Kateb, George. "Walt Whitman and the Culture of Democracy." *Political Theory* 18.4 (1990): 545–71.

Kaussen, Valerie. "Irrational Revolutions: Colonial Intersubjectivity and Dialectics in Marie Chauvet's *Amour*." *Tree of Liberty: Cultural Legacies of the Haitian Revolution in the Atlantic World*. Ed. Doris Garroway. Charlottesville: University of Virginia Press. 134–52.

Keane, John. "Monitory Democracy?" *The Future of Representative Democracy*. Ed. Sonia Alonso, John Keane, and Wolfgang Merkel. Cambridge: Cambridge University Press, 2011. 212–35.

Kelley, Robin D. G. *Freedom Dreams: The Black Radical Imagination*. Boston: Beacon, 2002.

Kostal, Rande W. *A Jurisprudence of Power: Victorian Empire and the Rule of Law*. Oxford: Oxford University Press, 2008.

Laclau, Ernesto. *On Populist Reason*. London: Verso, 2005.

Larrier, Renée. *Francophone Women Writers of Africa and the Caribbean*. Gainesville: University Press of Florida, 2000.

Lavine, Laurie K. "The Feminizing of the Trojan Horse: Marie Chauvet's *Amour* as War Machine." *Women in French Studies* 2 (1994): 9–18.

Lawson, Andrew. *Walt Whitman and the Class Struggle*. Iowa City: University of Iowa Press, 2006.

Le Bon, Gustave. *The Crowd: A Study of the Popular Mind*. etext.virginia.edu/toc/modeng/public/BonCrow.html. 4 December 2012.

Lee Boggs, Grace. *Living for Change*. Minneapolis: University of Minnesota Press, 1998.

Lee-Keller, Hellen. "Madness and the *Mulâtre-Aristocrate*: Haiti, Decolonization, and Women in Marie Chauvet's *Amour*." *Callaloo* 32.4 (2009): 1293–1311.

Le Guin, Ursula K. *The Tombs of Atuan*. London: Saga, 2012.

Linebaugh, Peter, and Marcus Rediker. *The Many-Headed Hydra: Sailors, Slaves, Commoners, and the Hidden History of the Revolutionary Atlantic*. Boston: Beacon, 2000.

Lordon, Frédéric. *Willing Slaves of Capital: Spinoza and Marx on Desire*. London: Verso 2014.

Lorimer, Douglas. *Colour, Class, and the Victorians*. Leicester: Leicester University Press, 1978.

Lucardie, Paul. "Let the Dice Decide! A Qualified Argument for Sortitionist Democracy." *Problems of Democracy: Language and Speaking*. Ed. Mary-Ann Crumplin. Oxford: Inter-Disciplinary Press, 2011. 103–19.

Lundahl, Mats. *Peasants and Poverty: A Study of Haiti*. New York: St. Martin's Press, 1979.

Lundblad, Michael. *The Birth of a Jungle: Animality in Progressive-Era U.S. Literature and Culture*. Oxford: Oxford University Press, 2013.

Lynd, Staughton. *Intellectual Origins of American Radicalism*. Cambridge: Cambridge University Press, 2009.

Mack, Stephen John. *The Pragmatic Whitman: Reimagining American Democracy*. Iowa City: University of Iowa Press, 2002.

Malcolm X. *The Autobiography of Malcolm X*. New York: Penguin, 2001.

Mancuso, Luke. *The Strange Sad War Revolving: Walt Whitman, Reconstruction, and the Emergence of Black Citizenship, 1865–1876*. Columbia: Camden House, 1997.

Marx, Karl. *Capital: A Critical Analysis of Capitalist Production*. Vol. I. Trans. Samuel Moore and Edward Aveling. New York: International, 1967.

———. *The Civil War in France. Writings on the Paris Commune*. Ed. Hal Draper. New York: Monthly Review Press, 1971.

———. *Grundrisse*. London: Penguin, 1973.

———. "Letters from the *Deutsch-Französische Jahrbücher*. Marx to Ruge." 23 December 2012. <http://www.marxists.org/archive/marx/works/1843/letters/43_05.htm>.

———. *The Poverty of Philosophy*. Trans. H. Quelch. Amherst: Prometheus, 1995.

Marx, Karl, and Friedrich Engels. "Contribution to the Critique of Hegel's *Philosophy of Right*." *The Marx/Engels Reader*, 2nd ed. Ed. Robert C. Tucker. New York: W. W. Norton, 1978. 53–65.

———. *Manifesto of the Communist Party*. New York: International, 1990.

McKean, Jacob. "A Fury for Justice: Lucy Parsons and the Revolutionary Anarchist Movement in Chicago." 17 October 2006. <www.waste.org/~roadrunner/ScarletLetterAr chives/LucyParsons/FuryForJustice.htm>. 4 December 2012.

Messer-Kruse, Timothy. *The Haymarket Conspiracy: Transatlantic Anarchist Networks*. Urbana: University of Illinois Press, 2012.

Mezo, Richard E. *A Study of B. Traven's Fiction: The Journey to Solipaz*. San Francisco: Mellen Research University Press, 1993.

Miller, Paul B. *Elusive Origins: The Enlightenment in the Modern Caribbean Historical Imagination*. Charlottesville: University of Virginia Press, 2010.

Miller, Peter. *The Smart Swarm: How to Work Efficiently, Communicate Effectively, and Make Better Decisions Using the Secrets of Flocks, Schools, and Colonies*. New York: Avery, 2011.

Mirzoeff, Nicholas. "For Democracy, Strike Debt: Resonances of Abolition in the Occupy Movement." *Social Text Periscope: Is This What Democracy Looks Like?* 4 March 2013. Web.

Mitchell, Melanie. *Complexity: A Guided Tour*. New York: Oxford University Press, 2009.

Montgomery, David. *Workers' Control in America: Studies in the History of Work, Technology, and Labor Struggles*. Cambridge: Cambridge University Press, 1992.

Montag, Warren. *Bodies, Masses, Power: Spinoza and His Contemporaries*. London: Verso, 1999.

Munro, Martin. "Avenging History in the Former French Colonies." *Transition* 99 (2008): 18–39.

Negri, Antonio. *Insurgencies: Constituent Power and the Modern State*. Minneapolis: University of Minnesota Press, 1999.

———. *The Savage Anomaly: The Power of Spinoza's Metaphysics and Politics*. Minneapolis: University of Minnesota Press, 2008.

———. *Subversive Spinoza: (Un)contemporary Variations*. Manchester: Manchester University Press, 2008.

———. *Trilogy of Resistance*. Minneapolis: University of Minnesota Press, 2011.

Nembhard, Jessica Gordon. *Collective Courage: A History of African American Cooperative Economic Thought and Practice*. University Park: Pennsylvania State University Press, 2014.

Nesbitt, Nick. *Caribbean Critique: Antillean Critical Theory from Toussaint to Glissant*. Liverpool: Liverpool University Press, 2013.

———, ed. *Toussaint Louverture: The Haitian Revolution*. London: Verso, 2008.

———. *Universal Emancipation: The Haitian Revolution and the Radical Enlightenment*. Charlottesville: University of Virginia Press, 2008.

Ness, Immanuel, and Dario Azzellini, eds. *Ours to Master and to Own: Workers' Control from the Commune to the Present*. Chicago: Haymarket, 2011.

Newborn, Jud, and Annette Dumbach. *Sophie Scholl and the White Rose*. London: Oneworld, 2007.

Newman, M.E.J. "Complex Systems: A Survey." *American Journal of Physics* 79 (2011): 800–10.

Olafson, Robert B. "B. Traven's Six-Novel Epic of the Mexican Revolution: An Overview." *B. Traven: Life and Work*. Ed. Ernst Schürer and Philip Jenkins. University Park: Pennsylvania State University Press, 1987. 141–48.

Orwell, George. *A Kind of Compulsion*. London: Secker and Warburg, 2000.

Paine, Gregory. "The Literary Relations of Whitman and Carlyle with Especial Reference to Their Contrasting Views on Democracy." *Studies in Philology* 36 (July 1939): 550–63.

Parramore, Thomas C. "Covenant in Jerusalem." *Nat Turner: A Slave Rebellion in History and Memory*. Ed. Kenneth Greenberg. Oxford: Oxford University Press, 2003.

Parsons, Lucy. *Freedom, Equality, and Solidarity: Writings and Speeches, 1878–1937*. Chicago: Charles H. Kerr, 2004.

Pateman, Roy. *The Man Nobody Knows: The Life and Legacy of B. Traven*. Lanham: University Press of America, 2005.

Payne, Kenneth. "B. Traven's Government." *Journal of English* 16 (1988): 79–89.

———. "B. Traven's Mexican Indian Utopias." *Antigonish Review* 104 (1996): 129–40.

———. "The Making of a Mexican Revolutionary: B. Traven's March to the Monteria." *International Fiction Review* 17.1 (1990): 41–6.

———. "*The Rebellion of the Hanged*: B. Traven's Anti-Fascist Novel of the Mexican Revolution." *International Fiction Review* 18:2 (1991): 96–107.

"Pittsburgh Proclamation" of the International Working Person's Association. *Freiheit*. 27 December 1890. Web.

Plato. *The Republic*. New York: Penguin Classics, 2012.

Plotz, John. *The Crowd: British Literature and Public Politics*. Berkeley: University of California Press, 2000.

Poe, Andrew. 2010. "The Sources and Limits of Political Enthusiasm." Diss., University of California, San Diego. 19 January 2016. University of California E-Scholarship.

Popkin, Jeremy. *Facing Racial Revolution: Eyewitness Accounts of the Haitian Revolution*. Chicago: University of Chicago Press, 2007.

Price, Kenneth M. "'Be radical—be radical—be not too damned radical!': The Origins and Resonance of Whitman's Signature Expression." *Walt Whitman Quarterly Review* 22 (Fall 2004/Spring 2005): 126–29.

Prince, Mary. *The History of Mary Prince*. London: Penguin, 2000.

Rabbitt, Kara M. "C. L. R. James's Figuring of Toussaint-Louverture: *The Black Jacobins* and the Literary Hero." *C. L. R. James: His Intellectual Legacies*. Ed. Selwyn R. Cudjoe and William E. Cain. Amherst: University of Massachusetts Press, 1995.

Rancière, Jacques. *Disagreement: Politics and Philosophy*. Minneapolis: University of Minnesota Press, 1995.

———. *Dissensus: On Politics and Aesthetics*. London: Continuum, 2011.

———. *Hatred of Democracy*. London: Verso, 2006.

Ransome, Hilda M. *The Sacred Bee in Ancient Times and Folklore*. Mineola: Dover, 2004.

Raskin, Jonah. "B. Traven's Revolution in Latin America." *B. Traven: Life and Work*. Ed. Ernst Schürer and Philip Jenkins. University Park: Pennsylvania State University Press, 1987. 226–33.

Rauwerda, A. M. "Naming, Agency, and 'A Tissue of Falsehoods' in *The History of Mary Prince*." *Victorian Literature and Culture* 29.2 (2001): 397–411.

Rediker, Marcus. *The Slave Ship: A Human History*. New York: Penguin, 2007.

———. *Villains of All Nations: Atlantic Piracy in the Golden Age*. Boston: Beacon, 2004.

Renda, Mary A. *Taking Haiti: Military Occupation and the Culture of US Imperialism, 1915–1940*. Chapel Hill: University of North Carolina Press, 2001.

Reynolds, David S. *A Historical Guide to Walt Whitman*. New York: Oxford University Press, 2000.

Robin, Corey. *The Reactionary Mind: Conservatism from Edmund Burke to Sarah Palin*. Oxford: Oxford University Press, 2013.

Robinson, Cedric. *Black Marxism: The Making of the Black Radical Tradition*. Chapel Hill: University of North Carolina Press, 2000.

Rogers-Cooper, Justin. "Crowds and Spinoza's Concept of the Political." *Meditations* 25.2 (Winter 2011): 37–59.

Rommel-Ruiz, Bryan. "Vindictive Ferocity: Virginia's Response to the Nat Turner Rebellion." In *Enemies of Humanity: The Nineteenth-Century War on Terrorism*. New York: Palgrave Macmillan, 2008.

Rosengarten, Frank. *Urbane Revolutionary: C. L. R. James and the Struggle for a New Society*. Jackson: University Press of Mississippi, 2012.

Said, Edward. "Always on Top." *London Review of Books* 25.6 (20 March 2003).

———. *Orientalism*. New York: Vintage, 2014. 3–6.

Sande, Melissa. "Cultural Memory for the Political Present: Examining Marie Chauvet's *Love in the Aftermath of Haiti's Earthquake*." *Otherness: Essays and Studies* 2.1 (August 2011).

Scharfman, Ronnie. "Theorizing Terror: The Discourse of Violence in Marie Chauvet's *Amour, Colère, Folie*." *Postcolonial Subjects: Francophone Women Writers*. Ed. Mary Jean Green. Minneapolis: University of Minnesota Press, 1996. 229–45.

Schmitt, Carl. *The Concept of the Political*. Chicago: University of Chicago Press, 1996.

———. *The Crisis of Parliamentary Democracy*. Cambridge: MIT Press, 1988.

———. *Dictatorship: From the Origin of the Modern Concept of Sovereignty to Proletarian Class Struggle*. Cambridge: Polity, 2014.

———. *Political Theology: Four Chapters on the Concept of Sovereignty*. Chicago: University of Chicago Press, 1985.

Scholnick, Robert J. "'Culture' or Democracy: Whitman, Eugene Benson, and *The Galaxy*." *Walt Whitman Quarterly Review* 13 (Summer 1996): 189–209.

Schürer, Ernst, and Philip Jenkins, eds. *B. Traven: Life and Work*. University Park: Pennsylvania State University Press, 1987.

Scott, David. *Conscripts of Modernity: The Tragedy of Colonial Enlightenment*. Durham: Duke University Press, 2004.

Seeley, Thomas. *Honeybee Democracy*. Princeton: Princeton University Press, 2010.

Shakur, Assata. *Assata: An Autobiography*. Chicago: Lawrence Hill, 2001.

Shank, Barry. "Jefferson, the Impossible." *American Quarterly* 59.2 (June 2007): 291–99.

Sitrin, Marina, ed. *Horizontalism: Voices of Popular Power in Argentina*. Oakland: AK Press, 2006.

Smith, Faith. "How the English Became English: Catherine Hall's *Civilising Subjects*." *Small Axe* 7.2 (2003): 159–67.

Sorel, Georges. *Reflections on Violence*. Mineola: Dover, 2004.

Sorensen, David R., and Rodger L. Tarr, eds. *The Carlyles at Home and Abroad*. Hampshire, England: Ashgate, 2004.

Spinoza, Benedict de. *Ethics*. London: Penguin, 1996.

———. *Political Treatise*. *Spinoza: Complete Works*. Ed. Michael L. Morgan. Indianapolis: Hackett, 2002.

———. *Theological-Political Treatise*. Ed. Jonathan Israel. Cambridge: Cambridge University Press, 2007.

Stone, Judy. "Conversations with B. Traven." *Ramparts* (1967): 55–69.

———. *My Search for B. Traven*. New York: Methuen, 1980.

———. "The Mystery of B. Traven." *Ramparts* (1967): 31–49.

Stovall, Floyd, ed. *Walt Whitman: Prose Works 1892*, vols. I and II. New York: NYU Press, 1964.

Summer, Kay, and Harry Halpin. "The Crazy Before the New." *What Would It Mean to Win?* Oakland: PM Press, 2010.

Surowiecki, James. *The Wisdom of Crowds: Why the Many Are Smarter than the Few and How Collective Wisdom Shapes Business, Economies and Nations*. New York: Doubleday, 2004.

Swammerdam, John. *The Book of Nature; or the History of Insects*. London: C. G. Seyggert, 1758.

Thompson, Alvin O. *Flight to Freedom: African Runaways and Maroons in the Americas*. Kingston: University of the West Indies Press, 2006.

Tolstoy, Leo. *War and Peace*. New York: Penguin Classics, 2005.

Toscano, Alberto. *Fanaticism: On the Uses of an Idea*. London: Verso, 2010.

Tragle, Henry Irving. *The Southampton Slave Revolt of 1831: A Compilation of Source Material*. Amherst: University of Massachusetts Press, 1971.

Traven, B. *The Carreta*. Chicago: Ivan R. Dee, 1994.

———. *General from the Jungle*. Chicago: Ivan R. Dee, 1995.

———. *Government*. Chicago: Ivan R. Dee, 1993.

———. *March to the Montería*. Chicago: Ivan R. Dee, 1994.

———. *The Rebellion of the Hanged*. Chicago: Ivan R. Dee, 1994.

———. *The Treasure of the Sierra Madre*. New York: Farrar, Straus, and Giroux, 2010.

———. *Trozas*. Chicago: Ivan R. Dee, 1994.

The Treasure of the Sierra Madre. Dir. John Huston. Perf. Humphrey Bogart. Warner Brothers, 1948.

Trela, D. J. "Carlyle's 'Shooting Niagara': The Writing and Revising of an Article and Pamphlet." *Victorian Periodicals Review* 25.1 (Spring 1992): 30–34.

Underhill, Edward Bean. *The Tragedy of Morant Bay: A Narrative of the Disturbances in the Island of Jamaica*. <archive.org/stream/tragedyofmorantbooundeuoft/tragedyofmorantbooundeuoft_djvu.txt>.

Unger, Roberto Mangabeira, and Cornel West. *The Future of American Progressivism: An Initiative for Political and Economic Reform*. Boston: Beacon Press, 1998.

Vargas Llosa, Mario. "Mexico: The Perfect Dictatorship." *New Perspectives Quarterly* 8.1 (1991): 23–25.

Wagner, Valeria, and Alejandro Moreira. "Toward a Quixotic Pragmatism: The Case of the Zapatista Insurgence." *boundary 2* 30.3 (2003): 185–212.

Walcott-Hackshaw, Elizabeth. "My Love Is like a Rose: Terror, *Territoire*, and the Poetics of Marie Chauvet." *Small Axe* 18 (September 2005): 40–51.

Wald, Priscilla. *Constituting Americans: Cultural Anxiety and Narrative Form*. Durham: Duke University Press, 1995.

Warder, Joseph. *The True Amazons: Or, the Monarchy of Bees*. London: John Pemberton, 1713.

Weinberg, Bill. *Homage to Chiapas: The New Indigenous Struggles in Mexico*. London: Verso, 2000.

Weisbuch, Robert. *Atlantic Double Cross: American Literature and British Influence in the Age of Emerson*. Chicago: University of Chicago Press, 1986.

Whitman, Walt. *The Journalism, Volume II: 1846–48*. Ed. Herbert Bergman, Douglas A. Noverr, Edward J. Recchia. New York: Peter Lang, 2003.

———. *Prose Works 1892*. Ed. Floyd Stovall. 2 vols. New York: NYU Press, 1964.

Winter, Sarah. "On the Morant Bay Rebellion in Jamaica and the Governor Eyre-George William Gordon Controversy, 1865–70." *BRANCH: Britain, Representation, and Nineteenth-Century History*. <branchcollective.org>. 4 December 2012.

Wofford, Eugene. "Who the Fuck Is Jacques Rancière?" *Critical Theory* 24 January 2016, 28 March 2013. <www.critical-theory.com/who-the-fuck-is-jacques-ranciere/>.

Wolff, Richard. *Democracy at Work: A Cure for Capitalism*. Chicago: Haymarket, 2012.

Worchester, Kent. *C. L. R. James: A Political Biography*. Albany: SUNY Press, 1995.

Wyatt, Will. *The Secret of the Sierra Madre*. Garden City: Doubleday, 1980.

Zogbaum, Heidi. *B. Traven: A Vision of Mexico*. Wilmington: Scholarly Resources, 1992.

———. "B. Traven Meets Frank Tannenbaum, Chiapas 1926." *Journal of Iberian and Latin American Studies* 2.2 (1996): 40–50.

<h1 style="text-align:center">INDEX</h1>

CPSIA information can be obtained
at www.ICGtesting.com
Printed in the USA
BVOW08*1213010517

482188BV00002B/2/P